# Archaeology

*The Discipline of Things*

Bjørnar Olsen
Michael Shanks
Timothy Webmoor
Christopher Witmore

UNIVERSITY OF CALIFORNIA PRESS

*Berkeley • Los Angeles • London*

University of California Press, one of the most
distinguished university presses in the United States,
enriches lives around the world by advancing
scholarship in the humanities, social sciences, and
natural sciences. Its activities are supported by the UC
Press Foundation and by philanthropic contributions
from individuals and institutions. For more information,
visit www.ucpress.edu.

University of California Press
Berkeley and Los Angeles, California

University of California Press, Ltd.
London, England

Library of Congress Cataloging-in-Publication Data

Olsen, Bjørnar.
   Archaeology : the discipline of things / Bjørnar
Olsen . . . [et al.].
      p.   cm.
   Includes bibliographical references and index.
   ISBN 978-0-520-27416-7 (cloth : alk. paper) —
   ISBN 978-0-520-27417-4 (pbk. : alk. paper) —
   ISBN 978-0-520-95400-7 (ebook)
   1. Archaeology.   2. Material culture.   I. Title.
   CC72.O46   2012
   930.1—dc23
                                        2012021917

Manufactured in the United States of America

21   20   19   18   17   16   15   14   13   12
10  9  8  7  6  5  4  3  2  1

In keeping with a commitment to support environmen-
tally responsible and sustainable printing practices, UC
Press has printed this book on 50-pound Enterprise, a
30% post-consumer-waste, recycled, deinked fiber that
is processed chlorine-free. It is acid-free and meets all
ANSI/NISO (Z 39.48) requirements.

# Contents

# Preface

This book is an outcome of a collaboration that has lasted nearly ten years. The births of children, conferral of PhDs, first jobs, international moves, promotions, a wedding: all are bound up in the completion of this project. It has been the proverbial journey, fostering intellectual challenges, development and unexpected partnerships, and is the manifestation of our collective destination. It began with Bjørnar visiting Stanford University in 2003 where all four of us were united in our unease with 'the state of things' in archaeology. Archaeology deals in the material remains of society, in things, their associations, assemblages, environments and contexts. While materiality and material culture have grown as objects of concern, things nevertheless are too often treated as secondary expressions of society, of social structures and cultural values. Different platforms and agendas have proliferated in seeking a social, cultural, or biological significance to the shape of things; what unites the diversity, even the incommensurability of most is an embarrassment that archaeology might primarily be about things, rather than other typical concerns of the social sciences and humanities such as norms and values, social structures and change, behavior and social psychology, historical agency, cultural geography. A question motivated us: where was the care for things in a discipline that is surely 'the discipline of things'? We wanted to write a book that would offer guidance to archaeologists in a *return to things*.

A very early iteration of this project was a presentation by three of us at Stanford Archaeology Center's workshop series in 2003. There quickly followed other iterations in the founding of a Symmetrical Archaeology Collaboratory, symposia at Theoretical Archaeology Group (TAG) Sheffield in 2005, the Society of American Archaeology (SAA) meetings in Puerto Rico in 2006, and TAG Stanford in 2009. There were resulting publications and additional presentations where we developed our ideas. Brainstorming for the structure and arguments began in earnest in 2007 and 2008 when Bjørnar was again visiting Stanford University. These many sessions around the whiteboard in the center's Metamedia Lab were fervent and memorable.

While circumstances dispersed the four of us, the spirit, ethos and aspirations of the Metamedia Lab—inclusivity, shared commitment, collegiality, creativity, openness, courage, and humility—were taken up in writing the draft chapters in a wiki. In step with a theme of the book, the work to manifest it has been collective and heterogeneous. Viewpoints, experience, and writing styles do differ, with a circulation of voices coming to the fore then receding to support in the background. Nonetheless, thoroughly collective, the book would not have been possible without all four of the authors.

Of course, there are many other essential ingredients that contribute to this collective work. We are indebted to many friends and colleagues: Susan Alcock, John F. Cherry, Douglass Bailey, Hein Bjerck, Ewa Domanska, Alfredo González-Ruibal, Ian Hodder, and Gavin Lucas. We thank Alfredo, Wendy Ashmore, and Michael Schiffer for their most pertinent comments to complete drafts of the manuscript. We are extremely grateful to Blake Edgar and Kate Marshall for their editorial guidance and support, to Peter Dreyer for his attentive work in copyediting the manuscript, and to Rose Vekony for her diligence in the proof stages.

Over the years, this project received generous support from Stanford University, the Joukowsky Institute for Archaeology and the Ancient World, Brown University, the Department of Classical & Modern Languages & Literatures, the College of Arts and Sciences, the Offices of the Provost and the Vice President for Research at Texas Tech University, the Institute for Science, Innovation and Society, Oxford University, the Institute of Archaeology and Social Anthropology, Tromsø University, and the Norwegian Research Council. We are grateful to Timothy Lenoir, the Jenkins Collaboratory, and the Information Sciences and Information Studies Group at Duke University for hosting Chris as a visiting scholar during the summer of 2011 and for providing a warm and inviting space for two of four when some final edits were being completed. We also thank Ian Hodder and the Stanford Archaeology Center for supporting

Bjørnar with work space and access to the research facilities during his two sabbatical years in Palo Alto. We also thank the Ruin Memories Project and the Norwegian Research Council for providing one of us critical support during the writing and allowing two of us to meet in Norway during drafting. Finally, Tim's gratitude goes to Amy Webmoor and Chris's to Liz Witmore.

*Tromsø, Palo Alto, Oxford, and Lubbock*

# CHAPTER 1

# Introduction

*Caring about Things*

This book is about archaeology and things. It considers the ways in which archaeologists deal with things, how they articulate and engage with them. The book offers a series of snapshots of archaeology as design and craft; archaeology is proposed as an ecology of practices, tacit and mundane, rich and nuanced, that work on material pasts in the present. We argue that a mark of archaeology is its particular kind of care, obligation, and loyalty to things. Our purpose in this introduction is to specify why archaeology should carry the moniker of the "discipline of things."

There is a growing litany of academic fields that now place emphasis on object-oriented approaches, taking things, their objecthood and materiality, seriously (Bennett 2010; Brown 2003; Bryant, Srnicek, and Harman 2010; DeLanda 2006; Domanska 2006a and b; Harman 2002, 2009a and 2011; Henare, Holbraad and Wastell 2007; Latour 2005; Latour and Weibal 2005; Preda 1999). It would certainly be disingenuous fully to disassociate ourselves from such academic kinetics, yet our novelty of purpose lies in revisiting, articulating, and developing what archaeologists have always done since the days of antiquarian science, and to emphasize how much archaeology brings to this new focus on things. Indeed, we even argue that archaeology offers an essential grounding to this *ontological turn*. This point is strangely absent from what is an increasingly pressing transdisciplinary discussion (cf. Latour and Weibel 2005; Preda 1999; Trentmann 2009; however, see Domanska 2006a).[1] This is not to say that archaeologists are not undertaking work that engages with the discussion (see, e.g., Alberti and Bray 2009; Alberti et al. 2011; Brown and Walker 2008; DeMarrais, Gosden, and Renfrew 2004; Harrison and Schofield 2010; González-Ruibal 2008; González-Ruibal, Hernando, and Politis 2011; Hodder 2011; Jones 2007; Knappett 2005; Knappett and Malafouris 2009; Lucas 2012; Meskell 2005; Olivier 2008; Olsen 2003 and 2010; Schiffer with Miller 1999; Walker 2008; Webmoor and Witmore 2008; Witmore 2004b; see also contributions to Hicks and Beaudry 2010). However, it is quite appropriate to suggest that archaeology is most often caricatured by other fields of endeavor as a circumscribed set of technical practices and interests that bear only indirectly upon the key terms of debate taken up in the ontological turn to things. On the other hand, archaeologists have not been as vocal as they could be in correcting such a view. There is an old and deeply rooted inferiority complex among some archaeologists, encapsulated in a self-image of archaeology as a second-rate, social science. This is often accompanied by an embarrassment that archaeology studies "just things," in contrast to the supposed cultural richness and subjective presence of text and voice. There is also even outright ambivalence and obscurity concerning the character and scope of archaeological practices.

We are far more optimistic. Indeed, we would go so far as to suggest that archaeology has developed an extended historiographical scope over the past few decades, offering a much broader scope than history itself (consider Foucault's use of the terms archaeology [1972, 1973] and genealogy [1977, 1984]). Archaeology encompasses the mundane and the material; its work is the tangible mediation of past and present, of people and their cultural fabric, of the tacit, indeed, the ineffable. It is this broad ecology of practices that we seek to understand better.

1. In a recent discussion exposing the roots of the turn, Frank Trentmann fails to list archaeology among the progenitors of the movement (2009). His inventory includes fields such as anthropology, science studies, material culture studies (we may acknowledge the archaeological connection here, not that many commentators do), and, perhaps not so usual, literary studies; it also includes older endeavors such as folklore and museum studies. Other examples of such a neglect of archaeology are just as revealing. The 1,072 pages of Bruno Latour and Peter Weibel's *Making Things Public* (2005) include the work of anthropologists, art historians, artists, architects, designers, engineers, legal historians, museum curators, philosophers, psychologists, sociologists of science and technology, and even English professors, linguists, and political theorists—but no archaeologists; not one.

## THE DISCIPLINE OF THINGS

One can read the notion that archaeology is the *discipline of things* in many ways. Our own reading is deeply practical; that is, centered upon *what it is that archaeologists do.* When one contemplates the hundreds of labor hours spent measuring, plotting, and drawing scenes on Corinthian perfume jars (*aryballoi*) by a practitioner interested in the development of ceramic design; when one considers the thousands of photographs deployed in documenting the excavations at Hissarlik in the waning decades of the nineteenth century, it seems trivial for an archaeologist to underline the point that words cannot provide an adequate expression for the ways the world actually exists. Words alone fail us with respect to matters of ontology. Therefore, we maintain also an elliptical drive to the expression "archaeology is the discipline of things," because we are not seeking to hammer out a fixed meaning.

The proposition that archaeology is the "discipline of things" does carry both rhetorical and etymological weight. Rhetorical, because in looking for the "Indian behind the artifact," many archaeologists (but by no means all), whether through embarrassment or an urge to engage with vanguard intellectual debates, have disregarded and ultimately forgotten the very thing they know best—things (Olsen 2003; 2010). Etymological, because one may translate *ta archaia,* one of the two components of the word *archaeology,* literally as "old things." Put this together with the second component of the word, *logos,* and one might speak of the "science of old things." Of course, the question of what both these components are is by no means straightforward (consider Shanks and Tilley 1992).

Practically speaking, the empirical fidelity of archaeology has always been to (old) things: Corinthian aryballoi, former Roman fortifications, avenues at Teotihuacan, abandoned Soviet mining towns, Sámi hearths, and mud bricks. As an empirical science, archaeology is concerned with the elucidation and analytic observation of immediate experience within which things play myriad roles, as do practitioners. These concerns play out across an iterative process of engagement and manifestation shaped by commitments to accuracy and adequacy of articulation and expression. Every science, as Alfred North Whitehead phrased it, "must devise its own instruments" (1978 [1929], 11). It has been in this very regard that archaeology has often labeled itself as a secondary science (applied or derivative), one that adds the products of forerunner disciplines and sciences (such as math and physics) to their accounts of the past (see, e.g., Nichols, Joyce, and Gillespie 2003).

However, the adjective "secondary" is not a scarlet letter of shame. Many of the so-called "secondary" sciences (e.g., education or nursing) are, in fact, sciences of care (Mol 2008). And here, we may draw a contrast with the "heroic" and lofty pursuit of the natural sciences (within archaeology, consider Gero and Conkey 1991). While not all archaeologists share similar perspectives, and neither do they necessarily share similar practices, there is nevertheless common ground—*things* draw the discipline together. Here we come closer to our reading of the discipline of things in the practical sense, that is, in terms of what it is that we do as archaeologists. From this angle, the phrase "discipline of things" underlines what is foremost a feeling of *care* and concern for legion material entities, from the monumental to the utterly mundane. Equally this moniker refers to how things themselves are "lures for feeling," as Alfred North Whitehead put it (1978 [1929], 87). We aim to place intuition, emotional allure and tacit engagement with things on the same footing as any intellectual rationale for the discipline.

Given the humanistic framing of so many archaeological endeavors, the notion of archaeology as secondary science is inadequate. From the big stories of urban development, the role of humanity in environmental change, or the rise of distinctive forms of complex polity, to the incidental details of animal figures in Scandinavian rock art, stems of clay smoking pipes, or the morphology of a human/bull cooking pot, archaeology has long delivered messages, whether analytical, critical, and/or speculative, that relate to the core of the human condition. It is also these big and small stories that make archaeology one of the most popular of the human and social sciences when it comes to public outreach and appeal.

From our angle, the phrase "the discipline of things" underscores a duty, an obligation, a need on the part of practitioners, to "always and consistently remember things" (Olsen 2003; 2010). Indeed, in their engagements with things, archaeologists are obliged to be *bricoleurs*. We collect bits and pieces, not because of an erratic whim (though, at times, this certainly is the case), but because of a commitment, a fidelity to the materials we engage. Bricolage is not without inevitable risks that may dull its edge. Theoretical incoherence, superficiality, trivialization, and redundancy can be the fruits of impulsive eclecticism, and their returns are depreciative at best. Weary of false beacons, the feral work of bricolage avoids proceeding haphazardly, by stubbornly going where it is led by its matters of concern.

John Dewey characterized the difference between science and art as one of statement versus expression. Statement, according to Dewey, "sets forth the conditions under which an experience of an object or situation may be had" (1980, 88). Expression, by contrast, does not lead to an experience; it constitutes one. Dewey's distinction is relevant on a number of levels, but here we underline it insofar as things demand numerous, often wild, angles of orientation of the archaeologist and archaeology. This is well evidenced in those crossovers with arts practice and vice versa (consider Dion and Coles 1999; Renfrew 2003; Shanks and Hershman 2009; Andereassen, Bjerck, and Olsen 2010). Playing upon the disjuncture between art and craft, we have suggested that archaeology is profitably seen as the latter (Shanks 1992; Shanks and McGuire 1996; Shanks and Witmore 2010; see also Schnapp and Shanks 2009). Craft suggests modes of activities enacted with an intense awareness, shaped through iterative engagement with materials and making, of the qualities of materials. In this, practice is not a compartmentalized mode of activity sealed off from theory.[2]

Here we may also connect archaeology as craft to the practice of design. Design we define broadly as a field of integration, of pulling together whatever is necessary to attend to a problem needing solution, of application of diverse fields of skill and expertise (typically engineering, psychology, materials science, and anthropology) with the interests, needs, or desires of an individual or group, of management of this process of making. It is a pragmatics of bricolage. It is also a field of rhetoric, where arguments are made for a particular solution, where what is designed is frequently an implicit argument for what is wished for. Both craft and design imply local attention, working in a humble way in a process that will deliver an artifact, an open process of constant and iterative improvement.

Considering its many, seemingly incommensurable islands of exclusivity, formed in the schisms between what was formerly recognized as culture-history, processualism, and postprocessualism, archaeology resembles an archipelago. Its diversity is born out in the lengthy roster of approaches it has generated, which include archaeometry, behavioral

---

2. Science, humanities, and art are riddled with economic, institutional, personal, and political crossovers.

archaeology, Darwinian archaeology, historical archaeology, social archaeology, heritage studies, and cultural resource management. Such variety is not without the potential further to indulge our differences along lines of divergence and turn away from a common struggle. We four are not concerned with what separates us, but with what pulls us together, that is, what matters for us. The strategy we follow in this book is not necessarily an attempt at integration (cf. Hodder 2011). We do not seek to smooth out disciplinary differences in engagement; rather, we believe our differences to be a strength so long as we focus on what binds us to a common struggle, shared worries, obligations, and mutual concerns, namely, *things*.

Things have repeatedly proved to be so bewilderingly variegated, distinct and unruly that no one field of practice can encompass them (Latour 1999, 176). Archaeology's larger loyalty to things necessitates such vast diversity. The ecology of practices that is archaeology is fully encapsulated by neither the arts and humanities nor the sciences. Indeed, in this we are better served by the old Latin meaning of the word *disciplina* as the instruction of disciples than by Michel Foucault's pervasive rendering of discipline. One could almost say that archaeologists are devout followers of things.

What then do we do with the designation "*old* things"? Antiquities, remnants, ruins, traces, vestiges; the bracketing of things in terms of an erstwhile existence, as the material past, has tended to fall into a scheme where the past is taken to exist apart from the present. That this separation has largely occurred through significant connecting chains of labor invested in typologies, classification, and standardization; that this has rested upon the management of legions of artifacts with the aid of instruments, cabinets, tables, rooms, and corridors in contract offices, universities, and museums is often overlooked. It is partially in taking archaeology's own achievements for granted that we forget how much work has gone into creating this divide between past and present. To assume that the past is gone accords the position of intermediaries, rather than full-blown mediators, to the things of archaeology. We run afoul of things when we assume a demarcated, disconnected past as *the ontological starting point* for what we do in the present. Archaeology does not discover the past as it was; archaeologists work with what has become of what was; what was, as it is, always becoming.

The remains of the past are all around us. We recognize the past as spatially coextensive with the very labor that attempts to articulate it. This labor relies on what things are willing to share regarding their prior involvements in the present.[3] Archaeology is certainly not the only field whose labor consists of myriad, ceaseless interactions with things; consider, for example, anthropology, design studies, engineering, ethnology, or museum studies. Making the claim that archaeology is the discipline of things has nothing to do with claiming privilege or exclusive domain; rather, it is to offer a competence and to seek to have it duly recognized. It goes to the heart of what archaeology is, and has always been, about. In approaching things, we do not seek to set forth a new theory that can be applied across diverse situations. We do not offer a series of boxes in which to place former aqueducts, long barrows, or 2,700-year-old perfume jars. Our charge, our task, is respectfully to return to things.

## APPROACHING THINGS

In his book *Archaeology from the Earth,* Sir Mortimer Wheeler insisted that which the archaeologist excavates is "not *things,* but *people*" (1954, v). Six years after Wheeler penned these words from his office in the Institute of Archaeology, University College, London (in 1952), Robert J. Braidwood observed in his obituary of Vere Gordon Childe, the Institute's former director, that he never forgot the "Indian behind the artifact" (1958, 734). These sentiments may serve to highlight what one of us (Olsen 2010) has described as an increasing embarrassment about studying "just things" among practitioners, for whom an Early Iron Age pit in Yorkshire, successive layers of plaster on a former wall in Iraq, or a rouletted dish from South India, for example, only are important insofar as they provide access to the human beings assumed to lie behind them. This conception of things as just means to reach something else, something more important, what we connect in chapter 8 with the notion of "an expressive fallacy," must be seen against the backdrop of the changes that had taken place in the human and social sciences, and perhaps most notably in anthropology (see chapter 2). In this new disciplinary regime, culture was seen as a separate, nontangible realm. "Culture is unobservable, is non-material," Walter Taylor (1983 [1948], 102) had already observed when Wheeler and Braidwood thus situated people behind things. In dooming the study of things to futility, anthropologists left little room for them, and archaeologists responded by claiming that it was not for the things that we were digging but for the people behind them.

---

3. Here, we are aware of the slippage between things as *archaia* and *pragmata* (Witmore 2012b).

Christopher Hawkes (1954) and Lewis Binford (1962) would push matters further by arguing that archaeology comprised more than the lower rungs of a ladder reaching up from material remains to immaterial cultural values and frames. Binford confidently asserted that while archaeologists could not dig up a "kinship terminology or a philosophy . . . we can and do excavate the material items which functioned together with these more behavioral elements within the appropriate cultural subsystems" (1962, 218–19). Archaeology was argued to be anthropology, and to get there it needed to reach *beyond* the artifact (Garrow and Yarrow 2010, 2–3; Olsen 2010, 23–26). And despite the self-proclaimed differences among those who came to be labeled postprocessualists, meanings, values, and beliefs remained locked in an exclusive province in which material things did not reside, although they provided access to it. Things "were indicative of and not essential to culture. . . . The whole productive idea of using artifacts to reconstruct the whole of an extinct society saw artifacts as leftovers, not as essential to the very existence of social life," Mark Leone (2007, 206) has pertinently remarked. For those who worried about the potential slippage of archaeology back into its embarrassing history of describing just things, there was the "corrective" of a social archaeology (Webmoor and Witmore 2008).

Of course, it would be disingenuous to claim archaeologists have not targeted the problematic of dualistic thinking. Archaeology is currently filled with attempts to "move beyond," "overcome," "transcend," and even "resolve" the myriad dichotomies that are basically variants of human and world. Along these lines, it has become somewhat dogmatic in certain areas of archaeology, material culture studies, and beyond to argue that people make things and things make people. The mantra of mutual constitution is at its very best a stopgap to balance the books, at worst a sleight-of-hand concession for those who ultimately maintain "the strong arm of humanism" (Webmoor and Witmore 2008). One of the premises of this book is that things do not reside in some separate realm or another domain of reality removed from the territory of society.

Mutual constitution, moreover, breaks down in several ways. First, it vastly oversimplifies things by ignoring the wider ecology of mixed and heterogeneous entities and relations that they draw together. Second, it forgets or ignores the bewildering variety of roles things play. Third, it disregards the qualities that things offer in a given situation. Fourth, it remains centered on the supposed primal rapport between humans and the world, thus it is "correlationist" (Meillassoux 2008). There are several observations to be made here.

First, interactions between kilns, reducing atmospheres, heat, clay, and slip are far too complex to be pared down to the hegemonic relationship between humans and the rest of the world. Our argument runs against the assumption that, as Gilbert Simondon put it, "technical objects contain no human reality" ([1989] 1958). The makeup of a Leica M3 camera gathers achievements far more diverse in space and time, far more heterogeneous in composition, than a look at its production in Wetzlar would reveal.[4] An immense genealogy of achievement in optics, geometry, high-temperature manufacture, leather working, and so forth, lay behind the making of the Leica. Moreover, the ontogenesis of this camera involves a kind of "internal necessity," as Simondon puts it, where the object self-realizes. That is, the Leica plays a role in its own formation; its design requires the presence and articulation of certain components for it to exist and work.

Second, a long-standing sentiment situates archaeological data as coarse and incidental by comparison to the richness of ethnographic accounts. Comparing archaeology to anthropology, Edmund Leach scolded archaeologists in 1973 for aspiring to address "How" and "Why" questions. He thought they should stick to "What," and even then, "in the last analysis, archaeology must be concerned with people rather than things" (1973, 768; also see discussions in Garrow and Yarrow 2010; Holbraad 2009). This sentiment, however, rests upon an assumption about the nature of the materials archaeologists engage with as of interest only in relation to humans. It also ignores the nature of archaeological practice, which is a process of co-emergence with the material past. The past is always the outcome of our practices, in which things that provide indications as to their nature play a part, and to no small degree. In this, the *how* is never separate from the *what*.

Archaeologists have become too timid in the face of anthropology, too eager for anthropological approbation (though see Garrow and Yarrow 2010; also Gosden 1999). There was never a need to await a confidence

4. Ian Hodder (2011) has developed what he calls an integrated approach to human-thing entanglement, which foregrounds the interdependences of things, humans, and other things. In attempting to take the things themselves seriously, Hodder lays emphasis on the ways things rely on humans and other things through chains of interdependence. While Hodder recognizes that things are collective achievements that draw diverse entities together, he does not recognize things' ability to make themselves.

gained through maturity to defend our practices. Archaeology does not operate under the same refrains as anthropology, because anthropology relies heavily upon the exclusivity of the human–world gap. Archaeologists need not take this as fundamental. Indeed, one of our premises is that, as practitioners, we do not work with a rule book that is separate from the material world; again, we are part of this world that we seek to better understand. Our achievement, as Isabelle Stengers puts it, should "not be abstracted from the practice that produced it" (2011, 376).

We treat notions such as past and present, and subject and object, as the purified outcomes of practice rather than the starting points: the past is accessed through archaeological (and other) practices. The real problem with such dualities is not so much one of oversimplification; it is rather "that human and world are taken as the two fundamental ingredients that must be found in any situation," as Graham Harman argues (2010, 146). Gauging the ontological status of a thing in anthropology has tended to rely on that overindulged two-fold of human and world. Though many practitioners, especially in the United States, work in departments of anthropology, archaeology cannot be encapsulated as anthropology (for a contrary view, see Nichols, Joyce, and Gillespie 2003). Archaeology has more freedom of movement in its ability to address object-object relations without falling back into the correlation of humans and the rest.

The rapport between human and wall should be no more or no less privileged than that between rain and exposed mud plaster. Material pasts are largely co-produced, not within an exclusive process of human selection, but through the interactions with anaerobic soils, microorganisms, moisture saturation, arid atmosphere, temperature, or even waves and beach cobbles (fig. 1.1). The differences in the ways an archaeologist and a stream of melt water negotiate an abandoned mining town are of degree, not kind. Rushing water washing against concrete pillars will "interpret" or "feel" the concrete surface as well as any hermeneut or phenomenologist (Harman 2010; Witmore forthcoming).

In revisiting the scope of the discipline of things, we have sought to avoid the modernist amnesia that tends to "overemphasize radicalism" or invest in "academic eliminativism" (Stengers 2010). Archaeology has arguably always been about the aforementioned concerns. Indeed, David Clarke pushed the envelope of empirical metaphysics by challenging practitioners to struggle with what they define as fundamental entities

FIGURE 1.1. Shipwreck, Hópsnes, Iceland, October 2008.

(1968; also see Dunnell 1986; Webmoor 2012a; Lucas 2012). Ever since the work of the first Danish "kitchen midden committee" in the mid nineteenth century (Klindt-Jensen 1975), archaeologists have had to take into account those other agencies that are involved in forming the archaeological record. We may look to contextual archaeology (Hodder and Hudson 2003), site formation processes (Schiffer 1976, 1987), or environmental archaeology (Dincauze 2000) for abundant examples where tremendous weight was placed on thing-thing interactions. Certainly, it would be disingenuous of us, to say the least, to claim such self-awareness on the part of archaeology as a whole. Working with things is full of wonder and confusion, creativity, and, yes, boring repetition.

Our task is therefore not so much to transform archaeology as to understand it. And, in seeking to do this, we aim to generate other kinds of narratives, more symmetrical accounts of archaeology and its common concern, things. We have called this project a symmetrical archaeology

(Olsen 2003, 2007 and 2012; Shanks 2007; Webmoor 2007 and 2012b; Witmore 2004b and 2007; also see González-Ruibal 2007).

## A SYMMETRICAL ARCHAEOLOGY

In returning to things and to questions of ontology, we necessarily revisit the question of how archaeology renders questions of agency, matter, and space and time. To boldly push with Clarke (1972) in contributing what one of us has called "an archaeological metaphysics of care" (Webmoor 2012a); to recognize the pressing need to reconsider our place in this world as human beings, as we have already suggested, we begin the task of imagining an archaeology that does not assume a transcendent, detached outside observer, but an immanent one, operating with/in the world, in medias res. This move from transcendence to immanence, from mastery to humility, does not imply a simple turn away from humanity; neither does it mean that we extend to things qualities that they formerly lacked. What we suggest is rather an act of recognition, to acknowledge the varied qualities always possessed by things, and thus the radical differences they make to the world—both among themselves and to humans. Based on such recognition, our task is one of *recomposition;* that is, of reformulating the compositional makeup of what it is to be human, where the human being is recognized as partially composed of objective reality.

Along the path of returning to things, we have followed series of guidelines, propositions that have aided our movements. It is worth pausing to set these out. It should be added that we place no empirical weight upon this vocabulary; it is simply meant to help us move with things.[5]

Where does one begin in dealing with things? Not from some "outside" position; it is neither about embodiment nor about domesticating and appropriating an alien or meaningless world. Archaeological engagements start in medias res: by jumping—or rather being thrown—into the thick of things, we seek to avoid predetermined dramas about how the world works in order to follow the connections wherever they may lead. Our dealing with things is grounded in an entangled ready-to-handness, a "thrown" condition that is enmeshed beforehand in a

---

5. Our debt to science and technology studies (STS) and philosophy is palpable, but our approach as archaeologists is quite distinct. Here we find allies, not as supports for our statements (not a second-string discipline), but as compatriots who recognize how anti-realist trends are ill equipped to deal with the world of today.

"Being-already-alongside-the-world" (Heidegger 1962, 85). This brings us to the notion of *symmetry,* which helps to remind us that the observer is in the world in the same way as that which is observed, and we may therefore describe them in equal terms (Webmoor 2007, 569). Ontologically placing priests, farmers, or shepherds on the same footing as walls, boundary markers, or goats is not to claim an undifferentiated world (Witmore 2007, 547). The entities of the world are of course different; in fact, they exhibit—between and among themselves—extremely varied modes of existence. What we claim is that this difference should not be conceptualized in compliance with the ruling ontological regime of dualities and negativities; it is a nonoppositional or relative difference that facilitates collaboration, delegation, and exchange (Olsen 2010, 2012).

Moreover, symmetry also implies that qualities and relations are on the same footing; that we should treat them symmetrically. Things are capable of making an effect, acting on other entities, not only because they are related, but also because of their own inherent properties. In other words, their ability to affect and act on us cannot be reduced to our inescapable enmeshment with them; rather it is grounded in their own specific thingly qualities (Olsen 2010). To avoid the trap of reducing things either to relations or to intrinsic qualities is an important feature of a symmetrical archeology (Webmoor 2012b).

Finally, another important aspect of a symmetrical archaeology is to take leave of the dominant paternalist idea that things depend on people and are of interest to us (and even exist) only insofar they involve humans. Symmetry involves an extended concern that includes how things exist, act, and affect one another apart from any human relations, whether or not this interaction eventually also affects human life. While there is no possibility of thinking humans outside the realms of things and natures, the other option is of course viable. Snow, ice, wind, sea, and penguins existed and interacted in Antarctica prior to being encountered by humans.

Things also exceed any ability to come to terms with them. No entity can ever encapsulate another, and this has implications for the nature of our empirical practice. A fortress, a ruined aqueduct, a hearth, or a perfume jar will always hold something in reserve, something that will not be brought forward in a given set of relations (Harman 2005; Olsen 2010). Things resist our attempts to articulate them. They are thus *irreducible to our representations of them.* This suggests that things are more than things-for-us; they hold and guard an otherness and integrity that require an attitude that does not subject them to sameness, but respects things for what they are in their own being (Benso 2000; Olsen 2012; chap. 9 below). This is not a restriction on interpretation, signification, or meaning; rather, and contrary to dominant isomorphic approaches in which things are reduced to human mouthpieces, to be sensitive to things' otherness and their utterances qua things may yield richer and far more compelling interpretations than those hitherto provided.

## THE ARGUMENT

This book is the result of a long collaborative effort between four archaeologists with different backgrounds, research experience, and interests. What we share is a sincere concern with things and an understanding of the fate and being of things as briefly outlined above. Thus we four find ourselves drawn together on these common grounds, in terms of what we do. Insofar as it is possible, we have emphasized what draws us together, the commonality found in our practices and modes of engagement. This gives us purchase on a series of important issues and questions to be addressed in this book.

The first question is why were things forgotten? Chapter 2 delves into the background to that amnesia regarding things in twentieth-century research by retracing how the estrangement from things (and various disciplinary practices) came about. As will be explored, the modern attitude toward things was characterized by ambiguity, entailing both contempt and desire. Ambiguity also positions things in the modern ontological landscape, whose topography has proved inhospitable to their needs for far too long.

There is a poetic irony in the fact that a discipline that assumes the importance of things for the study of the past has neglected them to such extent when recollecting its own past. Thus chapter 3 revisits the history of archaeological engagements to tell a difference story concerning the formation of archaeology as a recognizable ecology of practices, by which we are referring to archaeology as a specific community and a distinctive habitat (Stengers 2005, 2010). Here, as part of the diverse makeup of this habitat, the missing masses of showcases and diagrams, museum rooms and corridors, institutes and chairs, periodicals and diaries, theodolites and cameras, conference dinners and hotels bars, is reintroduced to form a thicker account of how archaeology became visible and normalized as a distinct disciplinary practice.

If what archaeologists claimed to do became the exact opposite of what they did, we take the opportunity in chapter 4, to dig deeper into the practices of excavation and fieldwork. Albeit archaeology's most distinctive feature, excavation has remained ambiguous in archaeologists' identity formation. Providing archaeology with its trivialized popular image of exploration and discoveries in remote places, excavation has been seen as a potential threat to "academic respectability." In chapter 4, we outline the distinctiveness of archaeological fieldwork and the role it has played in the formation of archaeology.

Chapter 5 attends to the question of documentation, and specifically the ways that visual media work to manifest things with fidelity. Moving through several case studies, from the chorographic anxieties of Sir Walter Scott to the mapping of the Teotihuacan metropolis, it builds an understanding of media, not as mimetic copies, but as active modes of engagement through which archaeologists co-produce the past.

Our media also afford the possibility of future action upon, and engagement with, the past, and this brings us to the question of memory practices. With the recognition that things present themselves in styles other than language or the visual, and are therefore not reducible to spoken or visual forms of translation, comes the responsibility to assess how we carry the material past into the future in terms of archival and digital practices. Chapter 6 sets out proactive, future-oriented practices; practices that underscore a new metrology for engaging archaeological media and highlight the importance of digital translation for manifesting things.

Working through Argos, Greece, and the wider area, chapter 7 shifts from a past held to exist apart from the present to a situation where pasts are understood as spatially coextensive. In putting to one side a modernist historicism where the past is situated as a series of successions and replacements, in favor of pasts as a gathered, multitemporal ensemble, we offer a different image of time as *percolation*.

Without the dominant character of the freestanding, autonomous human agent to hold the spotlight at the center stage of history, what then becomes its *subject*? In addressing this question, chapter 8 provides an alternative to both the myth of *homo faber* (thought proceeds action) and to the hylomorphic model of creation (form imposed upon matter) by taking a close look at the making of Fussell's Lodge, an earthen long barrow, and the design of an ancient Greek perfume jar. Two slogans capture much of our argument: we have always been cyborgs; and, making can belong to the most humble of things. Therefore, no entity has a monopoly on design. Chapter 8 culminates in a presentation of nine archaeological theses on design.

Throughout this book, we are making the case that things are not merely "enslaved in some wider system of differential meaning" (Harman 2002, 280), but possess their own capacities and inhabit their own compartments; in short, they have at least partial autonomy and transient essences. One radical implication of this proposal is to allow for an ethics encompassing things in their own being; that things are valuable in and of themselves. In this book's final chapter, we explore this issue and suggest *care* as a mode of getting on with things. Being a sensitive, responsive and nondiscriminatory way of attending to things, care involves far-ranging consequences for how we conceive of Stonehenge, an exploded bunker, rusted barbed wire, or a Greek perfume jar in terms of heritage and significance. Moreover, at excavation sites, in museums and laboratories all over the world, this mode has been essential to our disciplinary practices. It is more appropriate than ever to trust in our discipline's ability to confront any situation presented by things in our engagements with the material past. Thus, what is needed today, we conclude, is an archaeology that looks back at its own past with wonderment, approaches it without embarrassment or contempt, seeks to revitalize its important legacy, and folds this into a future vision for the care of things.

# CHAPTER 2

# The Ambiguity of Things

*Contempt and Desire*

Since the nineteenth century, industrial design and manufacture have delivered a mass of goods rooted in systems of technological knowledge fitted to an increasingly urbanized and global modernity. The constant offering of new products, combined with ever more effective marketing and advertising, have made the people of today seemingly more conscious about goods—about changes in design and fashion and the apparently urgent need to keep up with "the latest thing" in an age where the accelerating cycle of material replacement has outdated even last year's novelties. Still, despite the new awareness created by the irresistible attractiveness of the most recent iPhone, Acne jeans, or Mini Cooper, our everyday dealings with most things take place in a mode of inconspicuous familiarity. The bed, the fridge, the stove, the floor, the shower, the butter knife, the cup, the dishwasher, the car key, or the front door rarely become objects of conscious and reflexive concern. These quotidian realities stubbornly exist and perform as taken-for-granted elements of our tacit everydayness. Thus unless broken or missing, or in any other way interrupting our implicit expectation of service as usual, the demeanor of things is perhaps best characterized as one of shyness and invisibility. They largely escape our attention through their naïve givenness.

Curiously, in the study of society, too, there is a lack of concern with the masses of ordinary things securing our existence. Despite their indispensable presence, objects are largely ignored or confined to the margins when the "real" spectacles of life are accounted for in political narratives or sociological analyses. On the main social scene, they may provide a background, a context, a setting, but are otherwise denied any purpose or agency. "Much like sex during the Victorian period," Bruno Latour writes, "objects are nowhere to be said and everywhere to be felt. They exist, naturally, but they are never to be given a thought, a social thought" (Latour 2005, 73).

It is tempting to link things' marginality in the social sciences to their everyday mundanity. Being at the same time "the most obvious and the best hidden" (Lefebvre 1987, 9), such an intellectual amnesia may seem a predictable outcome. However, under scrutiny, the apparent obviousness of the argument is hard to sustain; what people are consciously aware of in everyday life does not determine the concerns of research. If so, it becomes difficult to explain why phenomena such as the unconscious, chromosomes, grammar, social structures, or germs have all become matters of great scientific or philosophical attraction. Without denying any connection between the two levels of taciturnity, this suggests that we probably have to dig deeper into the foundation of modern thinking, and even into the very political economy of this thinking, in order to understand the exile of things from twentieth-century social research.

In this chapter, we shall make such an attempt. By exposing what we consider significant intellectual layers of asymmetry, we shall try to explore the foundation of the paradox that things, despite their centrality in an industrial consumer society, despite being the most obvious, closest, and fundamental, even "what might be most distinctive and significant about our species" (Schiffer with Miller 1999, 2), have persistently been kept at arm's length when society was to be scrutinized and understood. There is more to this. Much as with Victorian sex, the modern attitude toward the thing has been ambiguous, simultaneously entailing ignorance and contempt, neglect and desire, knowledge and mystery. Thus, linked to the plot of silencing is a complementary story of how modernity also brought about a changed consciousness and ambiguous awareness of things. This ambivalence allowed for both a fear of things in their bewildering otherness and a redemptive longing for the atomized and humanized artifact, a longing for the comfort of things. In order to understand the fate of things in Western thinking, we also have to expose the roots of these ambiguities.

## THE IDEALIST LEGACY

Idealist models of mental cognition have had grounding impact on theories of human perception. According to a dominant conception, our experience of things is by and large a cognitive perception in which sensory inputs, mainly based on vision, are filtered and transformed by our mind and language. Ian Hacking has named such suspicion of all that is beyond or prior to thinking and discursive representation linguistic idealism (or the Richard Nixon doctrine), "only what is talked about exists; nothing has reality until it is spoken of, or written about" (Hacking 2001, 24). Another (but not identical) version of this doctrine is expressed in the famous phrase with which Ludwig Wittgenstein ends his *Tractatus:* "Whereof one cannot speak, thereof one must be silent" (1922). Taking this doctrine literally, an entity exists—and is rendered important to social analysis—only insofar as we as knowing subjects are consciously aware of it and are able to articulate this experience discursively.

Cartesian thinking constitutes a basal layer in the archaeology of idealism. This thinking left us with a notion of matter as passive and inert, while the human mind was seen as active and creative.[1] Matter and mind belong to separate realms, and the widening gulf between them became a never-ending source for modern epistemological inquiries about how (and if) our concepts of the world could correspond with the material reality "out there." The skeptical attitude that followed in the wake of Descartes's "methodological doubt" placed a seemingly irretrievable wedge between the material world and the human mind. The so-called external world, matter and nature, had no necessary immanent existence; actually, it may all prove to be a construction in our heads. If not unreal, matter was still mere surface without any powers or potential; all qualities and ideas about it have to be located in the thinking, self-aware subject (Matthews 2002; Thomas 2004a).

Immanuel Kant's efforts to reveal the a priori structures of experience also had a great impact on these issues for much of modern thinking. According to Kant, the thing in itself (*das Ding an sich*) cannot be grasped directly. Although things around us clearly exist, they are inaccessible to us as objects of experience in their own essence. Only things as they appear, as *phenomena,* are knowable "objects of sense"; we do not know "a thing in itself . . . in its internal constitution, but only know

---

1. This is what Alfred North Whitehead called the "bifurcation of nature" (1964); see discussion in chapter 8.

its appearances, viz., the way in which our senses are affected by this unknown something" (Kant 2001 [1783], 53, § 32). Kant's denial of any direct encounter with the material world meant that we understand the thing primarily in the way it is formed by ourselves, that is, by what we supply with our own thinking or reason (Andersson 2001, 81–93).

With things in themselves largely out of reach, they are, for Kant, shut off from our immediate experience and thus expelled from the knowable world. Only in their abstracted condition as objects of science could they still be admitted (Andersson 2001, 130; Olsen 2007).[2] This ontology denied any direct access to things and the rapports between them, and it later surfaced as a skeptical attitude whereby materiality is treated with suspicion and denied anything more than a provisional or transcendental existence. Moreover, creative engagement with the world became an asymmetrical enterprise leaving no role to the qualities and competences that could be said already to *dwell* in materials and nature, which humans in turn helped to release or make manifest in an act of co-production. Creativity, influence, and power became the current rare commodities, which only humans in themselves possess. The modern birth of humanity as the creative master subject coincided with, and in many ways presupposed, the simultaneous death of an active and purposeful material world. In short, this passage left us with a conception of matter as formless and basically meaningless (Latour 1993; Andersson 2001; Thomas 2004a).

TECHNOLOGY AND EVIL THINGS

That things became conspicuously present in the mundane world a short century after Kant ironically did not help their reputation. On the contrary, to most philosophers and social theorists the mass-produced, mass-distributed, and mass-consumed object of the late nineteenth century was a sign of an illusory world conveying a deceptive image of the world as thing-made (Brown 2003). Proliferating in the ruined landscape left by the onslaught of capitalism and industrialization, things, consumer goods, and machines, these cold and inhuman technologies,

---

2. This forms a basis for the rift between phenomenology—the philosophy of appearances—and science, where according to Heidegger, the world is progressively reduced to a shallow presence, whereby the interactions between menhirs and rain, goats and grass, are abandoned to the "calculating gaze" of the natural sciences (Heidegger 1994).

FIGURE 2.1. Rows of finished jeeps churned out in mass production at the Willys-Overland facility in Toledo, Ohio, in preparation for the invasion of Nazi-occupied Europe. Photo by Dmitri Kessel, June 1, 1942. Getty Images #50598573.

became the incarnation of our inauthentic, estranged, and alienated modern being (fig. 2.1).

Philosophers, social theorists, artists, and writers of the nineteenth and early twentieth century grew increasingly concerned with this process of withering and change: how mass production, factories, and machines replaced craftsmanship and manual labor, and how social relationships, including labor and exchange, become increasingly mediated by the "emptiness" of money and commodities. The firmly rooted and reassuring life worlds—that is, as in romanticism more generally, the rural life world of the peasant—were vanishing. To paraphrase Heidegger, the "monstrous" being of modern technology turned the world into a "gigantic petrol station"; in place of things social or "worldly" content, "the object-character of technological domination spreads itself over the earth ever more quickly, ruthlessly, and completely" (Heidegger 1971, 112).

Heidegger's conception of modern technology and mass culture typifies the nostalgia and pessimism to which modernity gave rise. The desertion of the countryside, the vanishing of village communities, family bonds, and traditional customs and values, created a sense of loss, of decay and death—also fostering historicism and projects of conservation. Losing the "nearness" of being, authentic "dwelling" became a nostalgic project—the caring for the heritage of the homeland and the people (Heidegger 1993; Young 2002). Such attitudes contributed to a kind of imperative of shortage based upon an arbitrary contrast between the authentic, singular, and unique as against the mimetic, mass-produced, and pervasive.

Similar anti-technological concerns were raised throughout the first and mid twentieth century by thinkers as different as Horkheimer, Adorno, Popper, Sartre, and Mumford. They all shared the conviction that the technology that was supposed to be our servant and improve our lives had instead become our master, depriving us of all freedom. This could be combined with an academic and elitist preference for high culture over popular culture rooted in mass-produced goods. Science and engineering were treated with intellectual suspicion or contempt, something that threatened humanity and which caused social theorists and philosophers increasingly to define creativity, emancipation, and authentic being as what escapes materiality. As in Sir Karl Popper's "nightmare of physical determinism": "It is a nightmare because it asserts that the whole world with everything in it is a large automaton, and that we are nothing but little cogwheels, or at best sub-automata, within it. It thus destroys, in particular, the idea of creativity" (Popper 1972, 222). Things were dangerous in their deceptive appearance; they were a threat against authentic human and social values. Whether intended or not, as humanism's other, things came to play the role of the villain, thus lending justification to them being ignored by disciplines studying what were seen as genuine social and cultural practices (Olsen 2003, 2010).

## AUTHENTICITY AND FAKES, CONTEMPT AND DESIRE

In addition to this technological menace, modernist thinkers also came to express a distaste for the inauthentic, the artificial. Mass-produced replicas and consumer goods replaced "good things"; evil things were substituted for things with "soul." Heidegger's care and concern, as in his famous essay "The Origin of the Work of Art," seem increasingly directed toward art and gentle things, the work of *poiesis*, while ordinary equipment is seen as determined by usefulness, part of the serviceable *Bestand,* or stock (a standing reserve), in which matter is used and "used up. It disappears into usefulness" (Heidegger 1971: 44).

This concern with technology and mass production in "the age of mechanical reproduction" (Walter Benjamin's formulation) gave rise in European thinking to a new and ambiguous awareness of things from the angle of shortage or loss: rooted in a past slipping away and dying, the real and authentic became increasingly scarce in their supply. The sense of this was well captured by the German poet Rainer Maria Rilke in a letter dating from 1925:

> To our grandparents, a "house," a "well," a familiar steeple, even their own clothes, their cloak *still* meant infinitely more, were infinitely more intimate— almost everything a vessel in which they found something human already there. . . . Now everything is intruding, from America, empty indifferent things, sham things, *dummies of life.* . . . A house, as the Americans understand it, an American apple or a winestock from over there, have *nothing* in common with the house, the fruit, the grape into which the hope and thoughtfulness of our forefathers had entered.[3]

Typifying this consciousness was a concern with mass-produced goods swarming the mundane world, providing ordinary people with affordable replicas of objects and materials otherwise reserved for the few and rich. The new and scandalous "preference for the unreal" became diagnostic of what the Austrian culture historian Egon Friedell (1937) termed "the common and principal era of material fraud." This preference manifested itself in a wide range of fakes: "white-washed tin presents itself as marble, paper mâché as rosewood, plaster as shiny alabaster. . . . A splendid Gutenberg bible is revealed as a sewing box . . . the butter knife is a Turkish dagger, the ashtray a Prussian helmet . . . the thermometer a pistol" (Friedell 1937, quoted after Christensen 1993, 27, our translation).

Another symptom of this concern for the vanishing real was a particular aversion against the new materials and designs that started to make an impact on the built environment especially from the nineteenth century on (fig. 2.2). Intellectuals and politicians increasingly complained about inauthentic architecture, the vulgar iron-and-glass arcades, exhibition halls, factories, and bridges constructed by engineers (Benjamin 2002, 33, Buck-Morss 1999, 127–29). Iron, for example, was distrusted by some architects because it was not immediately present in nature.

3. Rainer Maria Rilke, *Briefe aus Muzot: 1921 bis 1926,* ed. Ruth Sieber-Rilke and Carl Sieber (Leipzig: Insel-Verlag, 1935), 335–36, quoted in Heidegger 1971, 110–11.

FIGURE 2.2. A forest of wells, rigs, and derricks at the Signal Hill oil fields near Long Beach, California. Photo by Andreas Feininger, December 31, 1943. Getty Images #92925999.

Thus, when used structurally it was frequently faced with stone. Another argument used to denounce these constructions was that they lacked "ruin value," they could not produce gentle ruins of the kind left us from classical antiquity (Yablon 2009). John Ruskin, for example, refused to count iron constructions ("the iron roofs and pillars of our railway stations") as architecture, partly because the builders did not have true command over iron's "modes of decay" (2001 [1849], 68–69). Nearly a century later, the Marxist Ernst Bloch likewise claimed that the products of the machine age were unable to acquire an aura of antiquity: they "cannot grow old but only rot in the course of the years" (quoted in Yablon 2009, 8).

In *The Philosophy of Money* (1978 [1900]), the sociologist Georg Simmel sharply identified this ambiguity as a defining characteristic of the modern attitude to things. Technology and mass production were seen as depriving things of their social meaning, and thus fuelling hostility toward "mere" things, but at the same time, there was a growing interest in and fascination for genuine objects, Simmel noted: "a deep yearning to give things a new importance, a deeper meaning, a value of their own . . . the lively motions in the arts, the search for new styles, for style as such, symbolism and even theosophy are all symptoms of the longing for a new and more perceptible significance of things" (Simmel 1978, 404). To Simmel, however, this new interest in things was superficial and fragmentary, and actually served as an escape from the pestering of the present material world ("The flight from the present is made easier"). Thus the modern interest in exotic art, in antiquities, in turning objects into art, is a redeeming and "comforting stimulation for weakened nerves": "the present vividly felt charm for the fragment, the mere allusion, the aphorism, the symbol, . . . they place us at a distance from the substance of things; they speak to us 'as from afar'; reality is touched not with direct confidence but with fingertips that are immediately withdrawn. . . . In all this we discover an emotional trait . . . the agoraphobia: the fear of coming into too close a contact with objects" (Simmel 1978, 474).

In a similar way, another German intellectual, Walter Benjamin, explored how modernity came to impede this fundamental change in the conception of things. One of his concerns was how a "mimetic" and "auratic" capacity was giving way to a sublimated and intimate attitude. While the mimetic attitude implied a respect for things in their otherness, in their auratic own-ness, the modern gaze was isomorphic, subjecting them to intimacy and sameness (Benjamin 2003, 255–56). In his critical writings of 1930s, Benjamin was targeting this dominant modern conception of materiality, especially as displayed in the *intérieur* of the late-nineteenth-century bourgeois home. As a reaction against (or retreating from) the emerging cityscapes and the "cold and inhuman" works of engineers, the bourgeois home became a sheltered arena of aesthetization, intimacy, and the sublimation of tradition. Staged as inventory in this domesticated sphere, things had completely lost their otherness and individuality. They were sentenced to serfdom and became nothing but labels of privacy, faithfully mirroring their owner: "[t]he etui-man *[das Etui-Mensch]* looks for comfort, and the case *[etui]* is the quintessence. The inside of the case is the velvet-lined trace that he has imprinted on the world" (Benjamin 1999a, 542). In a wonderful passage, Benjamin writes of how modern people, "chilled in a chilly environment" (1996, 779), try to overcome their material estrangement: "Warmth is ebbing from things. Objects of daily use gently but insistently repel us. Day by day, in overcoming the sum of secret resistances. . . . we have an immense labor to perform. We must compensate for their coldness with our warmth if they are not to freeze us to death, and handle their spiny forms with infinite dexterity if we are not to bleed to death" (453).

## SILENCING THINGS: THE PROBLEM OF THE FETISH

It can be argued forcefully that the modern social and humanist turn against mass-produced goods and technology seriously contributed to things' nonsocial status. Although directed at mass-produced, inauthentic "evil things," this movement fuelled an implicit suspicion of the material, of things more generally. A very influential expression of this originates from Karl Marx's writings on alienation and reification, especially as developed in the notion of "commodity fetishism."

Fetishism is a concept that emerged in Western discourse primarily as a way of describing "primitive" religious practices, in which stones and statues were worshipped and treated as "real" gods. This phenomenon, which Western travelers and anthropologists saw as a "fallacious substitution," was developed by Marxist and psychoanalytical thinking into a more general conception of fetishism as misrepresentation or displacement. With fetishism came a "misunderstanding" by which qualities that can properly be ascribed only to the realm of humans were attributed to things (Christensen 1993, 39–41; Pels 1998).

In *Das Kapital*, Marx argues that the capitalist economy fetishized the commodity by ascribing to it an abstract intrinsic value (or exchange value). Operating in support of a wider bourgeois ideology, this fetishism masked the fact that the "real" value of goods stemmed from the social labor invested in their production. Things (as commodities) appear to have a value of their own, resulting purely from their circulation in a market. Thus they are alienated from their producers; they are divorced from the human toil and the social relations that gave rise to them through their production (Marx 1975, 324). This commodity fetishism is symptomatic of a more general process of reification or objectification in capitalist society in which human relations and cultural forms increasingly appear in the form of object relations. This fetishism works in a dual way by which social phenomena take on the appearance of things, as well as inanimate things are treated as if they had social qualities (Held 1980, 220).

Thus despite its iconic association with (historical) materialism, and the immense sociohistorical importance it assigned to ready-to-hand technology (as forces of production), Marxism paradoxically also came to fuel an aversion for things in modern social theory. Although primarily intended as a critique of how things lost their social value in the capitalist mode of production, Marxism de facto ended up providing social theory with an evocatively negative vocabulary that strongly contributed to their stigmatization: objectification, reification, and "instrumental reason." Much as a consequence, most later critics of mass culture and technology have tended "to assume that the relation of persons to objects is in some way vicarious, fetishistic or wrong; that primary concern should lie with direct social relations and 'real people,'" Daniel Miller observes (1987, 11).

Ironically, this critique joined forces with a long-standing bourgeois contempt in academia, and especially in the humanities, for dirt, manual labor, and working-class life in general. Academia was an arena for pure thought, to be kept apart, distinct, from the repugnant filth of trivial labor and production (a distinction even underlying the divisions of labor in archaeology and the separation of the field from the laboratory, the archive, the study (Berggren and Hodder 2003; Shanks and McGuire 1996; Witmore 2004b). Only aestheticized material, fine art, the exotic—and the book—were allowed access, keeping oily, smelly objects at arm's length (cf. Beek 1989, 95). The aversion to treating technological and applied disciplines and engineering as "real" academic disciplines rather than, at best, professional fields, is another aspect of this story.

## FORGETTING THE LESSON OF THINGS

At the same time as philosophers, writers, and intellectuals at large began to express their concern with an objectified, monetary and technology-driven modern society, things were excluded from being significant source material in anthropology and the social sciences. There is a striking coincidence in timing between the general intellectual reaction toward alienating machinery and mass production and the first cry against things as meaningful sources of social inquiry.

One powerful trajectory of this turn against things is seen in the development of British anthropology, which by the 1920s had reinvented itself as "social anthropology," a discipline concerned with processes and structures beyond and mostly inaccessible through things. Societies and cultures were henceforth to be accessed directly through the new disciplinary imperative of dialogue and participant observation—ethnography (Miller 1987, 111; cf. Kuper 1978). Things were no longer assigned any role in mediating the relationship between anthropologists and the cultures studied. Increasingly concerned with the reasons for the natives' "otherness" (i.e., that behind their seemingly strange and obscure habits and rituals, there was a "practical reason," an economic or social rationality), social frameworks needed full, immediate dedication. Things became superfluous or at best illustrations. "It led to the position that one should really be studying the framework itself (the social context = society)," Marilyn Strathern writes. "The artefacts were merely illustration. For if one sets up social context as the frame of reference in relation to which meanings are to be elucidated, then explicating that frame of reference obviates or renders the illustrations superfluous: they become reflections of meanings produced elsewhere" (1990, 38).

A very different development, but with similar consequences, took place in American cultural anthropology. As a key figure in the latter, Franz Boas came to manifest this new distrust of things. Whereas earlier in his career he had been deeply involved in collections management and museum anthropology, he began by 1905 to abandon these projects. One reason given by Bill Brown is that "he had become increasingly convinced that the most important elements of culture were irreducible to artifacts, that anthropological facts could never become artifactual—that the cultural Thing, let us say, was too intangible to be found in things" (Brown 2002, 118).

In this context, where the social (and soon the political and ethical) increasingly became flagged as a categorical imperative within the social and human sciences, studying things per se became a task in need of justification and a source of embarrassment, a reactionary heritage of a mindless antiquarianism that survived in the dusty storerooms of museums. In short, it left little honor for those practitioners within the discipline of things. And gradually a change could be discerned also in archaeological rhetoric: the material was only a means to reach something else, something more important—cultures and societies, the lives of past peoples, the Indian behind the artifact (see, e.g., Wheeler 1954, v; Braidwood 1958, 734). Social scientists, however, remained rather unimpressed with the attempts to reach these desired subjects of inquiry. Even after archaeology had become "new" in the anthropological turn of the 1960s, Edmund Leach, the leading figure of British social anthropology, for example, continued to lecture that in the "last analysis" archaeologists should be "concerned with people rather than with things" (Leach 1973, 768). Indeed, there may have been a certain tendency of granting "too much independence to the empirical world" over which "idealism had a nice polemical virtue" (Latour 1999, 147), as vividly expressed in the anthropologist Irven DeVore's harsh denunciation of archaeological practice: "In the past we were presented with lithic industries which, to judge by their descriptions, were copulating, hybridizing, evolving, adapting and producing offspring" (1968, 346). Still, the trump card of fetishism seemed always too close at hand. Thus when Daniel Miller in 1987 found it necessary to express his moral contempt of approaches to modern material culture in processual archaeology, fetishism became an argument beyond verification or explanation: "Such studies exemplify the kind of fetishism to which material culture studies are always prone, when people are superseded as the subject of investigation by objects, and become essentially labels for their movement or pattern" (1987, 143).

## THE FALLACY OF HUGGING A TREE

With the intellectual turn against things, it is important to understand why theories of fetishism were so smoothly and complacently accepted within modern thinking and why things, more generally, could be treated with such distrust. However, this is hardly sufficient for fully understanding the fate of things in modern social research. To take further steps toward a more comprehensive explanation, we have to ask a few basic questions: Why is it a priori wrong to blur the boundary between humans and things? Why is it a misunderstanding to ascribe personality and identity to things? What is the ontological justification for the persistent idea that action, influence, and power are qualities that only humans possess?

As hinted at in the beginning of this chapter, the answers to these questions are intimately linked to a wider effective history of the displacement of things in Western thinking since the seventeenth century (cf. Olsen 2010). The hermeneutics of suspicion that developed in the wake of Descartes's methodological doubt led to the perception of an all-too-significant difference between nonhumans and humans. In what follows, we shall try to show how this significant difference somehow predestined things to their subsequent intellectual dismissal and silencing.

However, in order to understand this difference as intellectually constructed rather than ontologically given, it might be useful to confront it with other ways of conceptualizing the world. Numerous ethnographic examples illustrate how peoples in different settings refer to animals as kindred beings with whom people can have social relationships (see, e.g., Hallowell 1960; Fijn 2011; Alberti and Bray 2009). Among the

Sámi of northern Fenno-Scandinavia, for example, as with most other circumpolar peoples, the brown bear was treated as a personalized being that understood human discourse and dispositions and was addressed as a relative. The hunting and consumption of the bear involved elaborate rituals terminating with human-like burials for the deceased bear (Fjell-ström 1981 [1755]; Myrstad 1996). Likewise, on their return from the mountains to winter pastures in the northern Swedish forests, the rein-deer herders are reported to have hugged and greeted the pine tree. An ethnographer observed a young Sámi girl hugging a big trunk saying, "Good day, pine, I greet you from the mountain willow" (Demant-Hatt 1913, 84). The Sámi also ascribed life to their drums (which were as-signed life-cycle rituals) and their supposedly "fetishized" stone "gods" (*sieidis*) (Kalstad 1997; Schanche 2000; Price 2002; Hansen and Olsen 2004). Nonhumans of various kinds, such as reindeer and lynx, drums and hearths, birch and alder, were different from humans, of course, but they were not considered as belonging to two distinct spheres. Personal-ity and identity were not regarded as exclusively human characteristics.

As discussed in detail by Tim Ingold (2000), hunter-gatherers rarely invoke absolute distinctions such as mind/matter or culture/nature in their being-in-the-world. Neither do they relate to landscape or nature as an external, "natural" world to be domesticated or embodied. In other words, they do not regard themselves as spiritual, cultural subjects struggling with an alien object world of nature. Quite simply, the abso-lute distinction between spirit and matter, culture and nature, does not have a place in their thought or praxis. Anthropologists, historians, and social scientists acknowledge these attitudes as expressions of native be-lief, of course, and affirm this cultural otherness. However, interpreting this otherness nearly always implies the application of some sort of sus-picious hermeneutics by bringing native thought to court, pitted against a preconceived (modern) ontology of how the world "really is" (that is, divided into nature versus culture). Thus analysis becomes an act of bifurcation and "purification" (Latour 1993), a sorting of the muddled worlds into the appropriate categories. Statements and practices that blur or cross the dividing line are interpreted and all too often shrugged off as "metaphorical" utterances, most commonly conceived of as social and symbolic appropriations of nature. The differences are to be found in disparate social groups, but the world is a singular underlying unity.

Following Ingold, such demystifying analysis usually involves argu-ments like this: "primitive people" make sense of their relation with things and the natural world by drawing on metaphors from their social life and their capacities as humans. They use their social experience to model their relation with the nonhuman world by which ecological or "thingly" relations appear as social ones (Ingold 2000; cf. Godelier 1977 for an illustrative analysis). Simple peoples themselves are, of course, unaware of their ontological blunders. They have not realized that their social relationship to nature is based on an illusion. However, as Ingold proposes:

> notice how the entire argument is predicated upon an initial ontological dualism between the intentional worlds of human subjects, and the object world of material things—or in brief, between society and nature [or rather societies and nature]. It is only by virtue of holding these to be separate that the one can be said to furnish the model for the other. The implication, however, is that the claim of the people themselves to inhabit but one world, encompassing relations with both human and non-human components of the environment on a similar footing, is founded upon an illusion—one that stems from their inability to recognise where the reality ends and its schematic representation begins. (2000, 44)

Thus the need of the anthropological analyst to draw the line, start purifying, and sort out the categories for their subjects of study (see Henare, Holbraad, and Wastell 2007). On the other hand, no suspicion arises when people establish intimate relations among themselves. These are social (or subsocial, i.e., economic, sexual, political, etc.). So we have one set of relations that are taken for granted as real, authentic, and honest; another set that are false, inauthentic, and delusional. The falseness seems to arise when we transgress a certain border, between the "us" and the "it," projecting relations prescribed for one realm onto another.

Why has this boundary become so obvious, so ontologically secure, that analyses can be grounded in them?

## A DIVIDED WORLD

In his manifesto *We Have Never Been Modern* (1993), Bruno Latour provides some suggestions that we find compelling. While modernity has been celebrated as both the origin and the triumph of humanism, as the birth of the human and the thinking subject (cf. Foucault 1973), there has been less talk about its less desired offspring: the simultaneous birth of things and "nature." Following Latour, the "birth of man" (and it is indeed gendered) presupposed the construction of—and simultaneous separation from—the nonhuman, in other words, it made imperative a fundamental divide. From this moment on, the human and the nonhuman were relegated to different ontological realms, which were assessed by different disciplinary fields. On the one hand, there are human and social sciences concerned with humans-among-themselves, and on the other, natural sciences studying the inanimate object world (Latour 1993, 13ff.). By this split, the power, interests, and politics of humans come to be placed at one pole, while knowledge about and over objects and nonhumans was placed at the other.

According to Latour, this first great divide caused another significant distinction, namely, that between "ourselves" (i.e., the moderns) and the "others" (i.e., the nonmoderns or premoderns). As we saw above, the premoderns did not understand the first distinction, but mixed everything together in an appalling stew of people and things, cultures and nature. It is because we are able to distinguish between people and things, cultures and nature, that we differ from them (Latour 1993, 97–103). Latour's cardinal point (drawing on the work of Serres, Whitehead, and others), is of course that this split reflects nothing but the modern "discrepancy between self-representation and practice" (Latour 2003, 38). The modern condition is more than anything a meshwork of hybrid relations and translations between humans and nonhumans; actually, the mess has never been greater! Thus—and this is the very paradox of this trope—we have never been modern. In other words, acknowledging the "symmetry" implied by all societies being mixtures of natures-cultures, humans and nonhumans, also discloses another principle of symmetry: that there is no ontological distinction between the constitution of our worlds and those of the "others" (Latour 1993, 103–6).

Still, the distinction between nature and society persists. Not because it is an ontological constant according to which knowledge or the sciences are differentiated, but because modernity and the various sciences continually create, maintain, and defend the opposition. Such distinctions are built into our very divisions of labor, into our categories of analysis. Scientific practice, in its modernist form, is thus also a purifying practice, in which everything that exists has to be placed within two distinct ontological boxes, categorized either as things or humans, objects or subjects. The more academic writing and being become enmeshed with things, the more exiled things become from intellectual discourses. As noted by Latour (2003), the true originality of the moderns was not to do away with things and hybrids, but rather to estrange themselves from their own practices, an estrangement that allowed them to do the exact opposite of what they were saying. It is only when you are so convinced that nature and society do not mix that you can mix them so thoroughly as to produce the mess in which we are stewing today. This was only possible by applying the same acts of purification that anthropologists have used to cleanse the illusions of those "others" who claim to inhabit a muddled world—encompassing relations with humans, animals, and things on an equal footing. In other words, the modern attitude consists of splitting the mixtures apart, in order to extract from them what came from culture (the social, the mind, the spirit) and what came from nature (Latour 1993, 78). The outcomes are then regarded as the starting blocks.

This desire for an immediate world emptied of its mediators has indeed assigned things an ambiguous position within the modern constitution. They are located outside the human sphere of power, interest, and politics—and still are not properly nature. Although prescribed for the nonhuman side, what came to be labeled as material culture ended up not occupying either of the two positions prescribed by the modern constitution; it was neither culture nor nature. And this, in all its simplicity, brings us to the core of the banishment of things from the social sciences: being a mixture of culture-nature, a work of translation, a work that increasingly mediates such relations, material culture became matter out of place—part of the "excluded middle" (see also Grosz 2002, 91–94) or rather that which was separated off by a second divide, as we shall show below (Latour 1993).

This exclusion—and the associated dangers of fetishism—might also be profitably related to the concept of the *abject* (Kristeva 1982). The abject is normally associated with the ambiguous border zone between (or rather outside of this separation altogether) the "me" and "not-me," a sign of ourselves as distributed and composite beings (or cyborgs), and thus something that the subject seeks to expel in order to achieve an independent identity (Brooker 1999, 1; Butler 1993, 243). Things, especially in their untamed and uncanny mode, may be seen as typifying the abject, leaving space only for the singular, aestheticized, and privatized objects offering comfort and consolation.

## CONCLUSION: ABJECT THINGS

This chapter has largely been concerned with explaining why things were neglected and ultimately forgotten among those studying societies and cultures. Some clarifications are, however, needed. It is, of course, not true that the academy—and public discourse in general—has forgotten things all together. As with the "folk" level, some objects have always been allowed to dwell and perform well within these discursive formations. However, with the partial exception of a few disciplines, they allow only for objects of a certain kind—usually objects that are emancipated from the networks of everyday trivia, dirt, and work. Thus, objects of art, conspicuous objects, have always been widely welcomed, talked about and discussed; although the opinions on their capacity to inform social science and humanistic discourses may vary greatly.

Although Simmel's diagnosis might be too harsh, that the attraction of these decontextualized, aestheticized objects reflected a fear of coming into too close contact with things, there is still little doubt that emerging modern technology, "empty indifferent Americanized" consumer goods, the iron and concrete of modern cityscapes, caused little but contempt in hegemonic intellectual environments. Perceived as *Gestell*, Heidegger's term for the monstrous and alienating technological framing of the world (Heidegger 1993, 325–32), modern material culture came to play the villain in academic and public discourses from the late nineteenth century on, a complacent and pervasive denunciation also based upon an all too arbitrary and socially biased contrast between the unique and mass-produced. Stigmatized as humanism's other, things seemed utterly unfit to inform the disciplines studying genuine social and cultural practices.

However, their exile was based on a more profound and grounding conception of things and nature as the abject of the modern human. The "Great Divide" launched by the modernist thought regime created an abyss that things were never assumed or permitted to cross. Social relations became by definition relations among human subjects and any attempts to include drums, reindeer, and birch trees were seen as highly suspicious. Such inappropriate attitudes were either condemned as an expression of fetishism or to be purified as primitive, backward, and archaic metaphorical statements and symbolic appropriations of nature. Things were relegated to the other side but were constantly and increasingly mingling and mixing with people. Thus they became a problematic and ambiguous category within the modern regime, an abject that blurred the boundary. Not properly situated, neither in nature nor in culture, they became matter-out-of-place, predestined to banishment. Despite the proliferation of hybrids in its midst and all nonhumans being enrolled in the very fabric of modern society, the modern regime came to acknowledge properly only those entities that could be firmly situated. In other words, the modern regime acknowledged entities as dwelling either in culture or in nature (Latour 1993). This was the prescribed fate of those entities that were inscribed with an unfortunate but pertinent and seemingly contradictory label: material culture.

# CHAPTER 3

# Engagements with Things

*The Making of Archaeology*

Histories of archaeology are typically compiled around key figures, traditions of thought or wider social processes. These histories, often rich in biographical details, philosophical influences, and social context, have provided insights into how and why archaeology came into being and on its subsequent development and configuration in the various parts of the world. These are all important and effective accounts, and they have been constitutive for the way we understand our disciplinary past. Thus we do not seek in this chapter to abolish the many excellent stories of archaeology. Our objective is rather to enlarge, nuance, and complicate these stories by addressing issues that are rarely accounted for when the disciplinary past is narrated.

A common trope, although one encountered with more frequency earlier, has been to present the birth of archaeology and its subsequent development as primarily the product of gifted individuals; of great minds struggling for truth and order (Daniel 1950, 1967, 1976; Klindt-Jensen 1975; cf. the intellectual genealogy of O'Brien, Lyman, and Schiffer 2005). Clearly, some scholars deserve more credit than others, but at the same time, we should inquire into the conditions that make possible the achievements of these key figures. What made their ideas and practices successful? Which allies were mobilized; what alliances were forged along the paths to such achievement? Another and increasingly popular approach has been to explain the states of archaeological affairs as intimately related to social and political conditions and needs.

Again, this perspective has produced a number of studies concerning the dynamics of scientific engagements and the often implicit conditions grounding them (e.g. Trigger 2006 [1989]; Patterson 1995). However, when social and political macro-processes have been positioned as the primary movers, we should ask for the utterly specific interlocutors and connections that remain cloaked underneath such processes. How, for example, do the methods of stratigraphical excavation, sectioning a ditch, and seriation, the use of graph paper, cameras, and Munsell-color codes, and the interest in experiments and reconstructions relate to often overdramatized enterprises such as nationalism, colonialism, and imperialism (cf. Diaz-Andreu 2007)?

We propose a different perspective. Without questioning either the acumen of the "big men" or the "social" context that contributed to their success, we seek rather to bring into view the many ordinary men and women with pencils, maps, trowels, and tripods in their hands (Callon and Law 1997). On the ground, hidden beneath the sociopolitical canopy, are humble things and instruments, networked people, libraries, funding agencies, review panels, professional organizations, museum magazines, collections, laboratories, and continually renegotiated standards of what constitutes scholarly and scientific knowledge. The aim of this chapter is to suggest how a recognition of these cloaked crowds may enable us to produce richer alternative accounts of how the discipline of things came into being, and how it has been stabilized into the ecology of practices (scientific and grounded) now recognized worldwide as archaeology. Needless to say, this chapter itself is not an attempt at creating the exhaustive account necessary to meet these aims. Given the scope of this book, our goal is the far more modest one of drawing attention to the many things involved in the making and "ontologizing" of the archaeological discipline.[1]

## ARTIFACTS, MUSEUMS, AND THE BIRTH OF ARCHAEOLOGY

How and when did archaeology as a discipline come into being? The term "archaeology," as Alain Schnapp has pointed out, was increasingly

---

1. For further work exemplifying more symmetrical accounts of archaeological history, see Lucas in press; Olsen and Svestad 1994; Shanks and Witmore 2010b; Witmore 2012a; Witmore and Buttrey 2008; also consider essays in Schlanger and Nordbladh 2008.

used in the first half of the nineteenth century to refer to the study of the material past, a shift in terminology from what had hitherto been labeled "antiquarianism," corresponding to "a modification of the role and purpose of knowledge of the past" (1996, 275). More precisely, according to Schnapp, the defining criteria for archaeology rested upon a trinity of combined principles—typology, technological evolution, and stratigraphy. While it is difficult to overstate the importance of the relations between these key principles as discussed by Schnapp, we suggest an answer to this question is that archaeology came into being when it became "visible" as a distinct "ecology of practices."

The notion of an "ecology of practices," as discussed by Isabelle Stengers (2005, 2010), implies a particular community and its unique habitat. It complements the Foucauldian notion of structures of discourse that enable the production of archaeological knowledge (as discussed in Shanks 1992 and 1996). In this chapter, for example, it encapsulates those infrastructures (museum collections, map rooms, spaces of interaction, libraries, laboratories), instruments, colleagues, vocabulary, media, and other diverse interlocutors, all of which are drawn to and thus gathered around a particular matter of concern. Archaeological practices are idiosyncratic and cannot be defined as just any other or indeed held to be derivative of other scientific practices. By passing into a new milieu, they become something else. An ecology of practices is more than descriptive. It intervenes. It aims, as Stengers puts it, "at the construction of new 'practical identities' for practices, that is, new possibilities for them to be present, in other words to connect" (2005, 186).

Visibility of archaeology as a discrete ecology of practices was achieved at that moment when it had acquired sufficient mass, density, and form, and had become properly networked and coherent. It is difficult to give a more precise date for this formation other than to say that it emerged at some point during the nineteenth century. True, burial mounds had been excavated, archaeological material collected, museums established, and monuments described and published prior to the professionalization of archaeology as a discipline. Even the Old World chronological imperative of a three-age system had already been suggested (Klindt-Jensen 1975). However, in contrast to these earlier discourses and institutions, archaeology, as an array of disciplinary practices, relies on a strong and increasingly self-confirming system of manifestations, requirements, skills, accountabilities, and modes of engagement.

For example, the vital difference between the earlier proposals for a three-age prehistory and the system that Christian Jürgensen Thomsen and his colleagues constructed was that the latter was not just a suggestion, an idea based on scattered observations and textual evidence (Jensen 1992; Olsen and Svestad 1994). Thomsen's three-age system could be demonstrated and proved by bringing in the masses of archaeological evidence that convincingly *spoke to the eyes.* It was immensely better constructed and networked than earlier proposals, an achievement made possible by the *centers of calculation* that had emerged in Copenhagen and in other metropolises where things and inscriptions were accumulating (Schnapp 1997).

Based on a new trust in the artifacts themselves and the material evidence from excavations, archaeology emerged as something distinct and partly in a long-standing opposition to disciplines based on textual accounts (cf. Momigliano 1950). As Thomsen stated in a letter to a Swedish friend in 1825: "For those who have derived their knowledge and their entire learning from books *alone* I have no sympathy. I have seen only too often what *utterly absurd errors* they fall into when they must put their wisdom to practical use. So, my good friend, let us by all means buy books and read them attentively, but never neglect to look with our own eyes" (Thomsen 1820, quoted in Klindt-Jensen 1975, 51; emphasis in the original). Things were more than illustrations of biblical genealogies and histories laid out in advance. They become a solid and unique source of knowledge about a deep past out of reach of textual evidence. Such a material-based knowledge of the past required masses of material, far more than the previous displays of selected specimens in cabinets of curiosity and *Wunder-* and *Kunstkammer* (Pomian 1990). The radical novelty of Thomsen's proposal was that it was implemented with great quantities of material gathered at the newly established Royal Museum for Nordic Antiquities. In his lecture on typology to the society for Scandinavian naturalists in 1898, Oscar Montelius thus emphasized the need of large collections in order to enable "correct results." He pointed out that both the natural scientist and the archaeologist had "to gather as large a quantity of material as possible and to arrange it so that the results are immediately apparent" (Montelius 1900, 267–68; our translation). Correct results, however, also required professional practitioners, a specific milieu, and exhibition space that allowed for the proper positioning of the displays vis-à-vis the observers. The material had to be ordered "in the right way by an experienced hand" (Montelius 1900, 268). Only in a modern museum was this possible.

FIGURE 3.1. Stone Age exhibition at the State Historical Museum, Stockholm, 1903.

The birth of archaeology was thus closely connected with the dawn of the modern museum. Moreover, it was through the emergence of modern disciplinary museums that prehistory and the deep past—the archaeological subject matter par excellence—were made accessible as something concrete and tangible. Although imagined by scholars and individuals, "prehistory" did not exist as any conceptual or tangible entity prior to the nineteenth century. Now even the distant past was made manifest. This manifestation was not only facilitated by the exhibited artifacts and their spatio-temporal ordering, but also by the very materiality of the museum buildings themselves. Prehistory was made accessible and public, it could be walked around, seen, pointed at, and spoken about. From the corridors to the cases, within these confined spaces the trajectories of the past, the sequences, and typological order became normalized and self-evident (Olsen and Svestad 1994) (fig. 3.1). The vast number of museums and exhibitions throughout the world provided typology, chronology, and archaeology itself with evidence and solidity.

## THE ORDER OF THINGS: MUSEUMS AS DISCIPLINARY ARCHITECTURE

To arise as a distinct ecology of practices, archaeology needed a political economy of knowledge; it required centers of calculation where things and inscriptions could be gathered and combined, making new knowledge possible (Latour 1986). Museums were such centers, as were the metropolises in which they were situated, such as Berlin, Boston, Copenhagen, London, New York, Paris, and Washington, DC. Clearly, modern museums and institutions did not just pop up instantly or out of nothing or from nowhere. They themselves were enabled by previous centers of calculation that, though different in numerous ways, constituted a crucial condition of possibility for the later achievements and restructurings. Scholarly and scientific societies and dinner clubs in London, for instance, were significant for the accretion, circulation, and exchange of information. The Royal Society's mandate to promote "physico-mathematical experimental learning" assembled a variegated, yet always exclusive, community of aristocrats, inventors, scientific enthusiasts, physicians, politicians, and, yes, antiquarians. Antiquarians like John Aubrey FRS (1626–97) were not only involved in a kind of eclectic information exchange as members, they also had access to an ever-expanding collection of the latest instruments—plane tables, alidades, and theodolites—and the associated skills for recording the megaliths of England.[2] This baroque sensibility certainly gave impetus to the rich documentation of ruins in the landscape. And these drawings and formative maps were circulated among scholars (learned gentlemen and their invisible technicians)—the Royal Society, for example, served as a locus for the accumulation of books in a library and the collection of charts in a map room (Witmore and Buttrey 2008).

The nineteenth-century museum, however, began to order things in a very different way. Museums sorted and combined objects from the material past into their proper compartments: here lithics, there metals, here ceramics, there sculpture. This was all the more important given the host of artifacts now in need of organization. Museums not only sorted

2. By 1830, the roster of cosmopolitan dinner clubs and societies in London included the Society of the Dilettanti, the Royal Society, the Royal Geographical Society, the Travellers' Club, the Athenaeum, the Royal Society of Literature, the Numismatic Society, and the Society of Antiquarians, and all constituted exchanges for research in the subject area of their mandate (Witmore and Buttrey 2008).

and classified the materials of the past; they also provided an itinerary through time. The "order of things" created through typological regulation contributed to the serial image of time moving between discrete moments. In fact, this synchronization of the past contributed to the modern spatial image of time through the alignment of artifacts and monument types made "present-at-hand" in museums and exhibitions. Showcases, cabinets, and galleries located artifacts and monuments in a hierarchical and efficiently visible spatial organization of continuities and discontinuities—that is, in a matrix of finely graduated and measurable intervals that revealed their typological and chronological identity (Foucault 1977; Olsen and Svestad 1994). From the Stone Age on, eras, periods, epochs—temporal blocks of time—were confidently presented. History was ontologized as series of *replacements*. Museums made spatial a very particular kind of corporal temporality (also see chapter 7), and this was enacted through ambulation. The museum building itself partitioned and thereby sequenced the past with plaster walls, corridors, doorways, glass cabinets, and shelves; it neatly separated, ordered, and showcased the past for our scrutiny while walking through the rooms, through gallery after gallery (Pearson and Shanks 2001 on museums, heritage, and performance, after Shanks and Tilley 1992, chap. 4).

More than boxes for sorting the past, museums were also architectures of engagement, nodes enabling serious speech acts and positive modalities. Museums were performative assemblies where various protagonists addressed one another. In the process of disciplining archaeology, they helped authorize voices and provided scholarly legitimacy. They granted the qualifying touch that helped to separate serious speech acts about the past from mere speculations (Olsen and Svestad 1994). For practitioners, there was also the wider possibility of visiting and participation. Tied to museums were spaces for producing, assembling, and holding groups of colleagues together. During the nineteenth century, this disciplinary architecture, including archaeological institutes and "schools," became historically effective in Europe and elsewhere, making archaeology possible as a scientific practice (cf. Foucault 1973, 1977). These institutions, likewise, did more than order artifacts. They also regulated entry to the discipline, controlled titles, and facilitated interactions with colleagues by hosting visiting scholars, conferences, and invited lectures. Moreover, they sought to perpetuate their existence. The influence of these institutions on research areas and orientations, the flow of information, and the regulation of our disciplinary demography was thus by no means inconsequential. Significantly, the Latin word *instituere* means not only "to teach" but "to set up," "establish," "ordain," "arrange," or "order."

## The Nineteenth-Century Museum

The modern museum thus implemented new spatial and corporal schemes for display and movements. In doing so, museums had to accommodate a new and far more numerous category of visitors: the public. Whereas earlier collections had been housed predominantly in buildings designed as palaces or in institutions with restricted access, the nineteenth-century museum was part of new democratic public sphere (Habermas 1971) and was seen as part of a wider project of *Bildung*— the German tradition of self-cultivation. When the new Danish state museum, the Royal Museum for Nordic Antiquities (later the National Museum) was decreed in 1807, for example, it was emphasized that the museum should "be run for the benefit of the general public" (Klindt-Jensen 1975, 49). To comply with the new demands for visitors and order, existing buildings were refurbished, reorganized, and made public.

In Copenhagen, the Royal Museum for Nordic Antiquities moved from the Royal Palace (Christiansborg) in 1853 to the rebuilt former residence of the Danish crown princes, where the National Museum still is located. In Oxford, the old Ashmolean Museum, dating back to 1683, was reorganized and extended with the building of the current Ashmolean in 1845 (the architect, Charles Robert Cockerell was the one of the excavators of the pediments of the temple of Aphaia on Aegina, as well as of the temple of Apollo Epikouros at Bassae). In London, the British Museum, founded in 1753 and flush with antiquities—including the Rosetta Stone and the Elgin and Phigaleian Marbles and recently acquired collections such as the Hamilton and Townley collections— arose from 1823 as a new quadrangular building following Robert Smirke's design.

As with the new Ashmolean and the British Museum, many nineteenth-century museums emerged as carefully designed and purpose-built structures. The National Archaeological Museum of Greece is exemplary in this regard. After the Central Archaeological Museum of Greece was established in 1834, the burgeoning materials from numerous excavations by the Archaeological Society quickly overflowed the Theseion, the temple turned church turned museum, known as the temple of Hephaistos, off the agora in Athens. Construction of the new Central Archaeological Museum (CAM) began in 1866 (the CAM was renamed

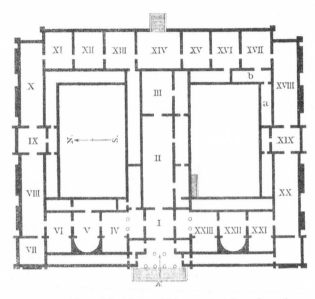

FIGURE 3.2. Map of the National Museum in Athens from the 1894 edition of Baedeker's *Greece: A Handbook for Travellers:* I. the Vestibule; II. Salon of the Mycenaean Antiquities; III. Salon of the Egyptian Antiquities; IV. Room of Archaic Art; V. Room of Athena; VI. Room of the Hermes; VII. Room of the Themis; VIII. Room of Poseidon; IX. Room of the Kosmetae; X. Large Room of the Sepulchral Reliefs; XI and XII. Reliefs; XIII. Room of the Sepulchral Vases; XVI. Room of the Votive Reliefs; XVII. Room of Miscellaneous Works; XVIII. Room of Vases of the Mycenaean Epoch and the Dipylon Vases; XIX. Room of the Red-Figured Vases; XX. Room of Red and Black-Figure Vases; XXI. Room of Terracottas; XXII. Room of Terracottas from Asia Minor; XXIII. Room of the Bronzes.

the National Archaeological Museum in 1881 by royal decree). Ludwig Lange's original designs were modified under the direction of Ernst Ziller, who supervised the construction. The layout—four wings arranged in a square around two open courts and a central hall—was something of a paradigm for nineteenth-century museum design (see Giebelhausen 2011).[3] Each wing consists of a sequence of salons, making for a linear progression by visitors through the collections (fig. 3.2).

3. More specifically, Lange's design, albeit a paired-down version, is reminiscent of Jean-Nicolas-Louis Durand's "ideal design for a museum" (Durand 2000)—a basis for Leo von Klenze's Glyptothek in Munich. Indeed, the subsequent eastern expansion would bring it closer to Durand's overall ideal design, even if the arrangement of rooms betrayed the symmetry provided by the series of stacked salons.

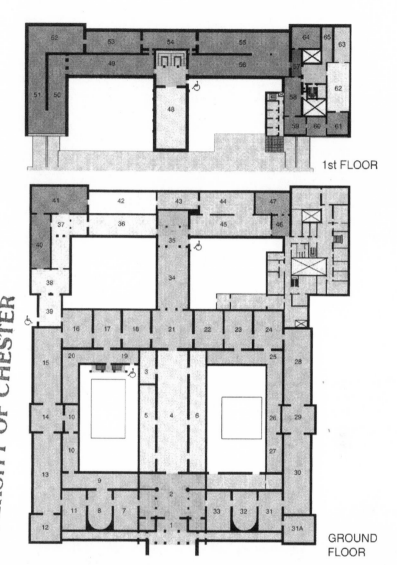

1st FLOOR

GROUND
FLOOR

FIGURE 3.3. Map of the National Museum in Athens, 2010.
Rooms 1 through 33 delimit the footprint of the nineteenth-century
National Museum.

The 1894 edition of Baedeker's *Greece: A Handbook for Travellers* describes the vestibule as providing access to three separate collections. To the north, one would find room after room of sculptured marbles— the Room of Archaic Art, the Room of the Athena, Room of the Hermes, Room of the Themis. To the south, a series of galleries contained bronzes and vases. The Mycenaean and Egyptian collections were arranged along the central hall. Rooms sorted collections by artifact type (sculpture, red-figured vases, metalwork) and period (the Mycenaean epoch, Archaic, Roman). The arrangement of objects in these rooms suggested something of their importance and choreographed a very particular engagement, to which we shall return shortly. Cases further sorted vessels by location. In Room XVIII, dedicated to vases from the "so-called Mycenaean Epoch" and the Dipylon Vases, for example, case 1 contained vessels from Troy, case 2, vases from Attica and other districts, and case 3, vases from Cyprus. The celebrated Dipylon vases held pride of place in the center of the room (*Greece* 1894, 102). Within this developing milieu, the significance of artifacts could be established simply through their physical proximity and disposition in relation to other things.

In 2010, aside from the east wing, which was added in the 1930s, the arrangement of rooms and corridors, walls and doors has changed surprisingly little (compare fig. 3.2 to fig. 3.3). Looking at two plans synoptically does not, of course, reveal the changes in lighting, arrangement of cases, seating, information boards, and artifact displays. Today, too, there is air conditioning, and attentive guards stand ready to ward off wayward hands and prohibit flash photography. In addition to the celebrated objects in the permanent collection, moreover, there are others that move in and out of storage (on changes to museums between the nineteenth and twentieth centuries more generally, see Dyson 2006, 133–71).

The assemblages of things that comprise museums make their own contribution to archaeological classification and to the very being of archaeology itself. While most scholars tend to emphasize texts, humble rooms, walls, and doors, seemingly mundane cabinets, shelves, and glass partitions serve to organize hundreds of Greek sculptural pieces, ceramic vases, and bronze objects in the National Archaeological Museum. Indeed, monumental achievements such as Thomsen's three-age system and the Union Académique Internationale's *Corpus Vasorum Antiquorum* (Corpus of Ancient Vases), a compilation of collections held in the world's museums, are the outcomes of interactions in comfortable atmospheres that spatially order things already displaced from another situation through archaeology and other means, such as the art market.[4] For practitioners, there was always the possibility of a more intimate involvement through the focused study of museum objects. For attentive museum viewers, there was always a compromise between observation and a more participatory relationship. Pedestals elevated works for eye-level contemplation. Sculptures or other objects placed in the middle of rooms allowed one to behold the piece from numerous angles. In some sense, the viewer can dominate the piece. Objects such as reliefs set against the walls invite, even demand, a pause. Thus, the question of whether an object is against the wall or freestanding offers yet another angle on its relationships, and this has an impact, however subtle, however overt, on what is articulated in print.

## NORMALIZING PRACTICES AND INSTRUMENTS

Archaeology emerged and was stabilized by many other modes of normalization. The increasing array of archaeological journals and monographs were important for its academic identity. As with museum display, distinctive textual tropes were developed for writing and imaging the past. Illustrations were standardized in terms of scale and style; linear perspective combined with optical consistency allowed something of the reality of objects and monuments to be easily transferred, compared, and, if necessary, combined with other media. Through increasing publication in disciplinary journals, in archaeological series, in books carrying its name, archaeology also acquired textual mass and form; in this way, archaeology became visible, pervasive, and distinctive.

Included in this trope or genre are the catalogue and the field report. The catalogue standardized description of artifacts and regulated what their essential features were. Though this also allowed for a range of normative aesthetic assessments ("elegant," "beautiful," "poor," etc), this took on the level of canon. The museum number, usually inscribed directly on surface of the object itself, was crucial for establishing the identity of the artifact. This unique key of identification not only distinguished the object from other similar objects but also identified the

4. Such displays were key to the further development of archaeological fieldwork; more will be said regarding fieldwork in chapters 4 and 5.

institution to which it properly belonged (and thus often its relative provenance). Through various numerical or alphabetical hierarchies, it also revealed its contextual relations to other artifacts. The field report acted to produce disciplinary distinguishing records, documents that over time, by being read and copied, delimited a certain way of representing temples and earthen mounds, walls and stratigraphy, soils and their characteristics. Thus the field report came to mediate practices of observation and modes of engagement, including photography, discussed below. Acting as the textual stand-in for a site radically transformed gave the site report a unique authority, and this kind of document often became the only "direct" encounter other archaeologists could have with a particular vanished site or one difficult to access.

The field report and, to a large extent, also the catalogue were, of course, directly related to the most distinctive of all archaeological practices: fieldwork, and in particular excavation (see chapter 4). Needless to say, the normalization of digging was crucial for the disciplining of archaeology. First, by becoming widespread. By the end of the nineteenth century, archaeologists could be spotted in the field literally everywhere. Second, by becoming standardized. Whether one was in Tanis, Teotihuacan, or the Thames Valley, how archaeologists excavated and recorded, though far from identical, were largely comparable; one's actions were increasingly routine, one's instruments were increasingly standardized, enabling peer circulation and judgment. Regular modes of engagement proliferated. Practitioners performed archaeology in a way that made it distinctive, generally comparable, repeatable, and consistent. It was also a matter of sheer scale in terms of familiarity and reach. In contrast to the solitary antiquarian strolling the countryside, archaeological fieldwork became a collective enterprise. Excavations needed the coordinated labor of people digging, sorting, and recording. Not only people—excavators, camera persons, material specialists, foremen, and native workers, whose roles were often hierarchically defined by task or even skin color (cf. Petrie 1904; also see Quirke 2010; Shepherd 2003)—but increasingly varied and sophisticated brigades of things, from wheelbarrows, scaffolding materials, and shovels to China ink, metal or glass-plate cameras, and prismatic compasses, were included in excavating collectives. In short, archaeology became *more* than what archaeologists did. These traveling people and things not only distinguished archaeological fieldwork from previous pre-disciplinary practices, they also distinguished archaeology from other disciplines—

even those that also insisted on fieldwork (the emergence of a unique habitat is a crucial aspect of an ecology of practices; Stengers 2005). As explored in more detail in the following chapter, fieldwork, and especially excavations, played an immense role in creating and normalizing an archaeological identity.

By the late nineteenth century, and increasingly throughout the following decades, archaeology became associated with an ecology of consistent and repeatable practices. Involved in this firming of practices was the increasing agreement around questions of what to observe and how to observe it, which again was tied up with skillful and habitual relations with instruments. As these skills and means became internalized as part of archaeological practice, they become black-boxed and increasingly invisible in the accounts of such conduct. However, and especially in the formative days of the discipline, we have rare accounts where trivial, mundane things are brought to attention. An example is William Matthew Flinders Petrie's recommendations of proper measuring instruments in his extraordinary 1904 textbook on archaeological practice:

> amongst the means of work the divided rod is indispensable, and it is all that is wanted for most small buildings that are met with. The tape is the most practical for distances of 10 to 50 feet; and the steel tape for accurate measuring of base lines, or long distances. The box-sextant is for very broken ground, and isolated details, or if working alone; and the theodolite for accurate work anywhere between the accuracy of, say, 1 inch on 500 feet and the refinement of a ¼ of an inch on a mile. The plane table may be convenient for approximate plans, and is simple and rapid to use. The prismatic compass is of use for the directions of single blocks or fragments of wall, and is handy for rough topography (generally with paced distances), or for underground passages. (Petrie 1904, 55)

These instruments and associated practices were not only argued for, many of them were already an indispensable part of the archaeological tool kit. Mutual agreement was established through the spread and repetition of specific modes of excavating and surveying. How to set up a grid system; what measurements to take, how to map and record: "For levelling, the handiest instrument is a short rigid pendulum, with mirror attached, to hang truly vertical. The reflection of the eye back to itself is then a truly horizontal line, and can be sighted on to any distance" (Petrie 1904, 58–59). Instruments played a stabilizing role in mediating those consistent and repeatable relationships that comprise routine archaeological practice, and also for producing standardized gazes, iterative engagements, and flat inscriptions.

Let us take a brief look at an example of how the propagation of certain instruments and their outputs, here visual imagery, modified the nature of archaeological work during this time.

*Photography and the Archaeological Image*

The birth of archaeology intersects with that of photography, as a number of studies have shown (e.g., Downing 2006). Probably the first attempt to use photography in the field was made by Richard Lepsius in Egypt in 1842, only three years after William Henry Fox Talbot's and Louis Daguerre's inventions (Fox Talbot's book *The Pencil of Nature* (1844–46) is remarkably archaeological in its subject matter: see Roberts, Gray, and Burnett-Brown 2000; Shanks 2012). Another early use of photography in the field was during Charles Thomas Newton's exploration of Halicarnassos. In December of 1856, prior to the removal of an extensive tessellated pavement believed to be Roman in date, Newton had the entire floor documented by photography in the following manner. A portable scaffold was erected above the floor and the camera, manned by an officer, Lt. Benjamin Spackman, newly trained in photography by the British Royal Engineers, was set up so as to obtain a planimetric view (fig. 3.4). This entire apparatus was then shifted from point to point until the whole surface was captured in this manner. What had previously required several hours of measurement with tapes and rules and drafting by hand was now transformed into several minutes of pouring an emulsion over glass and waiting for the exposure through mechanical reproduction (this is assuming, of course, that Spackman used the wet-collodion process—the exposure time was anywhere from 10 to 20 seconds).

When photography was initially enrolled in archaeological excavation, it was framed with respect to a recognizable set of practices conditioned by illustration. This conditioning was due to the fact that in the early half of the nineteenth century, illustration was the primary mode for inscribing a scene in two dimensions (Bohrer 2003; Witmore 2004a). The potential of photography in excavation would not, however, be realized for several decades after the new ocular performance enacted by gantry, camera apparatus, and Spackman on that cold December day. So while new equipment and personnel would become more familiar on

FIGURE 3.4. Charles Thomas Newton's photographic tower at Halicarnassus from id., *A History of Discoveries at Halicarnassus, Cnidus & Branchidae* (London: Day and Son, 1863), vol. 1, pl. XXXVIII.

archaeological sites from Hissarlik (Deuel 1977, 380–81) to Muldbjerg (Klindt-Jensen 1975, 77), it would take some time before photography transformed the nature of excavation beyond those necessary pauses demanded by camera and tripod. These transformations would be most obviously seen in the hygienic practices that arose in response to photographic verisimilitude.

Today, any experienced excavator is familiar with the lengths to which one must go for a photograph, from meticulously sweeping a floor surface to trimming every blade of grass to neatly cutting and delineating a stratigraphic sequence. However, when Newton was excavating Halicarnassos, illustration and drawing did not necessarily require a surface to be cleaned; of course, by this we do not wish to imply that some level of cleaning was not present. But if something was to be mobilized and transferred through the photograph, the details of surface could be viewed, so the photograph began to play an increasing role in how surfaces were prepared throughout the later nineteenth century.

Thus, by the beginning of the twentieth century, careful dressing of the excavated features to be photographed is recommended. Again, Petrie provides us with the apposite recommendations:

> Reliefs upon weathered stones should be dusted over with sand, and then lightly wiped until just the wrought relief is cleared, and the ground is left smoothed with sand. Stones in building should be brushed or scraped clean, so as to contrast with the earth. Joints in walls should be picked out or brushed so as to show clearly. Sometimes, as in a flooring of wood, the whole should be entirely brushed clean, and then the joints packed with the lightest-coloured sand so as to contrast well. A grave needs hand-picking, and then every bone brushing clean, and the ground between packing with dark earth to give contrast. All pottery and objects should be entirely cleaned around, and lifted to show a clear outline. (Petrie 1904, 76)

The reason for the lag time between the first uses of photography and routine cleaning and preparation of excavated features, surfaces, and assemblages for photography was connected with the ability to circulate the actual photographic prints in publication (see Rudwick 1976). And here, given the large numbers of plates needed in archaeological publication, cost was a major factor (Petrie 1904, 117–19).

Although photographs, as an alternative to photoengraving, had been matted directly into some books since the 1840s (Evans 1956, 292), actual photographs were not seen in a final excavation volume till Alexander Conze's *Archäologische Untersuchungen auf Samothrake* (1875). Even then, given the expense, such undertakings were exceptional, because photo matting could be undertaken only for small print runs. Lithography or engraving were more cost-effective options. However, these forms of reproduction reduced the near continuous detail of photographic grains of light-sensitive silver to engraved lines on neutral ground, much like illustration. With photographs so *inscribed,* no one could really see the subtleties of what had actually appeared on the ground glass screen of the camera in the field. It was not till later innovations, especially the halftone process, that the loss that occurred in the transformation of photograph to printed plate dropped below the threshold of human vision (Ivins 1953, 128). Succinctly, it was fine reproduction that necessitated hygienic excavation practices; the new photographic medium enabled the presentation of details that would be obscured by unkempt baulks or dirt-strewn surfaces. For a sense of the differences in published imagery, compare the lithographs of Newton's *A History of the Discoveries at Halicarnassus, Cnidus and Branchidae*

(1862–63) to the *Lichtdrucke* of Ernst Curtius's Olympia volumes (1890–97).

By the time of the publication of the Olympia volumes, there were numerous halftone processes for archaeologists to choose from—collotypes, chromolithography, autotypes, platinotypes, and heliogravures.[5] However, a decade later, Petrie claimed that autotypes, platinotypes, and heliogravures had "seldom come into the general run of archaeological illustration" (1904, 119). Notwithstanding, the further refinement of hygienic excavation practices is mediated by the fineness of detail seen in the showing of things within publication. It is Maurice B. Cookson who perhaps best sums up the mediating role of the photograph within the orthodox routines of excavation:

> no matter how correct the exposure and the development of the negative, no matter how carefully a print is made, a wall with mud still clinging to it, a floor poorly brushed, a pavement insufficiently washed, the badly-trimmed edge of a cut can completely ruin the finest of photographs from an archaeological standpoint. From experience, I know how heart-breaking it can be to scrape a stone floor hour after hour, or to wash the metalling of a Roman road pebble by pebble until I hoped that every stone would come loose and there would be an end to any photograph—but I know the pleasure the ultimate result has brought when the photograph of the finished work is seen. (Cookson 1954, 13–14)

While cleanliness was, for Cookson, a virtue to be held above all others, it was neither the floor nor the pavement nor the interpretation that suffered from poor brushwork or insufficient washing, it was the photograph (for further discussion of photography, illustration, dirt/ruin, and hygiene, see Shanks 1992).

## PEDAGOGY AND TURNING OUT TROOPS

Today, knowledge and serious speech acts about the past are inextricably linked to positions, titles, and university degrees. To become an archaeologist, you have to go through a long university education, and such is all but mandatory for one to attain a position as an archaeologist. This has not always been the case, and the emergence of a system of academic eligibility, which qualified the transformation of a novice into

---

5. The *Lichtdruck* is a hybrid process where collotype is applied to either glass or stone (Gernsheim 1969, 548).

a professional, ensures the formation and maintenance of competency and thus provides another component to the making of archaeology.

Prior to the nineteenth century, the academic study of antiquities, and of the past more generally, was largely undertaken by *polyhistors,* scholars who on equal footing mastered a number of fields in what we now define as humanities and natural sciences. Even later, this was to some extent the case, since digging and recording long remained hobbies for the affluent amateur and dilettante. However, gradually throughout the nineteenth century, the archaeologist emerged as a professional and specialized category of scholar.

The first chair in archaeology was established at the University of Leiden as early as in 1818 (Stoneman 2011: 275), and especially from the late nineteenth century on, chairs and positions as *archaeologist* were established all over the world. At first these positions were dedicated more or less entirely to research, including fieldwork; formal programs of education and degrees were primarily a twentieth-century development. However, when implemented, education and academic degrees became crucial for identifying the archaeologist, distinguishing him/her from those who lacked these qualifications. Later still, this proof of eligibility not only came to regulate access to positions but also to rank those entitled to compete for funding and research money.

A telling if implicit sign of the emergence of the archaeologist as a professional, specialized category of scholar is what seems to be an increasingly felt need from the late nineteenth century on to articulate archaeology's disciplinary achievements and simultaneously to distance oneself from earlier antiquarian exploits, amateur practices, and dilettante interests (Olsen and Svestad 1994, 15–16). Thus in his 1873 state-of-the-art summary, Hans Hildebrand wrote with confidence that: "The scientific study of the past has advanced beyond its earlier state. The viewpoints have become higher, the field wider, and one has learnt . . . to penetrate deeper. Archaeology in this state . . . is much more than a pastime for the leisure hours. It is no longer so that the dilettante is just a little more cursory that the scientist. . . . Between them there is a great difference, they work in different ways, on different levels and towards different goals" (Hildebrand 1873, 13, trans. in Olsen and Svestad 1994, 16).

Eighteenth-century antiquarianism was dismissed as the method of a "naïve-fantastical time," when "you could put the pieces wherever you liked" (Petersen 1898, 22–23), which needless to say was clearly no longer the case. As "the latest born of the sciences," as Petrie expressed it in 1904, archaeology had finally "struggled into freedom, out of the swaddling cloths of dilettante speculations" (1904, vii).

The identity of archaeology was further secured and supported by national and international professional societies and organizations. As the number of archaeologists grew, there was a need to meet for networking, collaboration, and research exchange. With proper organization, archaeologists could act as a united and coherent professional group in society, not least in relation to issues concerning heritage and legislation. Groups such as the Archaeological Institute of America (AIA) had already been formed by the turn of the twentieth century, but it may be significant for disciplinary demography that some of the largest and most influential archaeological organizations were founded in the 1930s, such as the International Union for Prehistoric and Proto-historic Sciences (IUSPP), the first archaeological "world" organization, established in 1931 (though with roots back to 1865), and the Society for American Archaeology (SAA) in 1934. Associated with these national and international organizations were scheduled meetings and conference publications, which gave a new face to this fast-growing disciplinary field. However, these meetings also served as means for securing internal cohesion in a discipline that was not only specialized in relation to other disciplines but was increasingly affected by its own subdivision into chronological and/or thematic fields. They provided venues for information exchange, including stories and social gossip, over food and drink, around tables and at bars. Furthermore, these professional bodies also established codes of conduct, ethics, and good practice for their members (see chapter 9), which provided additional glue, regulation, and consistent disciplinary behavior.

Another important infrastructure that contributed significantly to establishing and securing archaeology's identity and authority were the heritage acts and legislation that were implemented from the late nineteenth on, especially throughout the twentieth century. They provided identity to and formal justification for the search for archaeological heritage and also enabled the performance of professional tasks, thus contributing to the ecology of practices associated with archaeology. Excavating and inspecting monuments became activities restricted to specialists. Inventorying sites and structures requiring legal protection was of the essence. In most cases, to dig required permission and the certificate of eligibility that degrees and positions provided. Such legislation also gave rise to institutions managing heritage protection, planning, and rescue excavation. While museums and universities had long provided the given institutional habitat for archaeological pursuits, the postwar era has seen a tremendous growth in the number of archaeologists working in cultural resource management, including private companies and university-commercial hybrids. Thus our ecology of practices has evolved to meet the demand for an archaeology directly involved in modern programs of development and planning.

## CONCLUSION: MAKING ARCHAEOLOGY

The making of an archaeological discipline in the nineteenth and early twentieth centuries implied that archaeology was increasingly in the hands of professional practitioners—archaeologists. However, even if this holds true, it is too simple to accept it as confirmation of David Clarke's maxim that archaeology is what archaeologists do (Clarke 1973). By the first decades of the twentieth century, archaeology had become normal science in a far more comprehensive way than Thomas Kuhn's original term implied. In ways great and small, archaeology had become a distinctive mode of disciplinary existence, made solid and stabilized through a repertoire of standardized things, statements, and repetitive practices: museums, exhibitions, collections, archives, jobs, degrees, chairs, organizations, societies, journals, books, legislation, field practices, and instruments. As an ecology of practices, archaeology was clearly more than what *archaeologists* did.

More studies are needed to give detail to this sketch of the emergence of archaeology, and in this chapter we have only probed areas of the surface of an extensive disciplinary bedrock, emphasizing some of the crucial technologies and practices involved in the making and "ontologizing" of archaeology. While we have passed lightly over numerous issues in this short account, we have, nonetheless, provided some clues to how archaeology was materialized and stabilized through amassing legions of things and working on them in associated practices. If archaeology is the discipline of things, we have to acknowledge in the study of our own disciplinary past the array of roles fulfilled by these things, people, and other entities. It is somewhat paradoxical, and probably rather revealing, that a discipline focused upon things has devoted so little time, so little space, to its own instruments, equipment, and messy practices when recollecting its own past (Olsen 2003, 100).

There are other aspects to the story of archaeology that deserve attention along these lines. One is the crucial turning point when the discipline began to narrate its own past: the historiographic accounts of the settled controversies and the successful achievements that enlighten and justify archaeology's coming into being. As we have briefly explored above, this also involved the tried and tested strategy of self-definition through negation. Especially in the formative years, when, archaeology's identity may have been fragile, to denounce and distance oneself from earlier practices and scholars almost seemed imperative. From the angle we have taken in this chapter, we make bold to say that, contrary to the renowned enlightenment image provided by Clarke in his essay on the loss of disciplinary innocence (1973), archaeology was never childlike or naïve.

# CHAPTER 4

# Digging Deep

*Archaeology and Fieldwork*

Doing archaeology usually brings to mind the "down and dirty" of fieldwork. Fieldwork is done outside, away from the amenities of institutional or contract firm offices. Archaeologists labor hard to collect their data, their information. The artifacts and ruins from the past are brought to light and documented through expending time and energy in archaeological surveys and excavations. Over the course of the professionalization of the discipline, persevering scholars have plied new and increasingly more sophisticated techniques for the "prime directive" of archaeology: to maximize information collection while in the field. Why? Because, as the rationale goes, excavation destroys what it saves for posterity. Excavation, to reiterate the oft-repeated maxim, is "the unrepeatable experiment" (Barker 1982, 11). Even surface and reconnaissance survey are events that cannot be replicated (Cherry 1983). Although sound criticism has been raised against these probably too simplistic categorizations (Lucas 2001a and 2001b; Bradley 2003), the manner by which archaeology derives its primary data distinguishes it from both the carefully controlled experiments of the natural sciences, the questionnaires and participant observation of the social sciences, and the text- and archive-based humanities.

In this chapter we want to take a closer look at these "distinguishing qualities" of archaeological fieldwork. What are the distinctive characteristics of archaeological fieldwork and in what way has *working* in the field affected archaeological discourse and the archaeological community writ large? Notwithstanding increased attention to both practice and theory of field research, surprisingly little has been written about this most characteristic of archaeological activities (see, however, Carver 2011; Lucas 2001a; Yarrow 2003; Edgeworth 2006, 2011). Critical studies of fieldwork are few and largely comply with two basic tropes: on the one hand, there are distancing, irony-ridden commentaries that depict the field archaeologist as little more than an explorer and voyeur; on the other hand, there are more substantial but reductive analyses where fieldwork is largely seen as derivative conduct, either of grander sociopolitical enterprises or of theoretical discourses generated in proper academic settings. Although important insights have been produced, we want to take an alternative approach that engages with the distinctiveness of archaeological fieldwork and the impact it has had upon the discipline.

## IMAGINING ARCHAEOLOGY: FIELDWORK, STEREOTYPES, AND WOULD-BE ICONOCLASTS

As already stated, archaeology's disciplinary otherness and identity is closely associated with the act of doing fieldwork. Images of archaeologists working in the field fill the pages of introductory and popular texts (e.g., Barker 1982; Heizer and Graham 1967; Joukowsky 1980; Maschner and Chippindale 2005; Renfrew and Bahn 1996; Thomas and Kelly 2006; however, cf. Shanks 1991). From Århus to Austin, walk through the corridors of any archaeology department and you will see snapshots of faculty and students posing in a trench with trowels or prism poles, leaning over a draft board, or peeking into a total station—preferably with a background that indicates remoteness or exoticism. "Getting the hands dirty" in working with the instruments and materials of archaeology in faraway places attracts many to field research.

Admittedly fieldwork today is more often than not an encounter with ancient and other, exotic cultures, which is domesticated by attempting to control the encounter (cf. Chadha 2002). We can no longer entertain the notion that the conditions under which we conduct fieldwork are necessarily harsh and rugged. Urban rescue archaeology near a Starbucks coffee shop may match the comforts of academic life in general. Additionally, much pertinent critical work since the 1980s, deriving largely from feminist scholars and reflexive postprocessualists (e.g., Gero and Conkey 1991), has reminded us that the popular conceptions of the practice of archaeology are overromanticized. We are no longer "cowboy intellectuals," not that all of us ever were (Gero 1985, 342; see also, however, Holtorf 2005 and 2007). These acknowledgments notwithstanding, the image of the archaeologist as someone digging up the past still holds sway both within the discipline and among the public. The majority of archaeologists *do* regard fieldwork as an indispensable part of their disciplinary practice. Just look at the lists of "places excavated" included in biographies and résumés on university department web sites and in publications. Just read through the expectations for new archaeological faculty in job postings in the United States—field projects are requisite. Fieldwork is in many ways the ultimate archaeological mode of being-in-the world; stereotyped, perhaps, but one that holds true.

Still, there is latent ambiguity within the discipline with regard to the emblematic connotation of fieldwork. More theoretically minded archaeologists have recurrently voiced their opposition against conceiving fieldwork as the disciplinary "categorical imperative."[1] As expressed by Flannery's memorable processualist caricature, the Born-Again Philosopher (BAP), "I do *not* feel the need to break the soil periodically in order to reaffirm my status as archaeologist" (Flannery 1982, 275, actually paraphrasing Schiffer 1978, 247). His prospect of a not very cheerful field career had luckily been saved by the discovery of philosophy of science: "No more dust, no more heat, no more 5-ft squares. He worked in an office now, generating hypotheses and laws and models which an endless stream of graduate students was sent out to test; for he himself no longer did any fieldwork" (Flannery 1982, 266).

However, most processual archaeologists are actually quite dedicated to fieldwork.[2] Critical of previous, "traditional" approaches, they have called for reflexivity in terms of problem formulation and explicit procedures for hypothesis testing. Processual archaeology also introduced to the field an impressive array of techniques and strategies for sampling and recording (e.g. Watson, LeBlanc, and Redman 1971). Early postprocessual archaeology, on the other hand, seemed quite indifferent to what happened methodologically in the field, though later this changed (see below). One likely reason for this attitude was the various tactics of self-definition through negation that proved crucial to the ar-

1. Compare, for example, the recent discussion on the importance of excavation in *Archaeological Dialogues* 18(1) 2011; Harrison 2011.

2. There were, of course, exceptions. Consider Binford's long-standing distinction between applied and basic research.

chaeological science war of the 1980s. Due to the fact that many of the impressive methodological achievements that had taken place within field archaeology were a product of processual initiatives, fieldwork to the postprocessualists became strongly associated with positivist enterprises that stressed the primacy of objective data. Intellectually approached with a distancing, ironic flair, excavation was even compared to intellectual voyeurism and more interest seemed to be paid to exploring its metaphorical connotation than to considering what it actually amounted to in terms of material information (Bapty and Yates 1990; Tilley 1989 and 1990; see also Rosaldo 1986). To such would-be iconoclasts, digging anything represented a kind of academic embarrassment threatening to remove them even further from the theoretically savvy social science scene to which they eagerly aspired.

Even among more mainstream archaeologists, there has been suspicion and ambiguity, latent and overt, about the popular image of archaeology as the "discipline of the spade." Many scholars are worried by popular television formats, such as "Time Team," and the manner in which archaeologists are portrayed in programs on the Discovery Channel and the National Geographic Channel, because they think archaeological research is misrepresented (see, e.g., Clack and Brittain 2007). There may be something to this, but what also seems to ground these "worries" is a concern for "academic respectability," most notably the fear (but probably also some secret pride) of being associated with the heroic but anti-intellectual explorer image. Moreover, the archaeological toil of digging, removing soil and rock, being outdoors and getting dirty does not comply well with the image of an intellectual. Such work is held to be blue-collar. Taking into account the long-held bourgeois contempt in academia (especially in the humanities) for dirt, manual labour, and working-class life in general, the archaeological craft and its repugnant trivia may better not become too emblematic of an archaeological scholar (on the contrast between popular and professional, see Shanks and Tilley 1987, chap. 1; for an embrace of craftwork, see Shanks 1991 and Shanks and McGuire 1996).

INFORMATION, INTERPRETATION, AND PRACTICE

So what is it that is done when archaeologists excavate a site or survey an area? The answer may seem self-evident. They collect information about sites and landscapes "out there" in order to piece together the past. What if just as with the image of "fieldwork," though, we were to unpack this a little more and ask just what and how the work gets done. How do archaeologists actually "collect information" that can be "pieced together"?

What archaeologists do is usually captured in the form of a fairly standard sequence covering the practical and cognitive work of field research. These "flow chart" models, the direct outcome of the processualist call for methodological reflexivity, suggest how you can go about successfully conducting an archaeological project—or what to expect if you actually have a hand in the entire process. A typical example would be:

- Formulation of questions
- Research design
- Survey/excavation strategies
- Actual fieldwork
- Finds processing
- Analysis
- Synthesis and argumentation; presentation of results through publication

This linear, flow-chart model is convenient because it helps organize the field project into coherent and logical sequences of work, and it has been a basic component to teaching archaeology (see Fritz & Plog 1970, 411, Taylor 1983[1948], 35). In this model fieldwork is a *means,* an activity to obtain something (data, information) to bring home for further processing and interpretation. As currently invoked, the model is designed to optimize data collection while in the field by applying standards to excavation and recording. Fieldwork itself, as *practice* and *experience,* is mostly disregarded as a potential source of knowledge.

When postprocessual archaeology eventually turned its attention to the field, one major achievement was to challenge this "production line" conception of (field) research, running from "raw" data collection to analysis, interpretation and writing (compare figures 5.6 and 5.7 in Hodder 1999). The call for a "reflexive" approach implied extending, or returning interpretation to the "trowel's edge" (see, e.g., Hodder 1997, 1999, 2000, and 2003; Tringham and Stevanovic 2000; also Andrews, Barrett, and Lewis 2000; Berggren and Burström 2002; Chadwick 2003; Berggren and Hodder 2003). The field, in this argument, is not just an arena for mechanical data collection, but a vibrant scene of active individual engagements with the past (see also Tilley 1990;

Bender, Hamilton, and Tilley 2007). By encouraging widespread use of individual field diaries, new media, and the "documentation of documentation," the aim has been to make the interpretation process more inclusive, involving those in the field trench as well as later efforts of interpretation and synthesis off-site, in lab or office.

Fieldwork itself has also received more attention as an embodied experience, not least due to proposed phenomenological approaches to the archaeological past (Tilley 1994, 2004, and 2008). While mostly concerned with reconnaissance surveys (cf. Hamilton, Tilley, and Bender 2006), the range of tacit sensory impressions that one undergoes in the process of any fieldwork clearly adds an important dimension to how the site is understood (Webmoor 2005). As evocatively expressed by Colin Renfrew:

> the parched days under a hot sun in Greece, the pouring rain and sustained wind on the day at Quanterness [on Orkney] when, working together as a team, we had to backfill that west section in the course of a few hours, and never mind the weather. But also the sense of mystery and solitude when I was the first to enter, perhaps for thousands of years, one of the side chambers [of the passage grave] at Quanterness and stand up with the cold, damp sandstones all around me, and reach my hand above my head to touch the still complete corbelling of the ceiling. You don't find much about these moments in the printed excavation report, but they are an integral part of the reality. (Renfrew 2003, 39–40)

Although the various reflexive methodologies clearly represent a refreshing, important new attitude to fieldwork, the focus is almost entirely on the fieldworker as a conscious and subjective thinker rather than a skilled excavator or adept field walker (Chadwick 2003). Little emphasis has so far been paid to how fieldwork as a knowledge-constitutive enterprise also embeds a *positive* element of implicit or ineffable, nondiscursive skill, learning, and experiencing. If doing archaeology is *working* on "what remains" (Shanks 2007, 273), like embodied craftwork (Shanks 1991, Shanks and McGuire 1996), then the "knowing how" of this labor must be credited attention in addition to the preferred "knowing what." Introductory textbooks on fieldwork, however, mostly remain silent on these issues; for example, on how to survey in coniferous woodland or along raised beach terraces, or how to attune one's senses to the sharp edges, colors, and sound of flint flakes under boot. Little is documented of how to hold the trowel as you cleanse the surface of a Mesolithic floor layer or how to adjust your digging to the material requirements of a Sámi hearth. There are no how-to guides for these types of practical knowledge and perceptual-motor skills (but see Carandini 1991).

## TACIT KNOWLEDGE

This reticence may be seen as a natural outcome of the often-proposed imperative of tacit knowledge: "whereof one cannot speak, thereof one must be silent" (Wittgenstein 1922). Surely it is difficult, and probably futile, to attempt to teach or learn the necessary field skill satisfactorily through a classroom or textbook approach. Both surveys and digging can only be properly "learned by doing." Acknowledging this, however, is not a good excuse for ignoring these skills and the nondiscursive aspects of archaeological knowledge when analyzing fieldwork and the discipline more generally. These active engagements with the past rooted in tacit knowledge are more than emotions and empathy with the past. The direct and material engagement with the past through fieldwork and working with material remains brings forth a mode of familiarity and understanding of landscapes and things that cannot be achieved by a detached intellectual approach. The "having been there" aspect of fieldwork, its actuality, the conjuncture of past and present, is a mode of archaeological being that grounds an embedded understanding of the past.

Acknowledging this material impact, that sites and things relate to us, refers us back to earlier days of "inductive" archaeology, before the stress on theory and deductive research algorithms associated with the New Archaeology of the 1960s and after. Learning by encountering, by hand, from things, lost a clear role in the theoretical tropes of deduction, hypothesis formation, testing, interpretation, and textualism associated with the shift in conception to archaeology as an anthropological science, or to a more mature and professional discipline (from Binford 1962 and Clarke 1968 on). The mantra that all knowledge is theory-dependent made the practice and experience that emerged from our direct involvement with things and landscapes more or less irrelevant. Priority began to shift to the psychosocial and cognitive "work" that was needed before going to do research. This "intellectualizing" trend continued with postprocessualism (see, e.g., Gero 1996 on the gendered encounter; Wylie 1997).

There is another aspect of this that also deserves attention. The skills of fieldwork are learned principally through practice. This learning process takes place under circumstances very different to ordinary university teaching. On a field class, teachers, mentors, and students may live together, share bad weather, food, local conditions of living, and the challenges of the field. A large part of their leisure time is also spent together. This interpersonal "otherness" of the field is extremely important for socialization and bonding: ties are established, as are commitments and professional relations. Hierarchy and compliance are naturalized. Fieldwork is also a prime arena for "tribal songs" and effective disciplinary histories: anecdotes, founding stories, rumors, and enemy conceptions are being transferred to the uninitiated student. Through access to this unwritten knowledge—with the duties and restrictions it implies—one becomes a part of the guild. Fieldwork contains elements of a *rite de passage* into the discipline and discourse. Though they seem to be the emergent locale for many such activities, archeological conferences cannot supplant the material embeddedness of the field.

## BRINGING HOME: THE DISTRIBUTED FIELD

Interpretation and other activities that build knowledge are being located again in the field; there is also a blurring of the "field" as the site for experiencing and retrieving information about the past. The location of the field has always been transcended by "leakages" and points of transmission to other units and places that create long, complex networks that constitute the production of knowledge, embedded in the artifacts that make the discipline—plans, diagrams, reports, lectures, exhibitions (cf. Callon 1999 on such *technical* networks; also Witmore 2004b; more on this in the following chapter). Ceramic sherds, lithic material, soil samples, bone assemblages, dating samples, and attendant recordings have always been brought back, have always been key components of the dispersion of the field into museums, laboratories, storerooms, and archives. Boxes and bags of finds carry the names of faraway sites and fill up shelves in offices, storerooms, and archaeology departments. Even excavations have for a long time on occasion been conducted away from the field, when, for example, fragile and/or composite finds and samples have been stabilized and removed for excavation in a laboratory. This dispersal of the field involves a number of ontological, epistemological, and political issues. We shall address a few of them.

If interpretation is taken from lab and office into the trench and extended to the trowel's edge, we should also acknowledge that practice and embodied experience are not exercises reserved for the field. Thus, while bringing home the material involves dislocation, displacement in the sense that things, sites, and landscapes are partitioned and parted, the work and involvement with the dislocated constituents is not purely an intellectual task. Less strenuous perhaps, and clearly not interchangeable experiences, yet postexcavation work with the material is still a material encounter qualitatively comparable to those experienced during fieldwork (Lucas 2001a; 2001b, 14). Notwithstanding its numerous other epistemological and political issues, bringing home is also "bringing close"; it involves a careful and concerned "de-severing" of things (Heidegger 1962, 136–41). This manifests itself in a number of ways. The painstaking toil of cleaning, examining, and conserving artifacts by technicians and curators reflects a *care* for what things are in themselves and cannot be reduced to means to secure their new identity as scientific objects (we return to the issue of caring for things as mode of engagement in chapter 9). Likewise, the meticulous work of cataloguing finds, describing the characteristics, making drawings and sketches, "unconceals" certain properties of things and brings them close to us. The texture, form, size, weight, color, scars, and wrinkles of unearthed things are all accounted for. These are acts of domestication and categorization that may reduce the richness of things and contexts. Not every aspect of an artifact or location can be noted and compared with others. Nevertheless, immediate familiarity with things embedded in such work is indispensable for a *discipline* of things (cf. Ingold 2007).

Bringing home also raises important epistemological issues. What is brought back from the field consists not only of artifacts and ecofacts, but also their contextual settings. This is rendered as many inscriptions and mediations (photos, drawings, measurements). It has long been recognized that it is important to bring back from the field enough inscriptions to create a stable "record" of the site. The excavated site needs to be transformed into an articulated *assemblage* of artifacts, soil samples, and media, enough to create an adequate archive or a three-dimensional rendering of the site. As with excavation itself, this transformation is often described as destructive (cf. Lucas 2001b). Removing the things from their original "home" is seen as a process of loss, and fieldwork and postexcavation analyses become a means to minimize what is lost along the way. However, in epistemological terms, this process of bringing home (or removal) may also be seen as a productive enterprise that *increases* the potential meaningfulness of things (Latour 1986; Latour and Lowe 2011 on "the copy"). Being brought from a site "out there" to a museum is not only a matter of dislocation and disentanglement for the things involved; it also implies a relocation and reentanglement with similar or related objects from other sites. By entering new networks of association, new assemblages, the rim sherd from an early Funnel Beaker pot or the tang fragment of an Ahrensburg point achieves a meaning it could not have held as an individual specimen buried in the field.

Care and epistemological gains are, however, not the only and exclusive aspects of this trade. As addressed by a number of studies (Trigger 2006; Kohl 1981; Bandaranayke 1977), there is also the political economy of fieldwork and bringing home, the displacement, the movement of archaeological goods. Archaeologists in most countries consider their state borders as also defining disciplinary territory. They dig in their own country or region, with state and academic jurisdiction coinciding. Other archaeologists cross borders. Seen in the context of the global political economy, it is obviously not accidental from which countries border crossers come, and it raises questions of colonial and imperialist ideologies (Olsen 1991). Few expect the presence of Turkish, Icelandic, or Kenyan excavation teams or field schools in Germany, Britain, or the United States. "Bringing home" in archaeology is far from a reciprocal trade. While state-sponsored export of art works and other "displayable" cultural heritage objects has decreased (though not reversed), tracking the circulation of more mundane objects and media, those "raw" data transformed in order to travel and be processed into papers and other forms of intellectual capital, has largely slipped from critical concern in archaeology (consider, however, the activities of the World Archaeological Congress). Exporting the processed intellectual goods back in the forms of English-language books and papers reinforces the patron-client relationships (cf. Galtung 1974). Similar asymmetries are, of course, (re)produced on more national and regional levels all over the world.

The movement of archaeological goods, including the bringing home of data, thus raises ethical and political questions of equity; in many respects the global political economy of archaeological discourse and exchange is or has been unfair, rigged, and even exploitative. Typical justifications for the displacement and relocation of archaeological goods refer to conservation and treatment, and to raising the value of the intellectual capital through association with other goods and stronger research environments. In justifying the retention of the Parthenon sculptures acquired in the early nineteenth century from the ruin and mosque in Athens, the British Museum, for example, has emphasized the custodianship that they have received by virtue of being located in London, greater accessibility in terms of the open access to them afforded by this international museum, and the contextual enhancement in being displayed alongside other fine artworks in the collection.

Still, and despite the obvious problematic ethical and political issues raised by the asymmetry of this exchange, it would wrong to make such concern the only measure for how to evaluate this bringing home. As briefly exposed here, this is a layered and complex enterprise that cannot be subsumed to singular modes of judgment. Even if the removal of material from one part of the world to another cannot be legitimized only by referring to the care and treatment it receives at its destination, or by claiming that this new intellectual and material environment will increase its knowledge value, to completely ignore these aspects is equally debatable. As with humans, sometimes it is the case that things are better treated, receive more care, and have their potential more likely realized by being moved away from their home (though, in the case of the Parthenon Marbles, see St Clair 1998; also Hamilakis 2006; Jenkins 2001; Kehoe 2004; Lyons 2000).

## FIELDWORK AS COLLECTIVE ACTION

Archaeologists are not the only ones who do fieldwork; it is as much a methodological base for anthropology, animal ethology, and a number of natural sciences, such as geology. The tropes of "discovery" are also to some extent common: lost languages, lost tribes, lost lifeways and species, all rooted in a search for, or a rescue of a past that is no more. There is also the shared issue of going away to the field to collect objects, document their contextual information, and bring these data home. What then are the distinguishing qualities of *archaeological* fieldwork? In what ways, for example, is it really different from what *anthropologists* do in the field?

Let us begin with the simple distinction that archaeologists dig for remains, while social/cultural anthropologists observe people and what they do, often as participants. Excavation is a physical engagement. Data cannot be obtained without hard physical labor. Archaeologists (or, in some cases, their proxy workers) have to engage directly with earth and stone, and information cannot be gathered by pure observation. Additionally, while the social and cultural anthropologist typically works alone in the field, archaeological fieldwork is a collective task, which cannot be accomplished without many people and things. Excavation is what especially brings about this difference and is, in this sense, more

FIGURE 4.1. Excavations at Lovozero, Russia, in 2008 involve strings, stadia rods and baulks, trowels, brushes and clippers, buckets, scoops and sieves, rain gear, boots and knee pads, cameras, notebooks, and finds bags, as well as seasoned excavators and students.

central to the constitution of the discipline than surveying (but cf. Cherry 2011). From its beginnings, excavation has been a collective enterprise, involving all sorts of skills and labor, as well as shovels, picks, measuring instruments, and visual craftsmanship (fig. 4.1). Professional archaeology conspicuously enhanced such enterprise in the later nineteenth century and after, offering broader institutionalized infrastructures beyond the earlier amateur networks of antiquarians pursuing fieldwork and collection: museums came to organize great expeditions; universities came to run research programs; local and national governments have introduced legislative instruments to protect and promote the study of the archaeological past (see chapter 3). A significant difference to ethnographic fieldwork is that archaeology has continued to extend the scope and reach of its enterprise: ever more tasks are delegated to more people and more instruments . This collective enterprise operates, intervenes, penetrates the ground, and transforms sites.

There are several dimensions to this character of archaeological fieldwork as collective action. On the one hand, it is collective action in a very normal sense—in that it requires collaborative human work. Excavating a Bronze Age burial mound or a Linear Pottery long house requires large amounts of physical labor that cannot be effectively accomplished without sufficient crowds; a real workforce. It also requires an elaborate division of labor that has typically been mobilized through hierarchical organization and systematization of knowledge: digging, sieving, sorting, leveling, drawing, taking photos and field notes, directing and supervision, finds preparation, labeling, and so forth (Alexander 1970). This military style of organization is often claimed as stemming from a British school of field archaeology associated with General Augustus Pitt-Rivers (Bradley 1983, 3), and promoted through the popular descriptions of fieldwork given by another military man, Mortimer Wheeler in the middle of the twentieth century (1954). This may be an exaggeration. Military organization is only one example of the application of the efficiency of dendritic, hierarchical management systems (cf. Lucas 2001a, 22 ff.).

Moreover, the adoption of techniques and analytical methods from other disciplines and the increasing amount of material brought back from the field have both led to increased interdisciplinary cooperation as well as subdisciplinary specializations (Carver 2009; French 2002; Grant, Gorin, and Flemming 2008). Most, if not all, of these specialties relate to environmental archaeology and the natural sciences. This complexity and the multisited character of archaeological fieldwork is an old and typical state of the art. For example, in 1848, to investigate the shell middens of Jutland and Zealand, Denmark, a committee consisting of a geologist, a zoologist, and an archaeologist was appointed (Klindt-Jensen 1975, 71–73). When a second kitchen midden committee was appointed in 1893, an osteologist, a botanist, and an artist were added to the interdisciplinary team (Madsen et al. 1900). The number of relevant specialists has prompted increasing complexity in the management practices coordinating excavation and postexcavation analyses, synthesis, interpretation, and explanation. Specialists frequently work in laboratories, removed from the field setting, in specially equipped atmospheres, with the instruments, comparative collections, cold-storage facilities, administrative infrastructures, and archives necessary for the tasks at hand. Contemporary archaeology could not be accomplished without these laboratories and the work that they do.

Archaeological fieldwork is collective action also in the sense that it mixes many people with many different kinds of things, from both the past and the present. Archaeology is, to borrow Bruno Latour's phrase "an action that collects different types of forces woven together because they are different" (Latour 2005, 74). Digging, from the very beginning, has involved helpful tools (spades, hoes, trowels, trays, buckets, wheelbarrows, etc.) that ease the toil of removing earth and soil. Moreover, to be able to document a site, coordinates and measurements are needed, achieved through compass, string, measuring tapes, ranging poles, leveling instruments, theodolites, and total stations. It also requires reliable tools for inscription, including pencils, graph paper and boards, context sheets, notebooks, cameras, tripods, and now laptop computers (see Petrie 1904 for an early and detailed litany of these things). Finds need to be labeled, placed in plastic bags, conserved, described, and shelved when moved off site in vehicles. Standardization, afforded by accredited algorithms and classificatory systems, is essential for these collectives to be "cross-referenced," held together and shared (more on this in chapter 6). A set of Munsell color charts may be used to specify a shade of ceramic fabric, or the graphical convention of a Harris stratigraphical matrix may be used to convey relationships between layers and features. These standards are in tools, instruments, and charts, as well as conventions and agreements.

This takes us to another aspect of this collective character of archaeological fieldwork. Involved are institutions like museums and universities, funding agencies, CRM (cultural resource management) firms, and government departments that endorse standards and procedures, that accredit and authorize. A particular feature is that it involves *heritage*—legislation and institutions that link local municipalities and communities to the state and nation building through notions of locality, identity, cultural value, and belonging. Doing archaeology and crafting the past is a process of exchange, translation, intermingling, and swapping properties between entities and actions (Webmoor and Witmore 2008). Digging also involves landowners, heritage authorities, government agencies, and university departments. Doing archaeology binds together all of these diverse actors, instruments, settings, and stages (Webmoor 2012a; Witmore 2004b). We have called these *collectives* of people and things; they are sociotechnical mixtures or *imbroglios;* they are *heterogeneous assemblages* in that they combine radically diverse components (Shanks 1991; cf. Law 1987; we return to assemblage in chapter 8). They are the *blood flow* of archaeology (cf. Latour 1999, 99).

While stressing the genuinely rich diversity of special interests and skills brought together in archaeology's fieldwork, conventional accounts and histories of archaeology typically simplify this complexity. Like the practical skills of field research, both the many components of these collectives and the finesse to deploy them are little mentioned (see, however, Shanks 1991; Larsen et al. 1993; cf. Callon 1986). But attention to the network of flows and articulations, what we might perhaps term archaeology's *artereality*, has profound implications both for how we go about archaeology and how we construct archaeological knowledge, indeed, for how archaeology may contribute to interests that range far beyond the archaeological.

An opening point is that archaeology's artereality confounds any notion that research has a linear flow, as described above; it is instead continuous and reversible. We don't expect this to be too contentious: most archaeologists would recognize that fieldwork and archaeological practice constantly return to assumptions, premises, and orthodox explanations in new cycles of research. The heterogeneity of archaeological collectives calls on archaeologists to reach out beyond the narrow confines of this circuit, however. A stronger argument is thus that archaeologists produce the material past within their collectives and simultaneously emerge as archaeologists along with the past. Doing archaeology is part of our own self-construction. To conduct successful research, archaeologists become involved in heterogeneous engineering of *past, present, and future*.

To unpack this argument, we propose therefore to take a critical view of the management issues at the heart of archaeological practice.

## ARCHAEOLOGICAL MANAGEMENT AND CULTURAL PRODUCTION

We have touched upon aspects of the political economy of archaeology, the distribution of goods, the means of access, the powers and agencies implied by the connections forged in any archaeological project. Let's now focus on some logistical aspects of archaeological practice that come under the heading of "management," in the broad sense of how things get done, how projects are organized, how people and resources are coordinated in order to achieve desired ends (see, e.g., the hierarchical chains of command illustrated by Alexander 1970, 17, fig. 1, and Joukowsky 1980, 26, fig. 3.1).

Discussion of archaeological management specifies more or less standardized procedures that assume a neutral management structure (see, e.g., Alexander 1970; Barker 1982; Cooper et al. 1995; Webster 1963; cf. also the British Ancient Monuments Board's "Frere Report" [Great

Britain 1975]). Typical concerns are with efficient information flow (maintaining clarity in the application of a research design as well as simply ensuring order on site), division of labor, and human financial resource management. Professional and academic responsibility and codes of ethics are an overarching and prominent theme. All orthodox management models uphold fidelity to professional standards. Accredited by various national and international professional associations, these are designed to deliver particular discursive objects, reports and archives, and proxies for the past, as well as to regulate practice, ensuring equitable and fair representation of client and constituency interests, for example. There is some considerable debate on the latter as to how to deliver archaeological research that reflects the distribution of stakeholder interests in a particular archaeological theme or project—for example, the stakeholder interests of minorities might be swamped by more powerful hegemonic orthodoxies (see Webmoor 2007b and 2009 for critical discussions).

We have found little published discussion of alternative management models outside of the anecdotal (e.g., Dowdall and Parish 2003; Swidler et al. 1997). The World Archaeology Congress (WAC) offers a forum and pressure group, almost a professional association, particularly with respect to less well-represented stakeholder interest groups. But WAC stops short of offering a clear alternative management model, though embroiled in the cultural politics of archaeology since its inception. We might, similarly, look to the litany of excavation handbooks in archaeology for examples of good management practice. In his book *Excavation* (2000), Steve Roskams proposes a different division of labor and raises the pertinence of the Marxian emphasis on modes of production of archaeological knowledge. However, he doesn't address management issues. We might even ask whether there are *any* alternative management models in archaeology.

We are not suggesting that good management models do not exist. They are, to the contrary, already there in the best archaeological practice. We, however, suggest that making this explicit is essential for improvement. Consider the work of Archaeological Services Durham University (ASDU), an exemplar of good collective practice combined with an emphasis on management strategy.

Centered on the sequence of statigraphic relations between different contexts, ASDU, like most British archaeological units, has adopted the single context system, now widely used in excavation across Europe. Contexts are instantiations of events—what remains of past events—that

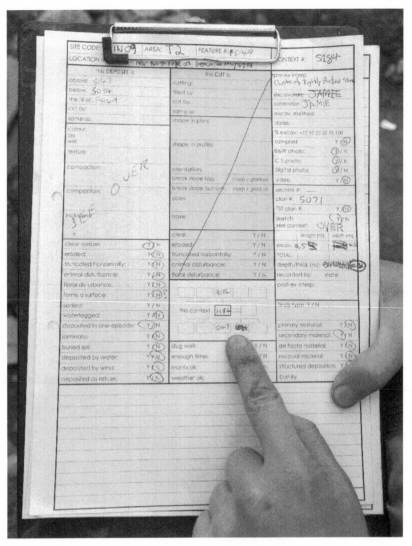

FIGURE 4.2. Archaeological Services Durham University (ASDU) pro forma context sheet, obverse of context #209, Binchester excavations, 2010.

can be differentiated from other events on the basis of various observable "traits." Contexts are manifest either as "cuts" or "deposits" and are recorded on what are termed pro forma sheets. The ASDU pro forma sheet for context #209 of the 2010 excavation at Binchester in County Durham, England (fig. 4.2), for example, records the deposit with a combination of sketch map (gridded space is provided on the reverse side of the sheet), diagram (Harris matrices), narrative, and boxes pertaining to descriptive details, including color, moisture saturation, composition, texture, and compaction. A guarantor of dutifully followed protocols, the context sheet is simultaneously a reference grid providing continuity to other contexts, features, finds, media (black and white or digital photos, color slides, video, plans), interlocutors (excavators, supervisors, JCB (backhoe), mattock, trowels, and so on), and other sundry details of the excavation process (whether the context was dug well, with sufficient time and in what weather conditions, and whether the supervisor is confident about the diagrammatic relation in the matrix).[3]

According to ASDU's manager, Peter Carne, the context sheets are designed, not only to accommodate necessary standards and protocols, but also to avoid predetermined terminology/classification as far as possible. ASDU takes a pragmatic line on excavation as an ongoing, developing project, however, and seeks to avoid limiting observation to ordered information sets as specified on the context sheet. The aim is to situate classification as the outcome of interactions with the materials, features, things, and other personnel on site. Routine procedures and abstract standards are not regarded as exclusive guides. Neither Harris matrices nor context sheets are to be treated as ends in themselves; nor are they intermediaries between the material past and final publication. Rather, such "records" are mediators in a larger process. As Carne puts it, methodology needs to arise within specific communities of practice, in which roles emerge in response to the engaged materials and experiences on site (Carne 2010). From this more organic angle, media are modalities within an archaeology understood as *lived,* kinetic engagement.

Carne's aim is to maximize fidelity to the co-creation of both site and community. In order to do this, one must look to the specificities of locality and community as they co-emerge in practice (fig. 4.3). Locality matters—since all sites are different, one has to dig in slightly different ways. Communities matter—the goal is collective achievement, where everyone plays a role in the co-creation of the excavation, rather than

---

3. A cascade of previous iterations of the ASDU context sheets, all vetted through interactions with other sites and archaeologists, lies behind this systematic configuration. Edward C. Harris (1979), the city of Winchester in southern England, the Museum of London Archaeology Service (MoLAS), and thousands of interlocutors have contributed to the development of systematic recording (see Lucas 2001a). That every single reference on the context sheet is something of a black box is taken for granted.

FIGURE 4.3. Excavation of Trench 1 at Binchester, UK, July 2010.

individual recognition. For Carne, this means setting standard management schemes aside. Excavation undertaken by a standard academic hierarchy, with professor at the helm, followed by a trail of PhDs, graduate students, and undergrads, divorces direction from data, leading more to the reproduction of academic/social relations than to a faithful portrayal of the material (Carne 2010). Linear flow charts, discussed earlier in this chapter, result in a production line where everyone is assigned a specific tasks and trained in specific techniques. The fidelity here is more to predefined products than to the idiosyncrasies of what is in the ground. By generating ordered sets of information about the material world, archaeology simultaneously changes that world into forms that are more accommodating to being rendered in such sets (see Lucas 2012; Webmoor 2005; Witmore 2009, 523).

Carne's management philosophy is one committed to excavation as community practice whose larger loyalty is to the materials, features, and things archaeologists work with, and with which they co-emerge. An undergraduate participant may become a meticulous and competent excavator, and an ill-defined area of stone may turn out to be the corner junction of a former wall (for more on archaeology and co-emergence, see Webmoor 2012a; Witmore forthcoming). Carne combines an approach that maximizes existing skills, knowledge, and practice, while recognizing what comes out of the ground as an active mediator of production. For this to occur, one's management practice should follow an agnostic and unassuming line, where position takes a backseat to engagement. Practice is something in constant need of improvement, and a commitment to the specific community involved is important.

ASDU's management model is both agile and subtle. It is both faithful to the idiosyncrasies of the materials and recognizes the importance of creativity in dealing with things. It emphasizes care, but not too much, which, for Carne, would lead one to discern things that are not there in excavation (2010). Its larger commitment does not center upon individuals, but on a community of practice with a shared obligation to the objects, features, and sites it engages. It is important for management to be grounded in the specificities of the site, rather than driven by discourse and hierarchical or academic relations arising from outside.

From the example of ASDU, which in a European context is quite typical, we suggest three key points for organizing archaeology: (1) good management recognizes the primacy of operating pragmatically in medias res; (2) good management emphasizes the documentation of the "place/event," that is, the *locatedness* of kinetic experience; (3) good management is local, that is, its fidelities are to the co-creation of community and specificities of site and not to rigid procedures and abstract standards. The values and larger loyalties of this management model are to care, authenticity, and genuine responsibility (Shanks and Webmoor 2012). Archaeology as craftwork is the iterative reworking of the past *and* the present with a view to sustainable futures. It looks to creative possibility and takes long-term perspectives on matters of common concern (Shanks 2007; Shanks and Witmore 2010a).

## CONCLUSION

This chapter has been an attempt to unpack archaeological fieldwork, when archaeologists work on what is left of the past in "the field." We have argued that archaeology is a unique kind of production within collectives—a co-production that involves indeterminate mixtures of people, things, institutions, flows of goods, standards, and agreements. Conventional accounts of what fieldwork is, how it is conducted, and who does it have narrowed our understanding of this defining activity of archaeology. The trend toward intellectualizing archaeological research overlooks the learned skills and tacit knowledge of working as collectives. "Reflexive" responses have begun to acknowledge some of the unspoken complexities and familiarities of this collective work. But they have not gone far enough in acknowledging and crediting the people and things that perform the practical and intellectual actions of research.

We can no longer separate how we know from what we know. Whether excavating a trench or surveying on the surface, "archaeological work" is an inseparable mixture of intellectual reasoning and practical, hands-on know-how. One of archaeology's most admirable skills is "thinking with one's hands" in following and being led by things. Modern science, in its Platonic tradition, has for too long elevated the contemplative activity of research above material practice. This division of activities and subsequent prioritization of one over the other is changing both in the field of science studies and within archaeology itself. Indeed, a history of archaeology recounted from the standpoint of field research would place less emphasis on brilliant individuals developing and applying scientific techniques than on the working out of solutions to particular problems with the aid of more or different colleagues, instruments, equipment, and media. The cognitive and the craft are mixed from the start in the collective activity that defines archaeology.

This argument has led us to suggest that a creative way forward for archaeology and, more broadly, for contemporary archaeological interests that engage the past in the present, is through reflecting directly and precisely upon how we engineer the collectives at the heart of archaeological practice. Learning from software development and design studies, we ask: what is it that we seek to produce? Is it enriched experience? Is it better stories about the past, attuned to changing circumstances? Is it continually new articulations of past and present, recognizing that the most profound innovation in archaeology is always premised upon an understanding of the long historical genealogies that have brought us to where we are?

# CHAPTER 5

# Things in Translation

*Documents and Imagery*

Archaeology abounds not only in artifacts from the past but in modes of documenting and studying them. In this chapter, we look at the way visuality works in archaeology, from the graphics, maps, and photographs themselves to the roles they play. Along the way, we question the stress placed in much discussion of visual media on their mimetic and representational qualities—that is, their fidelity to what they are taken to represent and their degree of correspondence to what is represented.

Looking at what might be called the political economy of visual media—the work they do in archaeology through networks of production, circulation, transaction, and articulation—also leads us to identify some of the implications of emergent digital media, not for more spectacular summations of data about the past, but as open forums for the co-production of pasts that matter now and for community building in the future.

## VISUALITY IN ARCHAEOLOGY

A basic premise of all archaeology is that archaeologists need to record and publish what they find. Through excavation, through the displacement of artifacts into collections, acts of conservation, or even in the course of surveying a site, as archaeologists, we simultaneously affect and change that which holds our interest. In this, there is often a rather peculiar trade-off: in working with things, in laboring toward their display, we participate in their destruction.

In the archaeological relationship between the things of the past and present that lies behind this idea of the "unrepeatable experiment" is a distinctive experience of immediacy—a notion of "discovering" the past in its material remains. This is the time of connection or engagement, the relationship of material duration and present engagement. Two terms that describe this temporality are "actuality" (Benjamin 1996b, 473–76), the juxtaposition of two presents, that of the past "as it was" back then, and that of the present, as we turn with interest to the past, and the *kairos,* or time of connection, between past and present (and that key opportune moment when the past appears to us).

Visual media are indispensable in the process of documentation, that is, the practice of transforming the things of the past into manageable, malleable forms. From reconnaissance surveys to excavation of features to laboratory analyses and interpretation of glyphs, the work archaeologists perform could not be accomplished without proxies of our vision of the past. This holds all the way from research methodology and project planning to information design and presentation of results. Understanding the past, making archaeological knowledge, is primarily about the process of making and using media.

Archaeology is about working on what's left of what was; archaeologists do not simply discover the past. The things we deem to be of the past are often on the move (see also chapter 6). Taking it up, sorting, classifying, counting, drawing, and measuring so that we can discern relationships, patterns, quantities, and changes are what archaeologists spend much of their time doing. This is an especially important part of designing quantitative information (Tufte 1997, 2001). But it is no less an integral part of engaging with the past through more affective means; the theme of the ruined past in the present, for example, has consistently proved to be a prominent component of landscape imagery in the West since the seventeenth century (Andrews 1999; Makarius 2004).

The archaeological process can be described as one that moves through a continuity of material worlds that run from ruins and remains to two-dimensional "proxies," those "stand-ins" for the material world that comprise the world of our media. It is more about crafting what remains of the past into "deliverables" (Shanks and McGuire 1996), into texts, graphs, maps, drawings, or photographs: this is the work of visual media in archaeology. Yes, there is, of course, the crafting of artifacts, material remains, and project archives, but much effort is required to produce the outcomes, those two-dimensional deliverables. It ought to be recognized as a highly skilled process akin to (reverse) engineering. Yet archaeologists tend to truncate this long sequence of workings on the past, these "serial orders of representations" that get us from the henge monument, the wall line, the abandonment level, or the storage pithos to the monograph, article, report, and web site (Lynch and Woolgar 1990, 5). Archaeologists mainly focus on the final products, particularly those that summarize and argue for a particular point of view or interpretation. We elide numerous transformative steps linking different media and their referents (Witmore 2004b). We "black box" the archaeological process as if there were only "inputs" and "outputs," with little inspection of the messy middle (Latour 1999, 304). Excavators, whether skilled or unskilled laborers, technicians, consultants, curators, and the many other specialists involved in archaeological engineering never act alone, however—archaeology's productive forces involve the actions of a complex host of characters. A political economy of media would recover the work done by our mundane plans, maps, photographs, narratives, and archives.

This elision is, of course, most often a practical necessity. Research cannot return every time to raw data sets, to first principles, to the minutiae of every project archive. We do have to rely on media that gather, articulate, and simplify the inexhaustible richness encountered in dispersed sites, collections, and archives. Our point is that unpacking the work puts stress upon the *process* of archaeological research, upon principles of traceability, upon this in-between, rather than the exclusivity of the ends, those ideas of verisimilitude or "seeing the past as it was."

## ARCHAEOLOGY'S COMMITMENT TO MIMETIC MEDIA

Archaeological work is connected to an ethical imperative to record authentically, with fidelity. Because archaeologists transform what remains of the past through their collective work, displacing and irrevocably transforming cuts, deposits, and features, they most often give epistemological primacy to the material remains: a drawing or photograph is considered secondary or a means to the actual things of the past, even though we could not construct knowledge of the past without such media. This makes visual media supplemental in a Derridean sense (Derrida 1976). The archaeological image is akin to a prosthesis—an artificial substitution to replace a loss or absence. The past cannot be known without media, and archaeology works in this charged middle ground—a fundamental point that lies behind our elucidation of the political economy of archaeological media.

The epistemological deferment to the "original" past accompanies a strong commitment in archaeology to a particular kind of representational accuracy, one that is technologically enabled and based upon a correspondence theory of truth. The translation of experience of archaeological remains, with all their complex qualities, into media frequently relies upon technologies (from geophysics to photography), instruments (from ground-penetrating radar to theodolites), and upon reproducible protocols and standardized procedures (from cartography and architectural surveys to cataloguing and finds drawing) that are taken to guarantee accuracy. There is often an early and thus enthusiastic adoption of media technologies in archaeology, whether it was the printed illustrated book, or systematic cartography, photography, and other forms of remote sensing, or more recently, architectural and virtual reality (VR) software. Consider again the work of Charles Thomas Newton with photography at Halicarnassus, for example (see chapter 3). Media artifacts produced with the aid of technology are most often evaluated in archaeology according to their degree of correspondence with what they represent, their mimetic qualities. These qualities are amplified in those cases where the human hand was removed from such processes. Consider Stuart Piggott's summary of the impact of photographic processes in the context of draftsmanship and illustration:

> From the beginning of printing all illustration (save in the exceptional circumstances where the original draftsman also made his engraving) interposed two interpreters between reality and the reader—the primary artist, and the craftsman who cut a block of soft wood across the grain, or engraved the end-grain of a hard one, or engraved, etched, mezzotinted, aquatinted or lithographed on metal or stone. With the introduction of the photographic processes, especially those of black-and-white line blocks, the original drawing could be transmitted in facsimile, or at most reduced in size, without passing through another person's mind. (Piggott 1965, 172)

We shall take a contemporary theme in archaeological visualization in order to examine the features of this commitment to "making increasingly accurate copies of what they depict" (Harman 2009a: 79). Since the 1980s, archaeologists have enthusiastically adopted software that enables 3D modeling and rendering. Coming out of professional architectural and engineering practice (computer-aided design) and the media industry (computer-generated imagery), increasingly affordable systems allow the creation of photorealistic simulations of ancient buildings and landscapes on the basis of archaeologically generated data. And not just on a computer screen; wearable media devices offer the possibility of more immersive simulations: Pompeii regenerated on a visor display, in the ruins themselves (see Raskin 2002; Siewiorek, Smailagic, and Starner 2008; Witmore 2004a, 2009). Accuracy can certainly and appropriately be correlated with the faithful witness of the photograph, because it effectively captures the style of things as they are seen. If the past is decaying and perpetually perishing, the attraction of an arrested or copied past to gaze upon is evident, even, as with photos of loved ones, comforting.

Virtual Reality experiences, typical of gaming and entertainment software, are making their way rapidly into archaeology and cognate fields (Forte and Sillotti 1997; Frischer and Dakouri-Hild 2008). In the last quarter of 2008, for example, Google offered 3D modeling of ancient Rome, superimposed upon their topographic and satellite imagery in Google Earth and based upon archaeological research and data processed at the University of Virginia. Visit Rome on your computer and you can fly through the ancient city of 320 C.E. Such visualizations complement CAD (Computer-Aided Design) simulations. Second Life, an online world, has grown rapidly since its launch in 2003 to become one of the Internet's most discussed manifestations of VR. It has several archaeological and "recreational" sites of antiquity. To explore the issues of VR in archaeology, in 2006 the Metamedia Lab at the Stanford Archaeology Center, in affiliation with Stanford Humanities Lab, undertook an experiment in constructing an archival facility in Second Life.

Life Squared, built on an island in the online world Second Life, is an archaeology of an artwork made by Lynn Hershman Leeson and Eleanor Coppola in 1972. In the Dante Hotel in San Francisco, Hershman Leeson created an installation of artifacts, traces, and remnants, posing questions of who had been there and what had happened. In 2005, Stanford University Special Collections acquired the artist's archive, which included what was left of the installation—texts, photos, artifacts. As part of the Presence Project (Gianacchi, Kaye, and Shanks 2012), an international interdisciplinary collaboration researching the archaeology of presence, the Daniel Langlois Foundation funded the reconstruction of the 1972 art installation at the Dante Hotel in 2006 in Second Life (fig. 5.1). This "animated archive" has since appeared at the Montreal Museum of Fine Art and the San Francisco Museum of Modern Art (Frieling 2008).

Life Squared thus addressed questions of how to treat archaeological or archival sources as the basis for the reconstruction, replication, or

FIGURE 5.1. Screen shot from Lynn Hershman Leeson's installation at the Dante Hotel, San Francisco.

simulation of an "original" experience and event: questions of how we might revisit the "presence" of an experience or event, in a "kairotic" connection, as previously defined. A context is the future of the art museum in the absence of a self-contained artwork (facing the question of how to curate "an experience"). Conspicuously, Life Squared is an experiment about modeling and simulation—core epistemological practices in archaeology.

An obvious option was to simulate the hotel of 1972 photorealistically so that avatars might rewalk the corridors as if they were there back then. Most of the VR experiences in Second Life aspire to photorealism. But we chose another option. In order to remain faithful to the fragmented remains, and in order to open up the 2006 experience to new associations (the actuality of the past), we traced out the surviving floor plan of the building and located the archived images and documents of the 1972 installation in a skeletal wire frame, reconstructed only to the extent attested by the sources. The fidelity to the original hotel of 1972 is highly selective; the hotel of 2006 in Second Life does not look anything like the original, yet it is empirically sound and contains nothing that cannot be verified. The result is something of a dissonance with the sunny photographs we have of the San Francisco street of 1972. Instead, it shares the ghostly light of Second Life of 2006 filtering through the digital ruins of a building hardly attested to now in any record or archive.

With respect to visualization, rather than a stand-for, substitute, or replica of the original, we chose to treat the "virtuality" of this online world as an opportunity for reiterative engagement, for people to come to a fresh participatory experience (Frieling 2008), connecting then and now. The intention was to open up the past to new interests and involvement, with avatars in Second Life revisiting and reworking the past on the basis of the surviving traces. A broader argument concerns the transitive character of information. Life Squared is based upon the premise that the information rooted in singular archives needs to be worked upon if it is to survive. Left in museum boxes in storage depots, sources will gather dust, molder, and decay. Information requires circulation, engagement, and articulation with the questions and interests of a researcher. "Inform" is a verb, not a substantive. Life Squared was explicitly treated as an experiment in "animating the archive."

Like an archaeological excavation, Second Life is a performance space indebted to visual media. We treated the space not as a representational medium, an animated 3D image, but as a prosthesis, as defined above, a cognitive instrument for probing this particular connection with the past. This shifts attention from visuality per se, the experience of forms and textures and the quality of the photorealism (aspiring to the response that "it surely did look like that"), to the specifics of how the traces of the past connect with the present, the avatar visiting the "hotel" of 2006 in a particular encounter located in the expectations and experiences of that avatar and his or her owner. This is to treat such a 3D world as a mediating space, and the construction of an archive as a co-productive project involving curator, the artifacts, and the visitors or users.

Another context for this project is the genre of theatre/archaeology, defined by Pearson and Shanks (2001) as the rearticulation of fragments of the past as real-time place-event, and sharing an interest in memory practices as part of a distinctive trend in contemporary fine and performing arts (Enwezor 2008; Giannacchi, Kaye, and Shanks 2012; Kaye 2000). This type of theater/archaeology is exemplified by Tri Bywyd (Three Lives), an ambitious assemblage of three portfolios of evidence put on by the performance company Brith Gof in the archaeological remains of a farmstead deep in a Welsh forest in 1995. Mediated by five performers, three architectures, an amplified sound track, various props, including flares, buckets of milk, a bible, a revolver, and a dead sheep, the three portfolios envision the "Welsh Fasting Girl" Sarah Jacob's death in 1869; an anonymous Welsh farmer's suicide in 1965; and the murder of Lynette White in Cardiff in 1988 (Kaye 2000, 125–38).

The explicit purpose of the work was to visualize and make manifest the subtleties of these archaeological/forensic narratives, but not to simulate or represent, or indeed to explain. The work's aesthetic, in common with much contemporary art, was not at all mimetic. "Three Rooms" (Shanks 2004) was another experiment in the documentary articulation of three forensic portfolios that eschewed any mimetic visuality, plot or character, but hinged on performance and the burden of work carried by memories and traces, albeit set in the long tension between urban and rural experience.

We needn't look only to the contemporary visual and performing arts for a critique of photorealistic mimesis. The impact of Foucauldian notions of discourse and the growth of the interdisciplinary field of media studies has resulted in a substantial body of critical reflection upon representations in archaeology (Clack and Brittain 2007; Joyce 2002; Molyneaux 1997; Smiles and Moser 2005). For instance, Stephanie Moser (2001) has brought discourse analysis to the visual conventions or visual language of archaeology. Timothy Clack and Marcus Brittain (2007) have taken a cultural studies approach, highlighting the manner in which popular appropriations of archaeological information have a "dumbing down" effect on representations. (On the other hand, they equally emphasize that archaeological representations must be communicable to an increasingly interested public). This critical examination of archaeological representation is important. Indeed, a self-critical orientation steers us away from historical and cultural biases—such as the portrayal of Pleistocene "man the hunter" or other conceptions based upon patriarchal, sexist values (Gero and Root 1990).

Such appraisals generally end by distinguishing between "popular" and "pedagogical" representations, on the one hand, and "inter- and intra-specialist" representations, on the other (Clack and Brittain 2007, 31). This seems to imply that representations geared toward popular communication inevitably stray from certainty, while others stick closer to the data. Of course, it depends on the image or graphic, but is there a datum that can be taken as the origin of a representation? Perhaps it is simpler to ask more broadly: just what are we representing with our visual media in archaeology?

## CORRESPONDENCE AND EVALUATION

Certainty and assurance also motivate archaeology's desire for photorealism. The belief in representing the things of the past, or, indeed, the past as it was, with fidelity, is coupled with the need to discriminate between different renderings. Expressions of archaeological epistemology have variously revolved around the notion of epistemic fit to the material past (Wylie 2002). In a concern to achieve more accurate or nuanced representations of ruins, vestiges, and artifacts, archaeology has moved in a historical trajectory in the development of its theory and methodology along with other natural and social sciences. Driven by ocular analogies, the pursuit of the "mirror of nature" (Rorty 1979) has involved the sciences in perennial questions of "representation and reality" (Putnam 1988). Philosophers of science have characterized such inquiry as the summum bonum of modernist epistemology. The reasoning and motivation is not misplaced: such a principle of representation as copy grants evaluative capacity to knowledge claims. Better representations are judged to match, hook onto, mirror, or correspond to an external reality. Therefore, better representations may be evaluated by peers as superior according to how they fit with the material world and the memories it holds of the past.

Such a conception of knowledge is very difficult to get to work. More specifically, knowledge claims do work; they just don't work by demonstrating any epistemologically privileged relationship with an external and removed reality. We sidestep the problem by refusing the radical distinction between the past and our claims to know it. This is not to question the reality of the past by asserting that we construct it. It is simply to question a modernist epistemological tradition that presumes an ontological rift between people and things, between internal minds and external reality, between the past and the present, between what we do (as archaeologists) and how we represent this practice. And if we sidestep such a deeply rooted epistemology, we avoid a theory of truth that rests on the correspondence of words with the world and bolsters a faith in representational proxies that "stand for" things.

In this shift away from questions of epistemology, the answer to the question of whether there is a datum, an origin to archaeological "mediawork," is clear. The idea of a "record" waiting to be passively recovered and represented is too simple. It begs the "Pompeii Premise," an assumption that there is an inert, static "past" to be represented, free from the kinetics of ever-present distortion (Binford 1981; Schiffer 1976).

Thoughtful archaeologists have been long aware that the "archaeological record" is something created through the work of making media. Transforming the dynamic and materially complex ruins in the landscape into media artifacts releases something of them into circulation as "immutable mobiles" that may be taken back to our laboratories, offices, and archives (Latour 1986; see also Lucas 2001a; Witmore 2006). These immutable mobiles are not copies, means to ends, or intermediaries. Rather, they are translations, the means and the ends, and full-blown mediators (see Latour 1987, 2005).

Several discussions regarding the complexity of archaeological science are relevant here: Michael Shanks and Christopher Tilley (1987) introduced the notion of archaeology's "fourfold hermeneutic" to capture something of these transformations; Lewis Binford (1977, 1989) and Michael Schiffer (1988) debated the character of the "middle-range theory" required to articulate past sociocultural processes from remains that had been subject to the transformation of natural and social origin; Linda Patrik (1985) and John Barrett (1988) contested even the reality of an "archaeological record" (now see Lucas 2012). The ethics of heritage interests and their impact upon what is left of the past are in the forefront of concern in archaeology's professional sector today. Visual media and representations occur throughout this manifold of operations performed upon what remains of the past.

Asking whether there is something that we are ultimately representing in our archaeological work, questioning the nature and origin of the archaeological record and determining our epistemic relationship to it, certainly provokes us. The particularity of archaeological work centers upon the "kairotic" temporality we have outlined, upon the relationship of artifacts and sites to social, cultural, and historical change, and upon the processes of decay and entropy that remains of the past undergo.

This transformative power of visual media is amplified through digitization. And the extraordinary power of digital media is perhaps encapsulated in geographical information systems (GIS) and VR software, which offer the potential of connecting data to spatial coordinates, fleshing out site and landscape, and rendering simulated pasts in photographic detail, all on the scale of world building—as complete a model of the past as possible; a "digital heritage" (Webmoor 2008). We might become enthralled with the "cool factor" and get caught up in a technological optimism aiming at such simulation and accept mimetic correspondence as achievable, at least in some circumstances (Solli 2008). But the epistemological conundrums remain, and we suggest that it is better to think of archaeological work in a different way, not as mimesis, modeling, simulating, or representing, but as a fundamental transformation or translation, work done in the spaces between old things and the stories they hold in the present—mediation.

Support for this view of representation in archaeology comes from a range of work in science studies and cognitive science. Early modern experimental science was wrapped up in "natural magic." Prescientific instruments were frequently popular parlor tricks. Magic lanterns, the camera obscura, and Robert Boyle's vacuum pump were employed for entertainment and edification.[1] Nevertheless, such popular technologies came to be valued for their capacity to augment the human senses and inscribe what they registered at the boundaries of human perception. Early demonstrations to gatherings of peers were intended to show the matters of fact under consideration through viewing and witnessing the instruments themselves. These ocular demonstrations relied upon common and shared experience for the settling of disputes concerning hypothesized entities and natural philosophy.

As considerations of nature became more abstract, delving into matters of cause and effect, instruments increasingly had to produce visual outputs. By the end of the eighteenth century, demonstrations gave way to recording instruments that mechanically translated relationships into visual media that were not modeled upon ocular perception. An example was James Watt's indicator diagram of 1796. A gauge attached to a steam engine physically translated the pressure in a cylinder into an inscriptional graph of volume versus pressure. These instruments translated a world not visible by the unaided senses into "self-illustrating phenomena." They produced visual media that were abstractions of physical processes. And ever-increasing amounts of background knowledge and assumptions were required to "read off" the invisible processes. They "showed" results, but through nonmimetic transformation.

Developing from the earliest diagrams of William Playfair and Johann Lambert, graphs, charts, and other visualizations, so common now to

---

1. We might further consider these points with respect to the figures behind the tradition of British empiricism. Francis Bacon and John Locke were distrustful of these instruments and the visual rhetoric that they produced (Hankins and Silverman 1995).

scientific endeavor, retain little physiognomic or iconic relationship to their subject matter. Instead, these visual media enable cognitive work to be performed. They have become cognitive prostheses rather than visual analogs for the world around us (Hankins and Silverman 1995; Tversky 1999). Visual media help us think and work as tools. They only "represent" in a very loose and often highly abstract manner. In step with the increased sophistication of instrumentation, our capacity for "intervention" comes to be the epistemic guarantor of our results.

Consequently, visual media are valued for their indispensable role in making modern science work (Carusi, Hoel, Webmoor, and Woolgar in press; Latour 1999; Lynch and Woolgar 1990). Emphasis has shifted away from debating whether information conveyed visually corresponds to the world toward information design and effectively expressing research with specific modes of engaging that information in mind (Tufte 1997, 2001). Correspondence is a difficult road to take with archaeology's visual media. It robs media of their active role, begs wearisome epistemological questions, and encourages a passive "past voyeurism" on the part of the public. Media, it cannot be overemphasized, are far from mirror copies.

## SIR WALTER SCOTT AND THE ANXIETY OF MEDIATION

Walter Scott (1771–1832) was a magistrate, antiquarian, musicologist, novelist, essayist, collector, landowner, poet, best-selling author in the new book trade of the early nineteenth century, and inventor of the historical novel. His focus was the borderland between Scotland and England, between past and present. The two volumes of his *Border Antiquities of England and Scotland* (1814), profusely and wonderfully illustrated with engravings in classic picturesque style, are subtitled "Comprising Specimens of Architecture and Sculpture, and other vestiges of former ages, accompanied by descriptions. Together with Illustrations of remarkable incidents in Border History and tradition, and Original Poetry." The work is a gazetteer of archaeological interests.

A long introduction takes the reader through a historical narrative of the Scottish border. On pages xviii–xix, Scott deals with the Roman frontier and Hadrian's Wall: "The most entire part of this celebrated monument, which is now, owing to the progress of improvement and enclosure, subjected to constant dilapidation, is to be found at a place called Glenwhelt, in the neighbourhood of Gilsland Spaw."

He adds a footnote:

Its height may be guessed from the following characteristic anecdote of the late Mr. Joseph Ritson, whose zeal for accuracy was so marked a feature in his investigations. That eminent antiquary, upon an excursion to Scotland, favoured the author with a visit. The wall was mentioned; and Mr. Ritson, who had been misinformed by some ignorant person at Hexham, was disposed strongly to dispute that any reliques of it yet remained. The author mentioned the place in the text, and said that there was as much of it standing as would break the neck of Mr. Ritson's informer were he to fall from it. Of this careless and metaphorical expression Mr. Ritson failed not to make a memorandum, and afterwards wrote to the author, that he had visited the place with the express purpose of jumping down from the wall in order to confute what he supposed a hyperbole. But he added, that, though not yet satisfied that it was quite high enough to break a man's neck, it was of elevation sufficient to render the experiment very dangerous. (Scott 1814, xviii–xix)

Was it that Ritson, a noted literary antiquarian, hadn't read the many accounts of the Wall published since the sixteenth century in that fascinating lost genre chorography? Unlikely. Had he forgotten? Or was it rather, as Scott suggests, that his "zeal for accuracy" meant he had to visit and witness the very structure in order to authenticate the written accounts of the remains? He clearly assumes that there was or had been a Wall: ancient authors and sources document it. What he disputes is that there is anything left. This tension between text and monument is very characteristic of antiquarian debate, and Ritson was renowned for his skepticism regarding claims for the authenticity of ancient manuscripts and historical documents.

Alexander Gordon's *Itinerarium Septentrionale: Or, A Journey Thro' Most of the Counties of Scotland, and Those in the North of England* was published through private subscription in 1726. It deals with Roman remains in the north and describes the surviving remains of Hadrian's Wall in great detail. Ritson may not have read it. He may have known it, but still doubted the description of Hadrian's Wall. We may assume that Scott had read it: his copy is still in his library at Abbotsford (fig. 5.2).

Gordon literally paces out and records every boot-marked trace of the Wall in his itinerary. He might not have jumped off the Wall, but you can almost hear every crunch of his boots through the pages of his expensive folio.

The book sets the "northern journey" in the context of accounts in ancient texts of the Romans in the north. Gordon knows his classical authors. The engravings are revealing. He illustrates many rectangular monuments in their various relationships with straight Roman roads. The monuments are all unexcavated and simply comprise earthen

FIGURE 5.2. Page 73 from Alexander Gordon's *Itinerarium Septentrionale: Or, A Journey Thro' Most of the Counties of Scotland, and Those in the North of England.*

features—tumbled-down, overgrown ramparts. Gordon's illustrations mark out nothing except rectangles and lines; though they have, significantly, been paced out. The engravings of sculpture show only sketched-in figures, focusing instead on the transcription of the inscribed text.

Ancient authors, epigraphy, and the antiquarian's boot—the topic here is the fidelity and authenticity of different kinds of witnessing of antiquity and its relics. This witnessing, representation, if you like, is in an indeterminate and debatable relationship to voice, text, image, and figure.

Scott's own writing represents a miscellany of voices articulating past and present. His bibliography includes: ethnomusicological collection of medieval bardic epic poetry; his own poetry; medieval historical novels (most notably *Ivanhoe*); the antiquarian gazetteer; historical novels dealing with Scottish themes in recent memory (such as *Waverley* and *Guy Mannering*); essays and nonfiction in various genres. Many of these were illustrated with the latest in steel engravings.

Scott consistently elides fact and fiction in his examination of traces in the present of the past (archaeological, memory, textual, toponyms, landscapes). Establishing the authentic voice of the past was a recurrent theme in literary antiquarianism in the eighteenth century, ranging from Thomas Percy's *Reliques of Ancient English Poetry,* an edited collection of antiquarian manuscript sources, to James Macpherson's creation of the wholly fictitious medieval bard Ossian (see Stewart 1994 for a fascinating treatment of this issue). A related interest is the transition from voice (oral poetry, verbal account, memory) to text (a new version of the old song, the annotated transcription/edition, the historical novel, historical narrative). A similar concern is evident in the efforts to relocate and translate experiences of ruins, monuments, and land authentically into the illustrated book—how the witnessing pace of the antiquarian, how sites and their names, how place-events become itinerary, chorography, cartography, or travelogue.

Conventional notions of media (as material modes of communication—print, painting, engraving, or as organizational/institutional forms—the media industries) are of limited help in understanding what Scott and his contemporaries were up to in mediating authorial voice and authentic traces of the past. We can consider the rise of cheaper engraved illustration, the popularity of the historical novel in the growth of the publishing industry, developments in cartographic techniques and instruments. But in order to understand how all this and more came to be archaeology—the field, social, and laboratory science—we need to rethink the concept of medium.

Scott, Ritson, Gordon, and their like are making manifest the past (or, crucially, are aiming to allow the past to manifest itself) in its traces through practices and performances (writing, corresponding, visiting, touring, mapping, pacing, debating), artifacts (letter, notebook, manuscript, printed book, pamphlet, map, plan, plaster cast, model), instruments (pen, paint brushes, rule, Claude Glass, camera lucida, surveying instruments, boots, wheeled transport, spades, shovels, buckets), systems and standards (taxonomy, itinerary, grid), authorized algorithms (the new philology, legal witnessing), dreams and design (of an old Scotland, of a nation's identity, of personal achievement). Making manifest came through manifold articulations. And "manifestation" was a complement to epistemological and ontological interest—getting to know the past "as it was, and is."

Visual media, in the conventional sense (print, engravings, maps), are involved, but also much more that challenges the premises of communication and representation underlying the concept of medium. What we are seeing, we suggest, is a reworking of ways of engaging with place, memory (forever lost, still in mind, to be recalled), history and time (historiography, decay, narrative), and artifacts (found and collected). The author's voice was being questioned and challenged. Who wrote the border ballads? Is this our history? Whom do you trust in their accounting for the past? Rational agricultural improvement was altering the traditional qualities of the land and ownership of land and property, which was being reinvented as landscape. The status of manufactured goods was changing rapidly in an industrialized northern Europe. That dinner with Ritson and the visit to Gilsland are establishing what constitutes an appropriate way of engaging with the past. It is only later on that Scott gets called a historical novelist, Ritson is marginalized as an irascible literary antiquarian, largely forgotten, and archaeology becomes the rationalized engagement with site and artifact through controlled observation, "fieldwork," and publication in standardized media and genres.

In this discourse over appropriate ways of engaging with the past, medium is better thought of as mode of engagement—a way of articulating people and artifacts, senses and aspirations, and all the associative chains and genealogical tracks that mistakenly get treated as historical and sociopolitical context. Scott presents us with a fascinating laboratory of such modes of engagement, one that runs from field science to romantic fiction through to what was to be later formalized as *Altertumswissenschaft* by German classical philology.

## A POLITICAL ECONOMY OF MEDIA

To recover the roles of media in archaeological work, let us now take a much closer look at a well-known example of archaeological surface survey and mapping. The aim of the Teotihuacan Mapping Project (TMP; fig. 5.3), begun in 1962 under the directorship of René Millon, was to provide the first complete map of Mesoamerica's first city, the entire area of which covered some twenty square kilometers. It was a prodigious effort, mobilizing a panoply of productive forces to transform the monumental ruin into media. The "TMP map" has become the media architecture for all subsequent research at the well-known site, and it anchors a rich and lively "heritage ecology" at the site today (Webmoor 2007a, 2008 and 2012a). To exhume how this influential piece of media became stabilized as the standard, and to unpack and clarify what we mean by transformation, we need to be utterly specific. We have to go back to April of 1962 (and again to September 1962).

Compañía Mexicana Aerofoto, subcontracted by Hunting Mapping of Toronto, flew over Teotihuacan and took photographs using a Wild RC5A high-precision aerial surveying camera with distortion-free lens

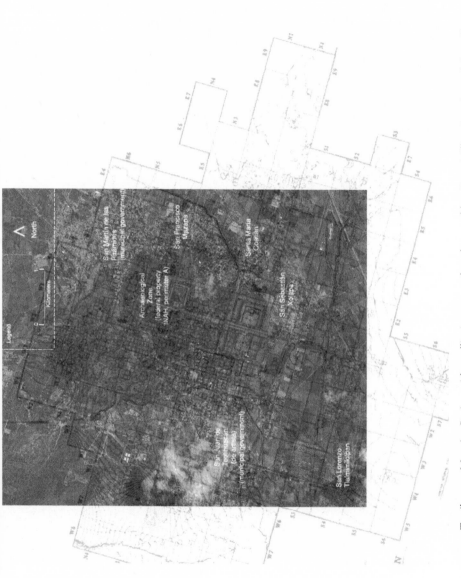

FIGURE 5.3. Teotihuacan Mapping Project with satellite imagery and modern pueblos. From Millon, Drewitt, and Cowgill 1973.

and a six-inch focal length. From 4,000 feet above the ground, the flight led to the generation of photographs at a scale of roughly 1:8000. These images would form the basis for photogrammetric drawings.

There were two stages to transforming the aerial photographs into maps: (1) from photo to photogrammetric drawing and; (2) from photogrammetric drawing to map. The aerial photographs contained too much information and detail irrelevant to the final map of the site's features, and in spite of all efforts on the part of the pilot and photographer, it could never be framed perfectly perpendicular to the ground surface. To reduce or to enable the identification of significant features and to compensate for oblique and irregular framing, ground control points were established at ten locations around Teotihuacan. These control points were located on the aerial photographs and the photographs were pierced with fine metal points. These metal points served to anchor the photographs to the ground. The 1:8000-scale photographs were transformed into glass plates. Cronaflex drafting film, which is dimensionally stable, was laid over the plates and permanent features of the site—architectural, natural, and modern infrastructural—were then penciled in. The Wild A8 stereo plotting instrument enabled the transformation of the glass plates into 1:2000 photogrametric drawings.

The mapping process moves from aerial perspective to photographs to glass plates to photogrammetric drawings, which were the basis for the TMP maps. Though many of those qualities apparent when walking the ruins of Teotihuacan have been lost—sounds, smells, textures, and kinetic experiences—much has been gained, especially when considered in terms of the project's goals. Spatial dimensions, so necessary for mapping an architecturally complex site, have been made the focus. Maintaining tight control over the establishment of control points and scaled transposition of glass plate to photogrammetric drawing meant that the accuracy of the final map was roughly 2.5m on the ground and usually within 1.25m. Feature boundaries, the line of house walls, the edge of pit structures, the orientation of steps, waterways (the Río San Juan, rerouted early in Teotihuacan's occupation, for instance), platforms, plaza dimensions, ancient roadways, and even, as a combination of all of these features, the directionality of the rigidly planned city are all particularly discernible. These properties of the ancient metropolis emerge against the backdrop of overgrowth and vegetation, crumbling walls and partially covered features, which superficially appear to dominate the photographs. The qualities of the site have been amplified, akin to the torqueing up (or down) of details, depending upon the scale of

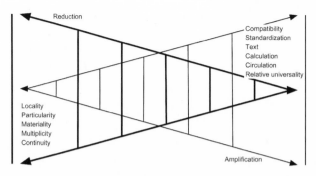

FIGURE 5.4. Circulating Reference. From Latour 1999, 70, 73.

map or photograph. There is an obvious trade-off in moving thus far along this chain of transformation from one medium into another.

Latour describes this entire process of moving across a series of small gaps as "circulating reference" (fig. 5.4). We no longer are talking of media mirroring nature, but rather of a heterogeneous set of instruments, actions, archaeologists, and others engaged in a series of coordinated operations articulated in order that the final map will do more than resemble the site: "it takes the place of the original situation" (Latour 1999, 67). It *stands in for* Teotihuacan so that it may be integrated with other information collected in the field—it must be fungible with graphical notation, statistical nomenclature, and textual narrative. Instead of a correspondence of the TMP map to the ruins of Teotihuacan, we have an actively manipulated transformation that holds something of the reality of the site and that may be circulated widely in order to be useful.

For practical use, the TMP personnel now have portable maps. These flat and mobile paper media are guides in predicting where other features and possible sites will be located and these may now be recorded and further mapped. Each step has transformed something of these visual qualities into a flat photograph, onto Cronaflex, and finally as paper.

In this movement, we have reduced Teotihuacan's particularity, locality, materiality, multiplicity, continuity, and ambiguity; but we have amplified compatibility, standardization, text, calculation, circulation (Latour 1999, 71; see fig. 5.4). None of these transformative steps, moving from one mode of engagement to another, from one visual media to another, can be described as a process of mimetic correspondence or a series of mirror copies. Or, if copies, then there meaning comes something closer to "copious" as suggested by the original Latin root *copia* (Latour and Lowe 2011). The aerial photograph is not a copy of the site itself, and the photogrammetric drawing at a 1:2000 scale is not a copy of the aerial photograph. Of course, they are closely related. But it is how they are related that makes for their usefulness to the TMP personnel. Each step in moving from matter to media is aligned with what came before and what will come after. With the metal pins piercing the aerial photographs, this alignment is physically apparent. With other steps, the alignment may not be so evident, but each mediation is carefully designed so that if one so wished, we could move back and forth by connecting up references circulated as media. Placing such reference trails for our visual media to follow is a basic element of the ecology of archaeological practices. Datum points, the Universal Transverse Mercator system, GPS coordinates, and the labeling of excavation corners facilitate such referencing. We usually focus upon these references in order to be systematic and consistent, for relocating sites and, most important, for reasons of provenience. Our information, our data, would lose much of their value if they were not linked up with these circulating references; yet our encompassing visual media only work by containing these references so that they can be linked "across" this chain. We "dig square holes" (cf. Thomas and Kelly 2006, 128) for the ease of translation into media that are fungible, combinable, and traceable to help ensure that these "chains of reference" don't break. Our work rests upon the traceability of this process, as does the question of accuracy (Latour 1986).

There is, however, still much more work to be done by the TMP crew (personnel, instruments, media, and supporting institutions) as they progress toward the two-volume, four-part compendium, containing over 147 maps (Millon 1973; Millon, Drewitt, and Cowgill 1973). The photogrammetric drawings based upon the planometric view of the site from 4,000 feet was tied to the ground of the site by physically substituting metal points piercing the aerial photos for the ground control points. It is so easy to overlook the seemingly mundane work that these unassuming pins do. Indeed, the task of superimposing images to the ground was delegated to these metal pins and, while they are absent in the final, flat map, it is these pins holding photo and drawing together that allow later sketches and locations obtained in the field to be placed on the map with the assurance of fidelity.

Following the precedent set while mapping the Maya city of Tikal, Millon chose to use a Cartesian grid-system comprised of $500m^2$ blocks

(Millon 1973, 7). This divided up the large site into manageable units, allowing Teotihuacan to be partitioned into ever-smaller blocks. In this way, all subsequent depictions of the site, from 3D "fly-throughs" of a virtual La Ventilla apartment compound to the stratigraphic profile of a trench in the *ciudadela,* can be hung on the scaffolding provided by the TMP map. It is a media architecture built for future generations. At the same time, the map is fluid and extensible. It can roll its grid outward infinitely to cover macro features; conversely, it can fold the micro details of burial offerings deep within the pyramid of the moon into its sliding scale. These are mercurial, hermetic media at their best.

The map itself now came to structure further survey, mapping, and engagement with Teotihuacan. What was to be the orientation of the 500m² grid? Looking at the 1:2000 photogrammetric drawings, Millon and the TMP crew could see that all of the structures of the pre-Hispanic city adhere to a citywide orientation (Millon 1993; Sugiyama 2005). This orientation was based upon quadrant dimensions, or more precisely a quincunx arrangement, accounting for the vertical dimension so important to Mesoamericans. With this orientation Teotihuacan North is approximately 15 degrees 25 minutes east of north. The crew chose the site's central avenue (the *avenida* or *calle de los muertos*) to serve as the centerline of the grid system and map, and thus orient the map to Teotihuacan north. The centerline for the map grid was drawn down the middle of the axis of the *avenida* on the 1:2000 drawings.

With this basis for survey, team member Raymond Krotser returned to the *avenida* and took measurements between prominent structures that were clearly distinguishable on the 1:2000 drawings (Millon 1973, 12). With the measurements in hand, he then plotted to the distances to see how closely they approximated their location on the ground. Krotser selected a final sixteen points, spanning 2,300m from the Pyramid of the Moon at the far north to an abandoned modern restaurant at the far south. These were marked on the drawings, and George Cowgill drew a "best fit line" (1973, 12). This was the "center line" on the drawings. And once established with reference to the *avenida,* it could be readily inscribed on the ground with the aid of paint and concrete and steel piping.

White lines mark the centerline along the northern half of the site. To the south the TMP personnel placed 50-centimeter-long, half-inch galvanized steel pipes driven into holes 20–30 centimeters deep and surrounded by concrete. They needed to be substantial so that they could serve as reliable witnesses in the future. Unlike the fragile marks on the drawings, these final steel rods will continue to stand-in for the orientation and layout of the TMP map on the ground. Larger versions of the steel tacks piercing the aerial photos, they are now tracers of this work on the ground. They anchor the grid to the material world; this is the work of suturing. Much of the responsibility of guaranteeing the precision and accuracy of the TMP personnel and of the final map is transferred to these durable markers. Once set, new measurements, a comparison of scaled distances to real distances, angles and triangulation to other enduring features can all be performed again (and again).

Aligned as paint, steel rods, and the site's architecture, with the centerlines of the primary axes in place, the 500m² blocks, which will form the basic units of surface survey, can now be drawn in and labeled on the 1:2000 photogrammetric base map of the entire site (Millon 1973, 18). What normally is placed first in the sequence of archaeological survey— field reconnaissance, taking measurements, and drawings—is actually secondary to the series of transformations that have just followed. With the map now anchored to the site, the field crews can begin a controlled ground survey. The maps of the TMP do not *stand for* Teotihuacan; they *stand in for* the site and provide a basis for further work to take place.

## MEDIATION, NOT REPRESENTATION

In our example from Teotihuacan, we have directed attention away from the communicative and representational function of media. We are arguing for a more performative appreciation of archaeology as work done with the things of the past, productive labor directed often toward building knowledge of the past, where such knowledge is an achievement, not a discovery.

That the "archaeological record" of sites and remains is an outcome of archaeological practice rather than a datum seems now well established (Hodder 1999; Lucas 2001a and 2012; Patrik 1985; Schiffer 1978). Something of the past is held in ruins and remains, in its archaeological traces, assembled through engagements with avenues and stone platforms, as well as operations performed with instruments, archives, through networks of institutions, and, of course, visual media. In this archaeological work, representation and "accuracy" come second to the critical need to move back and forth, to retrace the connections between the material remains, the evidence, and their stand-ins or proxies, the texts and visuals. This stabilizes the past, however provisionally, through connecting a host of humans and nonhumans. The measure of media is therefore their ability to afford such movement, such engagement, and to what extent they afford the possibility of future action upon and engagement with the past (we take this up in the following chapter).

One way that media may do this, somewhat ironically, is that representation can provide closure upon a piece of research. A convincing rhetoric of text and image (Gross 1990), a marshaling of evidence and study, can "black box" research such that it can be taken as given, work can move on, at least until the matter is reopened (Latour 1987). One aspect of such rhetoric involves visual media being treated as illustration, that is, they may act primarily as visual supports for statements made in a text (Webmoor 2005); photographs of an excavation, for example, may affirm the statements made about the structure of the site, rather than provide evidence for debate (Shanks 1997).

As corollary to this appreciation of active media(tion), the way media work with archaeologists, the paradigm of the archaeologist as custodian or steward of the past has been under serious challenge for some time now. As in the eighteenth century, this challenge is to do with shifting definitions (legal included) of cultural property. Archaeologists are again having to address the political matter of re-presentation—that is, advocacy and witnessing, who is representing (in a constitutional as well as communicative sense) the past, for whom, and on what basis. That the past is there as a datum to be represented is under question; though, of course, the traces remain, conspicuously prompting these questions and participating in arriving at potential answers. In chapter 8, we further elaborate the "expressive fallacy," introduced in chapter 2 above, that archaeological texts somehow "express" or represent the past. In chapter 6, we further consider these questions of manifestation in relation to memory practices and emergent digital technologies.

# Futures for Things

*Memory Practices and Digital Translation*

Chapter 4 took a closer look at the craft of archaeological fieldwork and made visible the collective and tacit labor that must be performed in order to translate the material world into the material past (the archaeological "record"). Archaeologists are keenly aware of the effort that is invested in crafting documents and imagery, and chapter 5 presented a range of vignettes to underscore the active and collective work necessary to relate material and media. Arguing against notions of "representation" as mimetic copy, with its philosophical pedigree rooted in correlationism (Bryant 2010, 277; Harman 2010, 22; Meillasoux 2008), we explored the question of translation and proposed an alternative practice of mediation. Emphasis was placed upon why the series of transformations and translations of local materials into stable and compatible forms capable of global circulation is most necessary for the discipline of archaeology. These modes of assembling material and media into standardized configurations are necessary in order to engage with a past. Otherwise, as developed in chapter 3, engagement with the material past would never have become a distinctive science.

All this sets the stage for this chapter, in which we begin asking to what ends we mediate the material past, following others concerned with the ontological consequences of our scientific assemblages (e.g., Barad 2007; Law 2004; Mol 2002). Our alternative to representational practice considers how we may assemble objects, documents, and imagery into stable pasts. It centers on a process of mixing, mingling, exchange, transaction, and swapping properties; of translation and co-emergence. It also takes into account the specificities of digital media, which offer different modes of manifesting things. These modes are richer, in light of particular questions, and they offer different possibilities for the translation, assembly, and stabilizing of pasts not predicated upon the conventions developed for analog representation. To develop these points, we have divided the chapter into three parts, respectively concerning memory practices, the noise of things, and digital media.

We begin with the issue of memory practices. In this, our focus is on what may be termed proactive, re-collective memory, which is more concerned with intentional and "inscribing" modes of remembering than with material and habit memory (for a discussion of the latter with respect to things, see Olsen 2010; also see chapter 7 in this book). Memory practices make explicit our materializing practices from the angle of how they facilitate the transportation of the material past into the future. Orderly information design is most necessary; to classify is human (Bowker and Star 1999). But these emphases must also be kept in check by struggling to re-member those qualities of things that cannot be conveyed in Euclidean space alone—that is, those qualities in excess, or what cannot be reduced or rendered into the conventions of realism and representation discussed in chapter 5. Notwithstanding that we may profit from mediating the qualities of things *qua* things, good memory practices come with an empirical obligation to iterative labor, including the retroactive verification of previous work (Witmore 2009). They imply an obligation to both determinacy and indeterminacy, to both signal and noise, to deal with what can be captured or documented through the conventions of media, and the background of indeterminate "noise," against which recognizable forms stand out.

The second portion of the chapter concerns the noise of things: their resistance to complete categorization and documentation. We treat language and visual media as specific mediating artifacts, rather than transparent windows onto the world. In so doing, we aim to flush out both the noncoherent qualities of the material world and the lives of things through two brief vignettes centered upon objects of archaeological concern in the northern Peloponnesus of Greece—the ruined citadel of Acrocorinth and the remnants of the Hadrianic Aqueduct.

The final section of this chapter considers digital mediation and translation, introduced in relation to potential futures for information design in archaeology in chapter 5. There we emphasized the practices, processes, and ambiguities of working on the past, in contrast to media as representational. From written texts to digital video, all media technologies transform our rapport with our worlds to one degree or another, thus effectively creating entirely novel objects of concern (Witmore 2009). What kinds of pasts, we may ask, can ultimately be realized in relation to the present with new digital modes of production? How do digital technologies graft onto analog techniques long established in archaeology? How does their suite of functionalities transform the material world differently from paper-based media? And how do the functionalities of digital media allow archaeologists to design and assemble things differently? In light of these questions, we address how digital media work and, in so doing, underscore the unique capacities of digital technologies to fold the requirements of a standardized and compatible "record" with the rich manifestation of ambiguities, the more ineffable qualities of things. In this, we aim to demonstrate how emerging media may be creatively deployed to fulfill the demands of good memory practices. Drawing on further examples from the Metamedia Lab in Stanford University's Archaeology Center, the final section of the chapter argues that archaeology can offer richer engagements with the past and the public in the era of digital technologies.

MEMORY PRACTICES

How we remember the pasts we generate as archaeologists is inevitably enmeshed with information design and infrastructure (Lampland and Star 2009). Both information design and the associated infrastructures of explication require data, metadata, and archival classifications and standards, and all of these rest upon shared commitments. As Geoffrey Bowker has meticulously detailed (2005), these commitments not only shape the kinds of pasts generated by scientific practices but also inscribe the horizons for future work. These points are especially pertinent for archaeology, for archaeological manifestation is simultaneously an act of memory. To manifest aspects of the material world is to articulate qualities suited to being rendered in those particular sets of information (again, this abstraction tends to filter out ambiguities in the generation of "explicit pasts"). What cannot be accommodated through these acts is doused in what the ancient Greeks called the waters of Lethe (the river of forgetfulness in Hades). Choices have to be made between what is recorded and what is left out; we cannot hang onto everything from the past; most has to be left behind. These acts of concomitantly making explicit ("committing to record") and relegating to oblivion, and how their manifestations are transported into the future, are what we term memory practices (after Bowker 2005; Webmoor 2012a).[1]

Memory practices are more than memory as it is commonly understood. They involve "legacy data" and enabling reiterative reengagement and recollection, so that information and accounts generated by archaeology will have longevity and be compatible with fundamentally different attitudes about and approaches to past and present. What will become of the information worlds generated by archaeology? How will they persist? We need to be able to stabilize material pasts with maximum usefulness, whether for now or for the distant future. This means that we should aim to mobilize what can be called variable ontologies, that is, leaving the past open to redefinition, reconstitution. In order to understand the importance of these acts, we need to further clarify what we mean by memory practices and how they differ from what we mean by memory.

For André Leroi-Gourhan, human memory, like the world of tools, was modified as the organs integrated within technical action were externalized as prosthetic devices (1993 [1964], 258). Just as the action of incisor teeth was transferred to the blade, that of the cerebral cortex was transmitted to specific media-relations (e.g., a card index within a researcher's field of vision; these points are echoed by McLuhan 1994 [1964]). Through this process of externalization, memory came to be stored within the wider ethnic group and within material culture.[2] Leroi-Gourhan divided the evolution of collective memory into five periods, beginning with oral transmission and cumulating in electronic serial transmission (emergent media; Pomian 1988 provides a complementary argument for vision). Eventually, this process of externalization would lead to co-intelligent entities—robot artificial intelligence and cognition, or even the "biological objects" Bruce Sterling calls "biots" (2005). In the contemporary digital era, the field of visual analytics has arisen to

---

1. Peter Sloterdijk has suggested that the "real fundamental term for modernity is not revolution, but *explication*," observing that the contemporary age "does not turn over objects or themes—it turns them out. It unfolds them, it pulls them to the forefront, it lays them out on a plane, it forces them to become manifest, it spells them out in a new analytic way and installs them into synthetic routines" (Sloterdijk 2008, 42).

2. Leroi-Gourhan's notion of externalization rests upon the assumption that memory is a kind ontologized mental phenomenon in need of externalization. His work stands in contrast to that of Bergson, and probably Merleau-Ponty, who have said that first and fundamental collective memory is pre- or nonlinguistic habit memory.

investigate the social and material augmentation of human cognition (Carusi, Hoel, and Webmoor 2012, 1–3).

Consider, for example, the exclusive oral transmission of memory. The voice is fleeting and such an exchange is always transient. Prior to written texts, collective memory required special groups who remembered. These groups cultivated a craft of association (we might point out the architectural mnemonics of the Roman rhetorician Quintilian or the memory palaces of the Jesuit priest Matteo Ricci [Spence 1985]), repetition, and mnemonic devices such as meter or rhyme. Writing, by contrast, pools otherwise fleeting events and provides them a spatial and material presence (we should note that initially these events were those not consigned to oral memory—Leroi-Gourhan notes that the Sumerians left records of debts, but no good recipes for minced lamb). Early on, the way that one read, the labor involved in passing through a manuscript, was conditioned by oral practices. Readers committed texts to memory "well enough to enable [them] to find their way around manuscripts with ease" (Leroi-Gourhan 1993 [1964], 261). As printed matter expanded beyond the threshold of recollection, references to the structure, indices, commentary, textual metadata became disembedded. Little by little, direct recall gave way to marginalia and footnotes. Eventually, tables of contents and indexes came to predominate as the modes of orientation and reference. Leroi-Gourhan discusses how new infrastructural arrangements—from index card systems for libraries to punched cards such as those used in the Jacquard loom to electronic, binary code and digital media—were devised to cope with the continued expansion of collective memory. With each new mode of externalized memory, profoundly different relationships with the past were generated.

Ours is an era in which different mnemonic registers are simultaneously juxtaposed and folded into each other within diverse and ever-burgeoning memory ecologies. The notes in the margins of any given text on our desks are medieval in date; the hygienic site photographs, along with the genre of the site report more generally, are protracted achievements that stretch out over the later half nineteenth century (see chapter 4); the calendar program some of us use to mark conference sessions was released on April 13, 2006, and the Java programming language in which the program was written appeared in 1995.[3] In each

3. Incidentally, the standard calendar we all share is based on two reforms, the first in 46 B.C.E. by Julius Caesar and the second in 1582 C.E. by Pope Gregory XIII (Holford-Strevens 2005).

case, memories are inscribed as a site report, in its margins, or in ordered boxes sustained across legions of Google servers. Should we need to retrieve these, we could walk to the shelf, thumb through the pages, or sign in to our e-mail accounts. Most of these actions are task-specific and individually located and would be of little use to any of our colleagues should these memories prove important in the future.

Today, mnemonic prostheses have proliferated and with them the costs of memory have plummeted. The thousands of notes, context sheets, and photographs, along with countless other measures typical of an archaeological excavation or a single season from a multi-year project, can now be stored on very convenient data-storage devices. Surely, with this combination of variety and lightness, humanity has never experienced better potential for collective memory. The range of detail, qualities, and nuances available for recall have never been more encompassing. And yet, despite all our hard work "committing to record," the future recall of these information sets is never guaranteed (Bowker 2005, 15). Moreover, with all the gains of every new memory prosthesis, there are concomitant losses, which often go unacknowledged (on the gains and losses between continuous and non-continuous media see Witmore 2009). With emerging media, any act of documentation always goes hand in hand with the need to curate (Shanks 2007; also see below). Archaeological entities and relations can be filed away and stored in dispersed locations, but to do so does not ensure longevity. Durability, longevity, preservation: these all come about through hard work, whether we are dealing with the field notebooks, permatrace drawings, and photographic negatives from a field survey conducted in the 1980s or with digital file corruptions. Along with every digital photograph, video diary, or sound recording we take comes an obligation to data management and preservation; these commitments require openness with regard to potential regeneration, reworking, remixing. Designing this digital heritage involves archaeology in a new political economy where the roles of "production" and "consumption" are increasingly merged (Webmoor 2008). Mundane technical issues such as data standards become paramount to preserving the past.

These points cast light upon the distinction between memory and memory practices: if memory is what is stored as various fields of media (in file cabinets, on library shelves, as .mp3 files), memory practices are how paths are designed to connect these various fields.

Collective archaeological memory and its associated memory practices are archival, that is, archival practices circumscribe how we approach things. These archives vary from singular collections of gray literatures with little circulation that are common in the world of contract archaeology to object-oriented databases that allow digital annotation. The range and diversity of archival collections mark our epoch as that of *potential* memory, as Geoffrey Bowker calls it. Here, "the question is not what the state 'knows' about a particular individual, say, but what it can know *should the need ever arise*" (Bowker 2005, 30).

This "information on demand" rests upon an underlying species of neglect. Databases and their underlying classification systems allow us to forget the idiosyncrasies of what is to be remembered. What is not "charismatic" does not get classified or stored (Bowker 2000). Furthermore, as Bowker puts it, what is stored in these dispersed archives comprises "not facts, but disaggregated classifications that can at will be reassembled to take the form of facts about the world" (2005, 18). Archaeological survey and excavation enlist media to enhance the qualities of standardization and compatibility for "data generation," for example, planning and surveying conventions, standardized finds classification, standardized color attribution, and even tab-delimited data matrices. The term "infrastructuring" foregrounds this transitive character of classification systems for "data storage" (Baker and Bowker 2007, 138). A database is far from a neutral matriculation of the world in media. We sort to sculpt information, though the capacities of things do constrain how we may assemble these collective pasts.

Currently, there are hundreds of initiatives to digitize and provide open access to archaeological and heritage archives. These initiatives range across a spectrum that extends from individual contract firms or projects to institutions (libraries, museums, or university archaeology programs) to government organizations to larger collective efforts.[4] Such archaeological databases aspire to enable other tasks through future data reuse. However, this reuse is constrained within the limits of the specified data standards. Indeed, reaching agreement on "standards"

4. In the United States, the high-profile Digital Archaeological Record (tDAR) and Digital Antiquity projects, funded inter alia by the National Science Foundation, aim at establishing consensus and convergence among archaeologists. ADS, a UK consortium of several universities and the Council for British Archaeology that provides a digital repository for archaeological information and ensures its cataloguing, storage, and longevity, is an excellent resource database for shared holdings of archaeological information from across the United Kingdom and abroad. See tDAR, www.tdar.org/confluence/display /TDAR/Home; Archaeological Data Service (ADS), http://ads.ahds.ac.uk; and see also, e.g., Hudson River Valley Heritage, www.hrvh.org/index.htm; MUSIT, www.unimus.no /arkeologi/forskning/sok.php (all accessed April 10, 2012).

is the motivation behind the Digital Archaeological Record's efforts to establish digital metadata protocols for archaeology (Kintigh 2006).

Of course, these standards are very necessary. We would not have reliable electricity, plumbing, mass transit, or health care without consistent standards (e.g., 110V 60Hz AC domestic electric power in the United States). Given the disjointed nature of archaeological data collection, in areas such as the Mediterranean, archaeologists are still far from attaining the coherent base necessary for comparing and combining data sets even on interregional distances—specifically, across the expanse of the Mediterranean Sea (Alcock and Cherry 2004). "The push to standardize presumes the ability to constrain a phenomenon within a particular set of dimensions, as well as the ability to dictate behavior to achieve the narrowly defined dimensions that stipulate its outcome," as Susan Leigh Star and Martha Lampland put it (2009, 14). Such constraints rely on different mnemonic registers, and just as there is a reality that standards and knowledge infrastructures strive to maintain, there is a politics of memory that they render invisible. Their performance is considered optimal insofar as they can be taken for granted (Bowker and Star 1999).

When we translate an event in archaeology, for example, a stone feature in a building's construction phase, we consign one form of material memory (trace or ruin) to yet other forms of material memory (this, of course, requires a particular object-orientation—on the material past as memory, see Jones 2007; Olivier 2008). At a general level, we bank artifacts in universities, museums, and storehouses, we database the final media translations of these, we relegate the mass of historical accounts of this process to a singular archive, a shelf or a box, which is rarely revisited, and we turn out a streamlined final report of this work. Let us briefly reconsider an example from excavation.

Throughout the preceding chapters we have drawn a distinction in terms of whether an account is centered on, say, the feature, a hearth, or the process of delineating such a feature through slight deviations in soil color and texture (mnemonic traces) at the edge of a working trowel. The narrative details of how the hearth came to be defined as such may be found in the excavation notebooks. The deviations in color and texture are translated into particular standards and classifications, which are often inscribed within the appropriate boxes on context sheets or transect forms (e.g., Munsell color 10YR 5/3, a classification based on hue, value, and chroma, or "sandy clay loam"). The relationship of the charcoal fill, stone lining, and surface cut may take the form of a series of stacked boxes in a Harris matrix. A photograph of the cleaned and measured hearth (extracted from countless others), or a carefully drawn plan, may find their way into a final publication. This is the point, in part. Final reports consolidate and allow us to forget the particulars (see, however, chapter 4); these, in turn, are held in reserve. The outcomes of events and processes are configured as objects of the past. This bracketing places the eventful nature of these exchanges, material relations enacted with specific people, instruments, and things, into separate registers. These particular processes are virtually invisible at the level of publication or in a digital database. Furthermore, the database often contains few clues about where these "metadata" are located.

All this brings us to the points we raised at the outset of this section on memory practices: shared commitments to standards, measures, categories, and classification generate the different object forms associated with the past; memory practices are ontologically generative. The way we organize the world translates into the ways we organize information and vice versa. In so doing, we inadvertently shape the horizons of possibility for future association with the things of the past. Consider the example of naming standards (the compatibility of which is the mission of organizations such as the UK Forum on Information Standards in Heritage [FISH]). A naming standard is a way of reckoning with things. Archaeologists may label a pile of unhewn stones a cairn, and in certain cases it might acquire further descriptive attributes such as "boundary cairn" or "field cairn." However, in other sets of relations, these same stones may be a quarry for materials used in the construction of a windbreak for a campfire or a platform to enable goats to reach higher foliage. We shall return to the question of the many lives things lead; it suffices for now to mention that standardized naming abstracts some attributes or characteristics from other potential relations that are constantly on the move from other times and other spaces. Such abstractions are what are carried forward in information design. Further work comes to depend upon the observation of a thing *as* a cairn even if one returns with doubt about this interpretation (in databases these named things acquire a modular character, enabling them to be shuffled around and further built upon).

These concerns are amplified in such cases as the hearth where what remains is no longer what it was. Archaeologists often only get one shot at translating the things and their relations that are displaced by excavation.[5] Here, reflexive practices have been deployed to address these moments, for example providing video documentation of the attribution of a material feature to a certain class of objects like a hearth (e.g., Hodder 1999), but such reflexive practice can only take us so far. Archaeologists can bring as many interpretations to an exchange videoed in the trench as there are personnel on a given project, and this is certainly good practice, but no one can know how the horizons of archaeological possibility will have shifted ten years from now. If history has taught us anything about this issue, it is that different information sets bequeath us radically different pasts. A globular jug excavated by Heinrich Schliemann at Tiryns can afford further relations in terms of style or design. We may speak of issues of chronology, trade, or craftsmanship by association, but no comparison can be made in terms of proximity to other pots and features, nor can we be 100 percent certain of its final contents through organic residue analysis. The strength of such material pasts rests upon an ability to expand through association (contextual, stylistic, physical, or chemical studies that expand the potential for articulating networks). It also connects with our ability to engage them in the context of other times and spaces.

Perpetual perishing does not stop with transformation into record. Memory wanes here as well. In the struggle against entropy (forgetting), memory practices need be reiterative and itinerant. It is certainly the case that with diligent work, a ceramic object or a standing menhir can acquire new attributes and go on to live new lives as an account, a data matrix, an entry in a global information system (GIS) map. Where such things remain there is a concomitant need for returning, remixing, and reactivating links between such translations and representations and the material. Materials that sit in storerooms are rarely revisited outside of dimensions set by systems of classification: stone tools, fine ceramics, animal bone, animal bone with cut marks, and so on. The possibility of returning to original material in a storeroom is connected with our ability to retrace the linkages we described in detail in chapter 5 with respect to Teotihuacan. Such traceability is the basis for accurate portrayal; being able to return to original materials is the basis for reassessing the fundamental components of our accounts of the past, even

---

5. Once displaced, things enter into new sets of associations with ordered shelves, labels, chains of references, and various translations; these, along with numerous protocols, are what comprise classifications and standards.

renegotiating the very nature of what remains, its ontology. We now wish to raise the question of how we can simultaneously stabilize the "past" and leave it open in these ways.

## THE NOISE OF THINGS

*La belle noiseuse* is a central theme in the work of the philosopher Michel Serres (1995a). Translated as beautiful commotion, ruckus, strife, all connotations of the archaic French word for noise, *la belle noiseuse*, for Serres, refers to the ceaseless fluctuation of background noise that prefigures phenomena, signal, explication. For Serres such commotion may well provide the grounds for being; *la belle noiseuse* is ontological foundation. Set against these grounds, archaeology is a sensibility, an orientation upon things. In other words, we do not begin with material pasts but with flux, with commotion, with noise, with things that, depending on our disposition and engagement, offer many different ontological possibilities. To bracket off a former hearth as being "of the material past" is to choose one among many other potential designations.

Archaeologists confront the material world by way of negotiation. At the table of these negotiations, as we have stressed thus far, are numerous mediators that condition the direction and scope of these negotiations. The disposition of things is to resist translation at every step. There is always more to be said about the things archaeologists find and work with. In chapter 2 we specified how things came to be forgotten for what they are on the other side of a gap set across from humans. The associated hierarchy of value elevated language over the material world, meaning over material. In this, certain qualities, those qualities that were conducive to being circulated in two dimensions as text and image, were elevated above myriad others, and these other competencies were quite simply ignored, as further detailed in chapter 4.

Just as we now recognize that language and vision are but particular mediating artifacts among many, we need to contend with the question of manifestation with respect to the myriad other qualities of things. While something from the past may be given an explicit, standardized description, we should also recognize that this by no means exhausts its many qualities, the inherent ambiguity and incoherence of things: again, there is always more to be said and done with the remains of the past.

## What Cannot Be Conveyed in Euclidian Space

It is no revelation to state that archaeological knowledge has over-whelmingly relied upon architectural drawing, the elements of which date to the sixteenth century (Ivins 1938). Its components are the standardized systems of plan, elevation, and section (collectively known as *ichnography*), and the rendering of architecture in perspective. Such architectural drawing amplifies our visual relationship with buildings and with things; such media are sensory prostheses (Shanks 2007; Webmoor 2005; Witmore 2006). They also direct attention to certain standardized aspects of buildings and things; they are sensory filters. As material forms, such two-dimensional media allow the transport of such buildings and things far from their location; we can take our plans and drawings from fieldwork back to the lab.

Of course there is much more to buildings than what can be translated into two-dimensional architectural drawing. Plan, elevation, and section assume perpendicular orientation. Perspective drawing is centered upon the eye of the viewer; it is ocularcentric, designed for the transference to paper of materials, architectures, landforms, and so forth, *as viewed by an individual*. There is so much more to buildings and things than what can be translated into two dimensions. How do we grapple with those qualities and attributes of buildings and things that are irreducible to the page as a mode of circulation?

Buildings and things are neither passive props nor static backdrops nor inanimate stages in the drama of life. Consider how we approach Acrocorinth, the second-oldest continuously inhabited citadel in Greece (see Andrews 2006 [1953]). With its concentrated defenses, the main series of gates is situated at the head of the western ascent (fig. 6.1). These primary defenses consist of three bastions with three gateways and a moat spanned by a single wooden bridge. Whereas freedom of movement was anything but the norm in 243 B.C.E., 1205 C.E., 1458, or 1612—consider the lengths Aratos of Sicyon, Geofrey de Villehard-ouin, Sultan Mehmed the Conqueror, and the knights of Malta went to gain access to previous Acrocorinths (Andrews 2006 [1953])—visitors are today permitted entry during open hours.[6]

6. Between the late seventeenth and early nineteenth centuries, it was at the first gate that visitors were required to dismount and wait for permission to enter—consent was not always forthcoming (Leake 1830, 3: 257–61).

FIGURE 6.1. View from top of Pendeskouphi looking northeast toward Acrocorinth in 2010.

After passing through the first arched gateway with its heavy, iron-covered doors, a small, two-room structure occupied by the guards, sits off to the left (fittingly, versions of this building provided shelter for guards in 1668). Suggestions as to how the interior space of this structure is occupied are present as plastic frappe containers in a burn bucket set by the door, muffled talk of local politics that turns to gossip, and wafting clouds of cigarette smoke.

Framing the approach to the second gate is a rubble terrace stooped under the weight of a dry grass-covered slope to the right; to the left is a retaining wall with parapet and loopholes. One must look up in order to observe one's surroundings, but to do so with any attentiveness demands a lull in one's progression. Otherwise, concentration, with all the senses, is directed at the uneven stones of the ascent. With another pause, one may discern how the terrace to the right ends abruptly at an angle in the gray limestone outcrop—angular, here and there, rough-textured, pockmarked, and stained reddish brown by iron-rich soils—a foundation/glacis for yet another wall crowned with weathered merlons (sections of parapet) and crenels (embrasures). Scaffolding for restoration work in August 2007 was no longer there in July of 2008. The retaining wall to the left, now an undulating relic of a former battlement, has also benefited from efforts at consolidation. Glance further left and up

FIGURE 6.2. View to second gate at Acrocorinth in 2007.

from this line and one sees the small castle built during the five-year siege under Geoffrey de Villehardouin (1205–1210), Pendekoufi, over the car park. From here, to the right, are the truncated heights of Pouka, the ancient Mount Apesas, and over the undulating middle ground in the distant haze of the west looms Ziria, otherwise known as Kyllini, the birthplace of Hermes.

Two hundred paces, by the Turkish travel writer Eviliya Chelbi's reckoning, is the distance between first and second gates (MacKay 1968). Halfway up, more or less, seemed, in 2007, to be a good place to pause for an impromptu photograph (fig. 6.2). The road steepens as one reaches the arched entry of the second gate. Ill-soled shoes slip here and there. Along the edge of the gateway, the limestone runs smooth, from thousands of steadying hands. Here one passes into cool shade, a welcome reprieve from sun in the early afternoon of a hot summer day—or this may become a refuge from sudden showers on a spring morning; weather creates new object relations, even novel spaces.

It is through the second gate that the first enclosure of the castle comes into view. Relic walls and rubble piles break through the loose cover of soil, stark and blackened by the fires of 2007. This open expanse of an enclosure does not align with the descriptions of Jacob Spon, George Wheler, or Chelbi. In 1668, Chelbi commented how here those "infidel Greeks" who were granted pardon and peace had 200 "ill-starred houses, with neither gardens nor orchards" (MacKay 1968). Such accounts assisted the imagination on summer afternoons in 2007 and 2008, but never in the same way.

After traversing a third of the distance through this enclosed area, as directed by the steep, tightly packed cobbled surface, the road jogs east toward the third gate. The stones of this road have been smoothed over in places by boot, sandal, hoof, paw, and wheel in numbers beyond reckoning. Formerly designed around the hoof, new acts of resurfacing have taken out many of the steps spaced in accordance with the gait of horse and donkey.

Flanked on either side by two great square towers, the southern of which is predominantly classical in construction—the trapezoidal masonry is perhaps fourth-century B.C.E.—the third gate is set within one of the most imposing wall façades of the entire castle. We may have little doubt that this monumental edifice, largely demolished, possibly even by Mummius in 146 B.C.E., only to be subsequently rebuilt, was a daily image for the Christians (non-Muslim Greeks) who lived in this section of Acrocorinth (Carpenter and Bon 1936). This gate, a point for inspections in the late seventeenth century, is another welcome refuge in the heat of summer. Water from the springs of Loutraki tastes better when savored in the shade of its vaulted passage; that is, so long as one waits. Low gusts of wind sometimes almost whistle through this cavity. Here, as a group passes as they walk toward the small chapel of St. Demetrios, one of us loses his bearings in thoughts of sitting in a taverna by the sea in Nauplion.

This short journey up through the gates of Acrocorinth brings us to a question: how do we manifest these movements? Kinetic experiences on the ground during the summers of 2007 and 2008 resist translation, as we have suggested. These pages are but one solution, combining media that date from the sixth century B.C.E., the sixteenth and nineteenth centuries C.E., and the recent past (still, see chapter 7). While we may suggest the style of the sounds, textures, or lived engagements through careful use of syntax and descriptive vocabulary, a sequence of digital photographs taken along the route and collated in a digital gallery would transport entirely different events, qualities, relationships, and so on. Were we to add thirty-second segments of sound, as streaming formats, to each image, entirely different sensory spaces would be provided for deliberation. Generating a video walk for subsequent visitors to the site would permit them the to walk the line with a particular disposition, however impractical. And yet Acrocorinth is a series of controversial spaces.

Acrocorinth is not the same place for an archaeologist, a site guard, for visitors to the chapel of St. Demetrios, a goatherd, or his goats.[7] The owner of the Acrocorinth Taverna by the parking lot (now closed) would have told you how he explored every crevasse of the castle while tending sheep as a child. The dark interiors of sally ports, cisterns, storage areas, and the keep have now been sealed up. Order a few beers and the conversation may lead to how the Greek Archaeological Service has not done enough to consolidate the walls, which are falling down on the eastern side of Acrocorinth. Without the accounts of Chelebi, Spon, and Wheler, one might never know that Acrocorinth once performed diverse nonmilitary roles—in politics, local governance, lordship, safety and security, agriculture, religion, community, and more. The variable, polysemic, ineffable spaces of Acrocorinth are made manifest by heterogeneous media.

Indeed, each new technological relation constitutes a different Acrocorinth.[8] The efforts of workers in the 37th Ephorate of Prehistoric and Classical Antiquities, a barrel cement mixer, bags of cement, and the Titan Corporation have contributed to the latest movements of

---

7. Such things impress themselves upon us and inscribe themselves upon our relations. This underscores the importance of actualistic studies, the richness of affective qualities—the past should not always be explicated in user's guides, it must also be *lived*. Experimental archaeology turns past relations into exhibitions, which in turn transform explicators into participants (even if the explication of participation is our goal).

8. Figure is sorted from ground, but this sorting is a matter of the associations. Maps, photographs, and the lines we write upon this page all transport something of our engagements with the high rock citadel above the isthmus. And yet, experiences defy displacement; the moment, colored by tacit association, matters and perishes.

Acrocorinth. Cracks once filled by lime mortar from nearby points of extraction are now filled by cement linking up quarries in Crete and Milos with cement factories and distribution centers throughout Greece. All these things, every stretch of wall, every merlon and former merlon, every gateway turned passageway, are, following Alfred North Whitehead, events or occasions, which aggregate within very specific sets of relation. They are, as the architect Bernard Tschumi puts it, place-events. Let us now further consider things as events and the implications for archaeological memory practices.

## The Realities of Things

Along the northwestern flank of Acrocorinth, the former channel of the Hadrianic Aqueduct extrudes from the slopes in two places: near the Church of Agia Marina and on the western flank of the Anaploga ravine, the latter at the lowest elevation along the former line, 191 m (Lolos 1997, 279). The aqueduct ran eighty-five kilometers from the springs of Kionia, which flow into Lake Stymphalos at an altitude of around 620 m, to the city of Corinth. Along its meandering course, a route overwhelmingly dictated by the contours of the terrain, the aqueduct incorporated three tunnels, spanned just over twenty gullies or rivers, and included at least two large settling tanks. Construction consisted of a vaulted channel (a *specus,* the average dimensions of which are 2.40 m in height by 2.20 m in width) with access points staggered at regular intervals (Lolos 1997, 281–82). The second-century C.E. peripatetic pilgrim Pausanias attributes the construction of aqueduct to the emperor Hadrian (r. 117–138 C.E.), and the water continued to flow down to the fifth century C.E., when it is believed to have fallen into disrepair. Corinth could no longer afford the upkeep of the aqueduct, which given the high gradient, 5.2m/km, which added to the turbulence of the water it channeled, the seismicity of the area, and the action of tree roots (most of the course was buried), would have required regular maintenance.

Such details of its design and execution, such specificities of gradient, course, and duration, were assembled by Yannis Lolos in the course of topographical survey and related research in the early 1990s (Lolos 1997). With sustained effort, Lolos linked up various remnants (noted on disparate occasions and distributed as numerous topographical texts) local memories, associations, and the visible vestiges of the channel. The fate of this single line was to break down into multiple remains, each of which went on to operate as a different entity. This latter observation forms the focus of our discussion here, but first there is more to be said about the taken-for-granted character of the aqueduct as an enduring object.

For archaeologists, despite the transient adventures that befall the various portions of the old course, the inner core of the extant channels, bridges, walls, tunnels, and settling tanks remains the Hadrianic Aqueduct. In other words, the sustained character of the aqueduct is based on an inner definiteness derived from its past, and this core resists myriad ephemeral relations. However, to subscribe to this common ontology is to bifurcate a thing into an underlying durable substance and transient relations (Harman 2009a). Here the continuity of the Hadrianic Aqueduct as an enduring object is regarded as given in advance. And yet all entities perish. This might be understood as the paradox of the "isotopy" of the past (Webmoor 2012a). Like unstable, isotopic elements, archaeological materials may be obdurate but their erstwhile modes of existence tend toward "radioactive" dispersion. Archaeologists struggle against this entropy when they work to stabilize certain object orientations.

For Alfred North Whitehead one cannot speak of an enduring object without taking into account how it is actively sustained and produced (see also Shaviro 2009). Rather than a stable, timeless procession of myriad remains staggered between Kionia and Corinth as the Hadrianic Aqueduct, we encounter a series or diversity of events, each a fresh and utterly specific creation. Water does not flow twice through the same aqueduct. Heraclitus's maxim holds not only for rivers, but also for all things, to follow Whitehead (Edgeworth 2011b).

In this, Whitehead's use of the word "event" needs further clarification. Here, we are not speaking of orthodox notions of event such as "the city of Corinth maintained an aqueduct," where the event modifies matter (Binford 1981, 199), where Corinth's, or rather administrators' and masons', actions (the event) happen to the aqueduct (a thing); on the contrary, *matter is the event.*[9] Because no thing exists irrespective of its relations, with every modification in a line of stone, mortar, or a sup-

---

9. Writing in *The Concept of Nature* of the red granite obelisk in London known as Cleopatra's Needle, Alfred North Whitehead suggested that to regard it as static or enduring in character was a matter of abstraction: "The more abstract your definition, the more permanent the Needle" (2006 [1920], 88). Cleopatra's Needle, for Whitehead, was itself an event; its persistence was not something that occurred *despite* the events around it, whether considered from the angle of physics, where it is continually gaining and losing molecules, or from the angle of an observant pedestrian who notes that it gets dirtier and is periodically washed.

porting arch, these things have transformed in some way. Whitehead would suggest that something novel, something altogether new is freshly created, even though this unique occurrence resembles what was formerly there. Whether these creations are radically different or strikingly similar will rest upon the new entities that enter the fold. With every new particle of silt, with every new crack, with every new cleaning or repair, the aqueduct, as a nexus of these actual occasions, transforms. Likewise, once the water ceases to flow, we can no longer speak of the multiple things that make up the line as an aqueduct. The sustained character of the aqueduct can only persist insofar as it is continually and actively worked at, and in this, things work to perpetuate themselves.

No longer the nexus of the occasions that once kept the waters of Kionia flowing to Corinth, the Hadrianic Aqueduct, as archaeologists know it today, then, comes about through the agency of lime mortar, the ancient Roman construction technique of *opus quadratum*, Pausanias's *Description of Greece* ('Ελλάδος περιήγησις), the Corinthian Ephorate of Antiquities, archaeologists such as Yannis Lolos, and so on. To understand things in this way, one cannot regard them as if they exist separate from their relations: indeed, for Whitehead, any attempt to do so results in what he calls a "vacuous actuality." It follows that the various things that formerly composed the Hadrianic Aqueduct will offer up different properties in different sets of relations.

For civil engineers in the late nineteenth and early twentieth centuries, a tunnel cut through the ridgeline of Mount Apelaouros provided a template for a subsequent irrigation channel supplying the Skoteini Valley. For a local farmer on the north side of Mount Stroggylo, a stretch of *opus quadratum* (42.50 m long, 11.20 m high, and 2.50 m wide) over the Xerias River is both a footbridge and a supporting structure for an irrigation line (fig. 6.3). For infrastructural planners, buried stretches of a vaulted channel were impediments to the construction of the new national road from Corinth to Tripolis. In every case, these relationships modify entities—an irrigation channel, a bridge, an obstacle to infrastructural development—and these are utterly specific to their associations. Such object orientations involve diverse spaces and times and underscore how with any such matter of concern, we encounter realities in the plural—this is why things are anything but mundane.

This is not to suggest that things are exhausted by or reducible to their relations. This point is so important that we need to expand on it briefly. The Hadrian Aqueduct would be nonexistent without the raw physicality of mortar, brick, and stone, combined with geometry, survey

FIGURE 6.3. Portion of the former Hadrianic Aqueduct over the Xerias River in 2008.

labor, and craft experience. These bits and pieces hold a great deal in reserve, thus giving the past a simultaneous presence and action (we return to this point in chapter 7). Moreover, the sustained character of the aqueduct is maintained not only by local personnel charged with such responsibility. The assemblage of eighty-five kilometers of continuous vaulting, channel, supporting terrace and ground, the myriad supporting arches, stone tunnels, and settling tanks perpetuate *themselves.* For us, the character of the aqueduct can be accounted for by neither the common ontology of substance nor a fully process-relational approach, as exemplified by Whitehead. The aqueduct endures as materials that change or are time-laden, as well as in its relationships with other things in its history. The core reality of things includes the consistency of qualities that have integrity even when they are affected and perturbed by relations in their history and environment. Complete change occurs when relationships outweigh the consistency of qualities. Integrity, however, is maintained so long as qualities are maintained, even if an aqueduct is no longer useful as an aqueduct carrying water from Lake Stymphalos to Corinth.

To conclude this section, the multiplicities that make up a former aqueduct suggest that such things are far more interesting than archaeologists have allowed. The most important implication for our archaeological memory practices, we believe, is that many of these events, many of these things, deserve to be *remembered*.

The preceding vignettes have exposed two paths. With Acrocorinth, a 2,600-year flow of performances, negotiations, transformations, a moving project (Ingold 2010; Latour and Yaneva 2008), the citadel is anything but a static backdrop to transient relations—nowhere along the line did we encounter a fixed relic of a castle; with every pace, with every pause, with every change in weather, various spaces opened up. Not all of these unfolding spaces were optical—suggestions of smell, sound, touch, taste, and vision, the styles of sensation, were bracketed within the narrative. Throughout the movement, things present themselves in ways other than the visual, and they are therefore irreducible to a Euclidian space, the page before you.

The Hadrianic Aqueduct, regularly presumed to be an enduring object, is also many other things. With a commitment to the realities of things, archaeology becomes a disposition, an orientation among others. It constitutes radically different objects of concern from the angle of past relations. At the same time, a recent irrigation channel, a barrier to movement, a terrace line, all these things should be considered and remembered—there are many more objects of concern to be *manifested* in a creative political economy of media. These issues bring us to the final section of this chapter, on *digital translation*.

## Digital Translation

In "old media's" prime, Wolfgang Riepl's 1913 law presciently stated that newer media never entirely replace or obviate the old; rather a mixture or supplementation of old with new media occurs.[10] Archaeology's

---

10. This is already apparent in the political economy of the academy with promotion and scholarship "impact" relying primarily upon analog publication. In terms of method-

digital heritage will incorporate "old" analog media. This is especially the case when data are achieved secondarily in a digital format versus "native digital" material. For example, the digitized maps produced by English Heritage for GIS require hachures to be hand-drawn over the digitally produced topographic maps. Or again, with finds drawings, while digital micro photogrammetry can render the features of an artifact, the skill of accentuating prominent and potentially important characteristics can only be done by hand. In both instances, digitization of the drawing or map comes later (Read and Smith 2009).

Taking a closer look at the work collectively done by media and archaeologists reveals discrepant nuances between manifesting the past in analog and digital form. For instance, the laborious and numerous steps needed to translate the material qualities of Teotihuacan into the TMP map (chapter 5) differ from how contemporary mapping projects combine LandSat, LiDAR, and Total Station images and measurements in a single GIS database—along with other compatible entries—which are then displayed in a digital interface. There is more going on than any one-to-one media turnover with the updating of equipment and instruments. Archaeologists are assuredly technophiles when it comes to instrumentation,[11] but chasing after the latest technology reaches beyond the attempt to stay "cutting-edge," or the cool factor of new gadgetry. The "digital turn" fundamentally changes how "data" are *achieved,* that is, how they are assembled, archived, distributed, and engaged with. In archaeology, these changes collectively shift the work that media do, how the archaeological "record" is assembled, the modes in which an archive may be engaged, and the overall political economy of the past.

For archaeology, manifesting digital heritage offers potentials and pitfalls for our memory practices. This is because of how digital media modify the nature of relations with the things of the past. These changes have to do with the functionality of the digital technologies, how they

---

ology and applications, there is, however, the opposite embracing of digital practices—indeed, the promotion of "e-Science" in North America and throughout Europe (see, e.g., Hine 2006).

11. The root of technophilia in archaeology lies with the very non-techy issue of epistemology. Lewis Binford (1989) tapped this desire most explicitly when, operating within the ambit of conventional correspondence theory, he addressed "pattern recognition work" and the subject-sieving role of technology and instruments in making second-order observations more objective (paradigm independent). For a broader treatment of the co-development of visualizing instruments and the notion of "objectivity" in the sciences, see Daston and Galison 2007.

may be deployed, and how they transform the material world into particular types of media. First, we offer several propositions to develop the centrality of memory work in archaeology.

The "archaeological process" is well described as the labor put into transforming the stuff of the archaeological imagination into manageable media (Witmore 2004b). These practices are media work. As we've already seen, archaeologists are especially adept at translating material into formats more amenable to circulation and calculation. Rather than an "internalization" of the material world in meaning, memory practices externalize in media our relationship with the past (examples of analog in chapters 4–5). Reasoning from these media may be lodged within a hermeneutic spiral of interpretation (Shanks and Tilley 1987a; Hodder 1999). But this is an incomplete analysis of the work performed—we even might say that it is undemocratic and elitist, because it elides the hard labor of many in favor of passive thought. Furthermore, interpretation of the "stuff of the past" is actually secondary and conditioned by this collective labor to achieve a "workable past."

Secondly, shedding the lenses of "anthropocentricism" and looking closely at memory practices reveals a diverse workforce (following on the arguments of chapter 4). This is no less true for digital media, which are fundamentally material. The steps involved in achieving digital media augment qualities that may be mistakenly taken for ephemera—the "ghost in the machine." But emergent media do not fade; rather they are configured as vibrant assemblages of humans and nonhumans—software engineers, server farms, start-ups, routers, IT staff, laser scanners, bandwidth, and bloggers. Readers of Bruno Latour will be familiar with applying such a nondiscriminatory appellation to the "actors" of analog media (Latour 1986). Digital media too are collectives. These sociotechnical networks perform digital media. They perform the archaeological for us to engage with; whether as publication, presentation, museum, or archive (Pearson and Shanks 1999). Digital heritage comprises ongoing events.

Let's develop these propositions by looking more closely at how assemblages of digital media change our engagement with the past. Again, Latour's circulating reference is a nice entry point for getting us around thinking in terms of correspondence theories of representation (1999; see fig. 5.4), and instead in terms of the many steps of aligned transformation that link contexts, excavation trenches, artifacts, field notes, laboratories, and archives to digital media. Yet although a serviceable schema for thinking through analog media, the notion of circulating

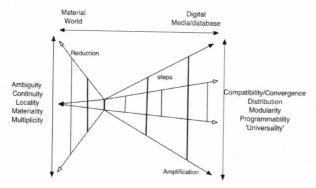

FIGURE 6.4. Circulating Reference and Digital "Infraphysics." How digital media work together: the pleat of mathematization into binary code precipitating a capacity to manifest multimodal engagements in the archive.

reference must be upgraded with respect to digital media (fig. 6.4; and see November, Camacho-Hubner, and Latour 2010). The take-home message of mediation we presented in chapter 5 is the same for analog and digital. There is, however, a new host of components, new networks of relations. The digital performs differently, and new qualities of the past emerge as these digital networks stabilize.

As with analog media (chapter 5), there are a series of aligned steps that traverse the supposed insuperable divide between world and "representation" in media. The components enlisted to affect these transitions, however, are new with digital media. Moving in either direction of this schema, we pass through steps such as "capture"/sampling, numeric coding, software rendering, storage, and display. However, not all the sequence of mediators are the same. The "fold" in figure 6.4 highlights a particularly important "obligatory passage point" of translation in this process (Callon 1986). Irregular in shape, the schema underscores the step of mathematization of the continuous material world around us into numerical (binary) code (Lynch and Edgerton 1988; Lynch 1990). This pleat is actually the folding of many micro-steps into this defining transformation of digital media; to capture or sample translates sight, sound, motion into discrete "units," whether pixels, scripts, polygons, or voxels (Manovich 2001, 30). It gathers up in a single operative step many of the labor-intensive actions that were required of analog media to amplify the qualities of standardization, universality, and comparability. To illustrate, Teotihuacan presented the TMP personnel and equipment with an imposing task of sorting out signal from noise. As we have seen, this took enormous collective effort and a myriad of aligned steps to move from aerial photographs to the gridded 1:2000-scale maps. The TMP collective had to work hard in order to establish discrete units in an otherwise continuous field of features (to sort and classify what we are calling the noise of things). Digital media collapse these many steps as they "break up" the continuous visual or auditory field into discrete units that are modular and fractal. While these units may be combined into larger and larger units, they retain their independence. So instead of the sandy loam transitioning uninterruptedly into clay loam in a profile feature—always posing the uncertainty of drawing a boundary—those grains and fine clay soils are already broken into discrete polygons in the digital image.

There is, then, a different work flow with digital media. Of course, with advances in technology the resolution of these "units" approaches the horizon of the continuous, seamless "data" of analog media and the world around, much to the chagrin of unemployed photographic film developers (cf. Witmore 2009). Nevertheless, the decision as to where to "break down" the stratigraphic profile into polygons remains relevant to archaeological interpretation and intervention.

These steps of sampling in modular units and the assignation of numbers to each unit—numeric coding—align with the next steps of rendering, programming, storage, transmission, display, and so on. In short, this is the computerization of qualities of the material world (Carusi, Hoel, Webmoor, and Woolgar in press). While a (conventional) ethnography of the initial bundle of micro-steps is more difficult because of scale—in the circuitry and processor of the device when activated by the user—the remaining steps take us to software start-ups, research and development brainstorming sessions, rows of storage servers in an air-conditioned "farm," and the wiring of DARPA (Defense Advanced Research Projects Agency) research centers into the early Internet (Weber 2004, 32).

The important point is that binary code allows wrinkles between poles of spectrum (viz., local/material/rich to the standardized/accessible). This capacity of the digital allows different sets of the rich detail and background noise of the material world to be included in our reportage. The digital affords fewer of the laborious steps necessary to transform its analog counterpart into wieldy, usable form (Gibson 1986, 137–38; cf. Coopmans and Woolgar 2007). In this way, the digital gives richer manifestation (more "continuous"), while compositionally more discrete (fractal, code) (Manovich 2001). This paradox of digital media is at the root of a series of other counterintuitive observations.

Most of us are already familiar with the benefits of this capacity of digital tools. There is, however, a farther-reaching implication. Apart from these sorts of conveniences, which arise from the affordances and composition of digital media, there is a more fundamental change. There is a new infraphysics (Latour 1993, 128). That is, assembled digital media have a different force, different action. One of these "strengths" is being more robust due to programmability and combinability, but robust in a specific manner. Drawing up qualities on both ends in the figure above, digital media allow for a rich manifestation of the past, while at the same time being more easily networked together in this binary "metalanguage." Digital media are ready-made networks. Mathematized into programmable binary code, digital media are highly fungible and reproducible; readily mixed and allied with other digital media formats. They are easily copied and dispersed. This is the sense of "force" or robustness: an ability to enroll many other bits of information and extend their network and capacity for engagement in so doing. In contrast to the recognizable architecture attesting to analog repositories, the strength of networked digital media is less apparent. There are fewer archives, museums, or filing cabinets. It is an unassuming solidity. Its network largely "underground," with rhizomatic branching formed through connections linking bytes of media content. None of which is apparent at the interface of the display screen.

Some paradoxes of the digital have been exemplified in the blogosphere. Archaeology has entered this realm of desktop publishing. The ease of setting up this new media platform is both a boon and a bane. Largely unedited and unfiltered, the archaeological blogosphere must be sorted through to find the signal in the noise. As with Geoffrey Bowker's potential memory, there is an abundance of information on demand. Publishing without "gatekeepers" has advantages, especially in terms of providing a channel for innovative thought and cutting-edge agendas.[12] In step with the amount of work—and time—required for analog and digital transformations, bypassing the many steps required of more formal analog publication offers much potential in accelerating debate and disseminating information in archaeology. These blogs are also mixed content networked together. A statement about the past may be

12. Or in expanding peer review in a postnormal science to expose political and academic scandals, such as the so-called "Climategate."

accompanied by images and graphs, but also by an embedded video documentary and a link to the online archive from where information presented was derived.

These networked media combine when the enthused amateur peruses the article, watches the video, examines the statistical chart and artifact drawings, and surfs away to explore some of the hyperlinked content. Then again, each of these media engagements remain largely distinct. Remove a node and the remaining networked content remains. The commercial server streaming the video crashes, but the text, hyperlinks, and images on the local server remain. The local server powers down, and the article and its content are still "searchable" and "indexed" or archived on a Google "cloud server" or by the Brewster Kahle Internet Archive. The rhizomatic infrastructure of digital information allows for far more durability than is assumed. At the same time, richer modes of engagement with the past are facilitated through digital media assemblages.

For instance, let's briefly compare the manifestation of what may be rather ephemeral archaeological material with the experience of presenting information from reconnaissance survey in analog form. A digital interface is designed to be a one-stop-shop mode of engagement: video-photos-documents-cartography mixed in a single screen. This was not possible with analog documents. Even with the best resources and planning, the material might have been conventionally published as a sequenced engagement (see Webmoor 2005 for archaeological maps). Digitally documenting the qualities of a Traditional Cultural Property (TCP) in the United States offers a richer engagement with the significance of such a "site," as they are legally defined (fig. 6.5). Indeed, as stipulated by the National Park Service's Bulletin 38, the determination of "significance" and the potential for listing on the National Register for future protection do not depend upon the presence of artifacts or other archaeological materials. The amended criteria of section 106 of the National Historic Preservation Act (NHPA) suggest that such sites ought to be valued for their relations with the surrounding landscape. This must not be mistaken for the wearisome assertion that such places are deemed important for purely social reasons (see chapter 9's discussion of heritage and ethics). To the contrary, being-in-the-landscape at such TCPs is very much a material encounter—wind, rocks, rain, lightning, the unremitting exposure of the Great Plains extending their flat surface to the horizon in every direction. Yet the analog documents submitted for compliance with section 106 offer little in the way of such

FIGURE 6.5. Digital interface with interactive photographs, video clips, notebook entries, and maps documenting a traditional cultural property (TCP) on the Comanche National Grasslands, Colorado.

material encounters. Structured around text, we are presented with narrative descriptions, bureaucratic checklists, photographs, and maps. We must even flip back and forth to find the relevant maps. There is cross-referencing and "linking" of the analog content, but the engagement is very different from the digital encounter. Without digitally-mediated engagements with sites such as TCPs it would be difficult to register those very qualities that define them as significant.[13]

This infraphysics grants digital heritage greater stability and malleability through networking. Assembling the past into digital heritage entails a network of many types of information. Linking, inserting, mixing,

13. Other examples of the material networking capacity of digital media could be explored through relevant proprietary software platforms. ESRI's GIS software, to take a prominent example, offers up images and video files linked to geospatial information when we query its database, albeit it is tethered to the map-maker's space (Witmore 2012a).

and embedding digital information together grants the final manifestation the character of an assemblage that holds on to its lines of formation: media are made more durable through heterogeneous alliances of information (we take this up again chapter 8). Viewed as a network of information, rather than as a singular, self-contained document, any "trial of strength" or contestation of the information claimed would require disputing and discrediting all the many allied media. Received notions of representation are no longer at issue. Digital manifestations urge us to rehabilitate the idea of "copy" as proof of fecundity rather than secondary (inferior) substitute (Latour and Lowe 2011, 279). Contesting a claim made by our surveying personnel on the Great Plains with their digital media would involve us in taking issue with multiple and converging types of information. The (nonepistemological) "cable of evidence" is immediately presenced before the skeptic with a digital format (cf. Wylie 2002). A new metrology is required for engaging digital manifestations, one that places emphasis upon the durability, "weight," or extensiveness, and temporality of networked hybrid media (see Webmoor 2012b on emerging metrologies).

Maps, charts, statistics, images, video documentation, and even "background noise" may all be near-simultaneous presences in supporting an interpretation. Students of other sciences have observed the amount of work involved in challenging a claim made in analog media (e.g., Latour 1986). This is because final professional publication in analog has the unfortunate effect of "black-boxing" or masking the many steps, the incredible work and effort expended, in getting to these final, "closed" representations (Amann and Knorr Cetina 1990; Latour and Woolgar 1986; Lynch and Woolgar 1990). All of the traces, the telltale signs of translation, performed by "inscriptional devices," have been swept clean. "Information archaeology," tracking down these traces and way-finding with them to discover the original datum points can be daunting indeed. Practically speaking, it is a huge expenditure of resources and time to do so.

Digital media would seem to completely obscure their sources, giving the appearance of the perfect black box, inscrutable to all but the most computer science–savvy users. By truncating transformation to the key step of mathematization and hiding any traces behind circuitry boards the intermediary steps of translation are not disclosed. Yet unlike the analogues in analog, digital media leave traces of the work they've performed through metadata "signatures." For instance, reading an offline document for publication in a familiar program like Microsoft

Word or Apple Pages makes tracking changes less apparent. Of course, this option can be selected for, as in Word, but the output as a printed document elides the many versions and changes that the document underwent before its text, images, hyperlinks, and statistical charts were all imported and arranged in the final form of a closed document. Contrast such conventional document preparation with online documents, or documents prepared in "cloud computing." A familiar online, browser-accessed authoring environment is Google Docs. Again, the blogosphere or other online authoring platforms—part of the new media of Web 2.0—offer examples. MovableType, WordPress, or Blogger, all popular blog software and service providers, integrate a track-changes function into a "recent activity log." A timeline results, giving our information archaeologists a timeline of how the "final document"—or blog entry—was engineered—an *ichnography*. What was posted, who modified the text or added a graph, who left a comment, how an image was resized, and so forth. We leave digital traces (Neuhaus and Webmoor 2012).[14]

The manuscript for this book was prepared through a wiki, a particular type of new media that manages content such as text and image and facilitates collaborative authoring. Looking at a function typically in a wiki called "versions," we can see how the manuscript came together through time. All changes made by specific authors are highlighted. Tracking changes this way opens this publication to the messy process underlying its final manifestation. Remaining an e-book or digital-only manuscript—not simply digitized as a .pdf that can be downloaded—this text could continue to transform and change as comments were made, omissions or errors rectified, additional images or videos embedded. It would be a much more cumulative and collective work, simultaneously revealing the work of producing it while resisting closure as a final, black-boxed document. Online documents are ongoing, open works.

Digital media such as collaborative, open documents dissimulate their vulnerability. Rather than inscrutable black boxes, they have built-in measures to reveal the networks of media, researchers, and software behind their deployment. The networks supporting their manifestation are more readily discernible. This "circuitry" can be mapped, tracked,

---

14. It is in fact the commercial potential of our everyday traces left on the Internet that have embroiled Facebook, Google, and other social media companies in legal controversy. "Scraping our profiles" for this information economy involves selling our (online) personal preferences and habits to private companies (Neuhaus and Webmoor 2012).

and followed to the sources. In principle they permit digital media to be more easily contested. At the same time, however, the democratic values that infuse the design and function of digital media contribute to a disarming effect. One of the strongest functions or values of digital media is inclusivity and participation. Again, what would seem to be a weakness of digital media enables stronger assemblages.

Digital media are highly malleable in a specific and unique sense, and in distinction to analog. Selections of digital media—video clips, sections of photographs, GIS maps, audio recordings—can be removed from one network and combined into new networks of media. This is an example of what Lawrence Lessig has called "remix culture" (Lessig 2008). This fungibility or combinability encourages user-generated content. The networks of digital media that make them good black boxes also make them more easily opened. Their content can be entirely or partially user-generated, and they can be creatively remixed and re-presented. More durable, not deconstructed and criticized, but reworked, taken up in different networks, redeployed. In archaeology, we are already seeing this malleability in terms of treating data in nonproprietary ways, with the transparency of "data," the maintenance of open archives, and the take-up of open source software (Weber 2004; and Richard Stallman's radical Free Software Foundation). All of this is part of the more general ethos of digital democracy and the ideal of freeing-up information. This new manner of producing and sustaining archaeological engagements with digital media transforms archaeology's political economy. At the same time, it has a strong intellectual current in the manner of questioning operational and theoretical assumptions in archaeology. It is an "open paradigm" (not in the Kuhnian sense, but in the etymological sense of *paradeigma,* meaning example or pattern—to bring to light constituent relations)—an open way of working/thinking with things.

These new modes of co-creating and engaging with digital heritage change our roles as specialists, our identity as "stewards of the past." An animated archive would open memory practices to digital design, in a shift from author-generated content to a mix of specialist and user-generated content. This is richer capture made "stronger" with linking more networks of humans and nonhumans. Open source and Creative Commons are movements to facilitate such ease of digital alliance making.

An understanding of our digital heritage, with respect to how we assemble the past and the discipline's own material legacy, questions the role of archaeologists as stewards or custodians of the past. The primacy of the "user" in digital media moves us toward a new cultural heritage with a logic of mixing, co-creation, and participation. Broader circulation and increased interaction with heritage brings with it a political economy that blurs the roles of production and consumption (Webmoor 2008; Shanks and Webmoor 2012). We begin to "crowdsource" our memory practices. Users simultaneously create, contribute, download, consume, and distribute. Thus, our memory work is now less stationary, immutable, and authoritative.

We underscore this point: the nature of engagement with the past changes in digital media. Digital media may at first it may seem to distance us from the past. This is due to their perceived immateriality. In fact, digital networks are anything but immaterial. Interactive, responsive, and animated, digital heritage responds rapidly to engagement. Whether this is posting commentary in on-line publications, downloading and reworking statistical figures, annotating archaeological maps in Wikimapia or Google Earth, or contributing site images to a photobank, the assembled "record" responds in real time.

The future archaeological record may be better described in biocultural terms as a media or informational ecology: a circuitry of archaeological material, institutions, archaeologists, analog repositories, and digital databases innervated by user engagement. Jenkins's (2006) "media convergence" means more devices and user-end engagements with the past. "Everyware," ubiquitous media bring ubiquitous engagement, ubiquitous pasts (Webmoor 2008; Witmore 2009). With the past becoming pervasive with digital media, we must attend to the issues of "legacy data" and "potential memory" for future pasts. The promise of digital memory work, of the democratic (ontological) composition and use of the past, is cogently summed up by Peter Sloterdijk (2004, 43,45): "Anthropo-technology is characterized by cooperation rather than by domination, even in asymmetrical relationships . . . [an] inter-intelligently condensed net-world."

A complex informational ecology emerges with new media (Baker and Bowker 2007). Durable in its connections with other media manifestations, this ecology is also fragile, or at least untested, in this very dependence upon other technologies. We don't want to contribute to extinct or "dead" media. For digital media, this is really an issue of media lifespan and server stability (critical for the controversy over digitization of library holdings, museums, and especially primary digital material). Digital media will not survive by accident (consider Bruce Sterling's

"Dead Media Manifesto").[15] We know, for example, that the lifespan of information carriers is limited: a web site is dependent upon server stability (or at least the Brewster Kahle Internet Archive or Google's indexed web content), a CD is roughly ten years, miniDVs have already been replaced by internal hard drives and memory cards (Shanks 2007). Moore's law with processors suggests that the technology for maintaining digital media will become exponentially more stable. Storing information in digital-only formats is still in its infancy. It is too untried for organizations such as the National Science Foundation (NSF) to embrace this method of archiving (Kintigh 2006). Just as analog media in deteriorating archives require attention, the networks constituting digital information and documents and sustaining their preservation require curatorial work to maintain. This creates new responsibilities for sustaining our digital heritage, new rules for manifesting the past.

## CONCLUSION

This chapter expands on an understanding of things in light of the qualities we translate through media, both paper-based and digital. It focuses on three key themes: (1) memory practices; (2) the noise of things; and (3) digital translation. Our aim in exploring archaeological memory practices is to emphasize how things of the past are transported into the future. Discussion of the noise of things accentuates the variegated qualities and lives of crumbling walls, bastions, towers and gates, reused arch supports, stone circles, and obstacles to further construction, underlining what else might be made manifest and thereby remembered. The final section examines the potential of digital media for translating and assembling those qualities of the material past that are left behind by conventional, paper-based modes of documentation.

The things of the material past are inexhaustible in terms of their qualities, affordances, allure, and potential. They are also "isotopic" and must be cared for in curated networks of artifacts, institutions and media - whether analog- or digital-based. Any empirical fidelity to this richness demands a combination of practices that are orderly and consistent *as well as* open and creative. In this chapter, we have made a case for

15. Bruce Sterling, "The DEAD MEDIA Project: A Modest Proposal and a Public Appeal," www.deadmedia.org/modest-proposal.html (accessed April 10, 2012). Curatorial necessity now accompanies every act of translation we undertake. Longevity requires the work of translation, iteration, or, as Timothy Ingold (2010) puts it, *itineration*.

the past to be kept alive through an immanent, kinetic engagement, one that is ultimately in service of life. In this, entropy and endurance are the bedfellows of time, witnessed in the intertwining of ephemerality and repetition, of perpetual perishing and incessant novelty, of never-ending accumulation and duration; the isotopy of the past (Webmoor 2012a). We now turn to this issue of time and how the things of the past endure as much as they transform.

# CHAPTER 7

# Timely Things

*From Argos to Mycenae and Beyond*

Archaeologists tend to regard time as linear. It is along the time*line,* the modernist image of time par excellence, that "time" is ordered into a succession of events or laminar phases. Most archaeologists take it for granted that the Iron Age commences with the end of the Bronze Age; that the Bronze Age brings about the end of the Neolithic. This image of a series of successions and replacements, where one era is irrevocably lost and supplanted by a new one, runs to the heart of the discipline. Mortimer Wheeler offers an archetypical image of this linear time. In drawing a distinction between a timescale produced by vertical excavation and a specific phase generated through extensive horizontal excavation, Wheeler enlists the metaphor of the railway timetable and train (1954, 126–27). Vertical excavation (synonymous with a "culture-scale" for Wheeler) allows one to deal with an area in depth, but, deployed without recourse to the horizontal, it is a "timetable without a train." Likewise, any horizontal excavation bereft of a deeply excavated stratigraphic profile is a "train without a timetable." Emphasizing the complementarity of these practices, Wheeler sought a properly running train system with a clear timetable whereby we might know when the trains were running, "where they started," "their intermediate stopping-places," and "their destination." Set in motion along its track with the measured precision of timetable, Wheeler's locomotive metaphor is exemplary of linear time and its chronology.

Of course, we readily accept that the things around us do not all share the same temporality. It is long been recognized that entities may transform at different rates or have different life spans with respect to temporal duration (Lucas 2005). Consider some features and places from the Argive Plain of Greece: a limestone escarpment erodes over the course of hundreds of millennia; an olive tree lower down the flank of this ridge persists for several centuries; the late Byzantine church of the Panaghia in Aghia Triada continues to stand, while, not sixty meters distant from the church's northern door, the exposed mud-brick walls of a nineteenth-century farmhouse wash away with every rainstorm (Bailey 1981, 1983, 2007; Ingold 1993; Lucas 2005; Olivier 2001, 2008). Whether the life of a tree or the perishing of a building, these processes are often situated within a unidirectional passage temporality. Here the "arrow of time" subsumes the more chaotic relations of time per se.

Modernist thought introduces a radical gap between past and present. As if splayed out upon the butcher's block, time is cleaved apart at supposed interruptions. Whether clock time or processual time, the present, as the locus of the modern, is forever advancing along the track, leaving behind all that has come before. Historical events, previous eras, all are safely situated at a distance. The powers of archaeology are focused upon seemingly remote pasts; pasts that have forever passed; pasts that are assumed to be separate from those living today. This image of linear successions vastly oversimplifies time (the notion that time passes results in a complacent attitude toward the abolition of the past; see Olivier 2008). Indeed, it would be more precise to regard this image as a particular form of historicity. Archaeologists may have paid homage to this form of historicism from the inception of the discipline (Lucas 2005; also see McGlade 1999), but it is thankfully beginning to break down. We are beginning to recognize that time is much more complex and chaotic, and that archaeology has a major role to play in this complexity.

All around us the things of the past defy the presumably unbridgeable distances held firm by the rigidity of a unidirectional line and the seemingly unbridgeable chasms left in the wake of revolutionary gestures. Here, in the northeastern Peloponnesus, a Hellenistic route follows the line of a Bronze Age road; there, a Geometric cemetery (strengthened with the aid of governmental legislation and the perseverance of Ephoria archaeologists) bars a homeowner from adding a room for his in-laws in 1986; here, thirteenth-century Frankish fortifications play a role in a desperate battle during the Greek War of Independence six centuries later, contributing to the birth of the modern nation-state; there, the wall of a fourth-century B.C.E. temenos, or sacred precinct, provides a backdrop for a tool shed in Hermion. Time passes and doesn't pass. In this, something of pasts endure (Bergson 1998 [1907]; Olivier 2001, 2008). The great walls of Tiryns still stand. The route of a late-nineteenth-century railroad is still traveled by crowds on summer holidays. The Byzantine church in Aghia Triada still resonates with the celebration of the Virgin's Assumption every August 15. Something of these pasts is gathered and extended in the present (see Olsen 2010, 109, on the possible etymological association of the word "thing" with the root *tenku*, suggesting "duration"). Formerly distant, abandoned or forgotten pasts can even become proximate again. Freed from its covering of earth, a theater can once more gather a throng. A ruined castle can again provide defense against a siege. A Bronze Age road can facilitate modern access to a famous citadel.

With the democratic ontology we are laboring to articulate, we need not hold to a modern historicism that strives to maintain a radical chasm between past and present by attributing a separate and derivative position to things. Given that the past is no longer past, we are now obliged to question what happens when collectives enter into simultaneous exchanges with *ta archaia*, the old things. Our task in this chapter is to suggest another path along which we hope to make tentative steps in the direction of understanding time as a percolating diversity (Prigogine and Stengers 1984; Serres with Latour 1995; Shanks 1996b; Stengers 2010; Witmore 2006, 2007; also Olivier 2008). Moving from the city(s) of Argos to the citadel(s) of Mycenae, this chapter explores a range of relational possibilities between material pasts in a storied Greek land. Through the rich textures offered by empirical vignettes, it works through different angles on the sheer complexity of time. In this, our task cannot be hurried. Let us now expand on many of the points introduced here through the fabric of Argos.

## ARGOS, GREECE

It is quite possible, even probable, that for six thousand years, Argos (fig. 7.1) was never *un*inhabited (Kelly 1976; Piérart and Touchais 1996). It may be, as residents claim, the oldest city in Europe. The earliest materials suggestive of occupation that have been discovered thus far are Neolithic. In casting off on our discussion of time, let us begin with the chronology of these six millennia of continuous human occupation at Argos.

FIGURE 7.1. Argos as seen from its acropolis, the Larissa, in 2010.

The Neolithic of the Argolid spans over three thousand years, from roughly 6850 to 3600 B.C.E. The "Bronze Age," subdivided into early, middle, and late, lasts from 3600 to 1000 B.C.E. The early "Iron Age," commonly broken into the Protogeometric and Geometric eras—each again segmented into early, middle, and late—stretches to 700 B.C.E., the beginning of the Archaic Period. After the Archaic, the Classical, with its celebrated "heights" of human achievement, commences around 500, or 480/79 B.C.E., to be exact (dates marking the defeat of the Persian Great King Xerxes at Salamis and Plataea; in this, Argos remained neutral). The Hellenistic Period is commonly reckoned as running from the death of Alexander the Great in 323 B.C.E., or, on occasion, from the victory of Philip II at Chaironeia in 338, to the catastrophic defeat of the confederated Peloponnesian city-states of the Achaian League and the annihilation of Corinth by the Romans under Lucius Mummius in 146 B.C.E. The early, middle, and late Roman periods span the centuries between 146 and 650 CE (the period from 400 to 650 B.C.E. is also known as Early Byzantine). We could continue with outlining the key markers of this linear history, but for our purposes let us jump ahead to a definitive break.[1] The first modern Greek government fixed its seat at

1. From here, the medieval period persists for as many as 850 years (see Jameson, Runnels, and van Andel 1994). Given their "ill-defined" nature and the downturn in materials, its early centuries have been dubbed the "second Dark Age." After a few years of strife in the wake of the Fourth "Crusade" (1204), the Morea passes to the Franks (Geoffrey I Villehardouin captures Nauplion and Argos in 1211–12). Then, in 1394, the Venetians take possession of Argos (Nauplion had been taken five years earlier); then the Ottomans capture Argos in 1479; then the Venetians once more reclaim the Morea in 1685; then the Ottomans do so yet again in 1715. During the Greek War of Independence, Argos hosted the first national assembly in 1821 (the assembly of Epidaurus took place in December of the same year [Finlay 1877, 239]), and Nauplion fell to the Greeks in 1822.

Nauplion in 1828. The capital was moved to Athens in 1834,which is taken to mark the beginning of the "modern period" in Greece (see, e.g., Finlay 1877; Jameson, Runnels, and van Andel 1994).

Age, epoch, era, period, phase, these "blocks of time" are stacked in a linear, ordered sequence: early, middle, and late (a key trope of linear narrative; see White 1973; also Hodder 1993). The events these boxes contain are situated according to their intensity (consider the formative image of Greeks development from "archaic" to "classical" and its associated prejudices). Within this temporal framework, time, it is regularly maintained, passes from the earlier phases to the succeeding ones: the Frankish Morea (Geoffrey I Villehardouin captures Nauplion and Argos in 1211 and 1212) precedes the Venetian (the Venetians take possession of Argos in 1394); the Venetian precedes the Ottoman (Argos is captured by the Turks in 1479). These successions mask what seems to be an unambiguously transitive flow. In this, the farmers, shepherds, and merchants of Argos progress from beginnings to ends along an irreversible line marked out by episodes of "progress" or "regression." This linear temporality, we argue, does not equate to time.

Indeed, this image equates more to a particular species of temporality, which passes continually from the past to future, thus leaving behind an irreversible succession of discrete moments, a geometrical line punctuated by instants. A common component of this passage temporality, chronology has served as a supposedly external parameter for sorting eras, periods, or epochs and thus ordering time with respect to a series of dates and well-defined distances (Shanks and Tilley 1987, chapter 7; see Ramenofsky 1998 for a discussion of the utility of any distinction between absolute and relative chronology; summary in Lucas 2005). These chronometrics are the composite result of decades of painstaking work with ancient texts, historical accounts, ceramic typologies and sequences, all subsequently reappraised, refined, and finetuned. And yet, on some level, by treating time as an external parameter that can be specified in calendar years, chronology often assumes that it is everywhere laminar, geometrically rigid, and measured. Archaeologists employ years to give an indication of scale even with unspecified episodes in a relative chronology or ordinal system. Moreover, as we have repeatedly maintained, *things* do not always *work* in this way— they are far more complicated, and this too holds with respect to time. Here, we need carefully to distinguish such a linear, passage temporality from time. This is tied to acknowledgment that our chronometrics are more about information management than about time (Bowker 2005; Shanks and Tilley 1987 on chronometrics).

To understand this, let us now consider what was covered by this linear temporality with respect to space—not as a sequence of spaces, but as simultaneous spaces.

Entering Argos from the direction of Nauplion, one crosses the Corinth-Tripolis railroad at the interchange with the Argos-Nauplion line. The latter, Corinth-Argos-Nauplion interchange, was completed on April 15, 1886: the Argos-Myli extension on August 4 of the same year (Matzaridis 1996; Society of Friends of the Railway 1998). After 2000, new tracks were laid on concrete ties. The old one-meter-gauge track lies stacked in separate piles of rails and ties along the wayside. Nearby, a World War II machine-gun box from which bored Italian soldiers once monitored this interchange sits abandoned in the partial shade of a eucalyptus tree. Its doorway is largely choked up with soil and construction debris; inside, it is littered with plastic bottles and broken glass.

Continuing along Nauplion Street, one passes a series of concrete apartment blocks, the first of these was constructed in 1962. At 24 Nauplion Street, a dilapidated abandoned joiner's (carpentry) workshop sits within a walled enclosure centered upon an adjacent house. Shelves retain the order of how grease cans, saw blades, and nail bins were left; the mud-brick walls, now exposed under a collapsed roof, recede a little more with every rain (fig. 7.2). In the rear, a neglected orchard of citrus and olive trees is overgrown with weeds. Such compounds were pervasive features of Argos in the nineteenth and early twentieth centuries.

From Nauplion Street we take Vas. Sofias west to the main square, Plateia Aghiou Petrou. The cathedral was completed in 1859. Two hundred meters north, at 48 Korinthos Street, excavations in 2000–2001 revealed several stone chests aligned in a row and covered with stone slabs. Of these, four contained between 120 and 150 inscribed bronze plaques from the late fifth and fourth centuries B.C.E. (Whitley 2003–4, 19–20). Across Plateia Aghiou Petrou to the west is the archaeological museum. Within its concrete and rebar walls (completed in 1957 and 1961) are several galleries housing diverse materials: the ground-floor gallery is filled with lines of cases containing Bronze Age and Geometric pottery; the first floor holds Roman sculpture; the lower level, Early Neolithic to Late Bronze Age materials; the outer terrace, fifth-century C.E. mosaics (see also chapter 3). From here, we could continue with the neoclassical houses of (British) Major General Thomas Gordon, Demetrios Kallergis, and Demetrios Tsokris, the classical/Hellenistic/Roman agora, the Hellenistic theater, the old castle of the Larissa, the Helladic

FIGURE 7.2. Abandoned joiner's workshop on Nauplion Street, Argos, in 2007.

(Bronze Age) remains on the Aspis hill, and so on, but our point can now be made: spatially, Argos is a gathered, multitemporal ensemble. This holds for all the realities of Argos, all its times (for complementary discussion of amassing pasts and multitemporalities, see, too, Olivier 2001, 2008; Olsen 2010). Still, there is far more to the issue of time than situating these locales and materials by date.

Consider now the temporal composition of some of these old things.

Returning to the derelict joiner's workshop at 24 Nauplion Street, let us ask a simple question: what time is this building? Late nineteenth century? Early twentieth? Post–World War II? Yes, it may be one of these; or it may be all of them. Even so, this is only a partial designation at best. Rather than date it by its construction, by specific interactions that transpired with the workshop, or even by its subsequent abandonment and ruination (in using these latter terms, we must already be thinking in terms of a particular temporality), let us consider the derelict structure bit by bit.

The walls of the workshop are plastered mud brick, a building material that requires extraction, molding, drying, setting, and maintenance, a set of distributed practices dating back to the Early Neolithic in Greece (see Perlès 2001). The plaster on the walls, the ceramic tiles, and the post-and-lintel structure of the doorways and windows—some still with their glass panes—possess similar temporal depth. Glass windowpanes date back to Roman times and were further improved in medieval Europe (Macfarlane and Martin 2002). Their history involves numerous, dislocated transactions distributed across three continents and four millennia. We could continue in the same way with the electric wiring that connects us, not only to early-nineteenth-century experiments in telegraphy (Black 1983; on the connection to later developments in electrification, see Hughes 1983; Schiffer 2008), but also to the copper age, or with the mode of roof construction or with the elements of design. However, we have said enough to reemphasize the point: whether considering the buildings or infrastructure along Nauplion Street; whether dealing with a 1947 Leica IIIc camera or the 2006 model rental car we are driving around Argos (Serres with Latour 1995, 45), gathered in these things are aggregate mixtures of accumulated achievements, which both date to different periods and have various durations or fluctuations, and yet are nonetheless simultaneously present.[2]

But there is far more. Let us shift again from these things as multitemporal assemblages to the collective relations they enter into.

On December 12, 1821, the Greek national assembly met in the Hellenistic theater (*Greece: A Handbook for Travellers* 1894, 256; Finlay 1877, 239).[3] Freed from much of their former blanket of earth, the stone bleachers of the theater would once again accommodate the masses.[4] The theater is a semi-circle of concentric bleachers carved out of the hillside. In such theaters, intelligibility is afforded by acoustic design. On that mid-December day in 1821, the Greek military commander Dimitrios Ypsilantis employed this Hellenistic theater as a device for gather-

2. We are not talking about the old historical notion of the continuity of tradition; rather, this is very much an issue of translation and circulation as things.

3. The Fourth National Assembly, convened by Ioannis Kapodistrias, met in the theater of Argos on July 23, 1829 (Miller 1966, 104).

4. The remaining portions of the ancient theater at Argos were excavated intermittently in the nineteenth and twentieth centuries.

ing crowds and broadcasting to the throng. This was an orchestrated scenario (note the double etymological connection here to features of the theater) that the material past had a part in shaping.

A few months later, a force of volunteers would defend the Larissa against ten thousand Ottoman troops under Mahmud Dramali Pasha (Finlay 1877, 291). Until this ragtag bunch frantically rushed up the hill from the town below, the old castle of Argos was regarded as a ruin (Leake 1830, 2: 395). However, in this course of the mêlée the former ruin took on new characteristics. In the most desperate hours of the siege, the efforts of ancient Greeks, Franks, Venetians, and Turks (all complex collectives) in the form of bastions, towers, and an inner and outer enceinte (along with a few hundred reinforcements from Lerna under Ypsilantis himself) would lend their aid. One could similarly detail other such polychronic exchanges: between the castle and, for example, the Argives and Villehardouin, the Venetians and the Ottoman Turks, the *condottiero* Bertoldo d'Este and the pasha of the Morea, the Turks and the Venetians under Francesco Morosini, and, yet again, the Venetians and the Turks (see Andrews 2006 [1953]). And in these situations 1212, 1397, 1463, 1686, and 1715 are merely coordinates for much more complex temporal folding, for much more intense episodes of turbulence spawned by such heterogeneous, polychronic transactions.

Nineteenth-century town planning dominates the movement of gas-guzzling automobiles in the town center; classical designers play a delayed role in shaping Argos's Roman Odeon (Ginouvès 1972); fifth-century remains are located in a network of relations with legislation and personnel of the General Directorate of Antiquities: there are countless examples where agencies of one time make others do something in another. Likewise, tens of dozens of inscribed bronze plaques recirculate financial details of treasury of Pallas (Athena), dating from the late fifth and fourth centuries B.C.E.—such movements constitute reverse temporal fluxes; what was distant is now proximate. And all are to be found in dynamic, multitemporal sets of relations. When considered from this angle, time doesn't simply pass: it percolates (Serres with Latour 1995; Pearson and Shanks 2001; Witmore 2006 and 2007).

Thus far, our movement has been from the purified and ordered to the more jumbled and chaotic; from a line to a sheet to an aggregate mixture to a more turbulent notion of percolation. In this passage, we have, in a manner of speaking, reversed the sorting of the archaeological process. Indeed, the proposition that archaeologists are separate from their fields of study is the artifact of a particular historicism (and empiricism, as discussed in chapter 2), and that separation, we contend, must be regarded as the outcome of our ordering practices (Olsen 2010, 126–27). This point has implications for our understandings of time.

Let us revisit, once again, this image of modern historicism. Just as earlier temporal blocks were partitioned from one another by conquests, upheavals, and abandonments, we, living in the present moment, hold ourselves to be separated once and for all from the premodern by scientific revolutions, epistemic breaks, and paradigm shifts. Michel Serres compares this idea to medieval diagrams where the earth was the center of the universe (Serres with Latour 1995, 48). Reminiscent of these diagrams, this modernist image of time places those alive today at center, which corresponds to the cutting edge. Unambiguously unidirectional, isotropic, and invariant, this partial image of time treats the past as that which was lived.[5] Likewise, discussions of entropic time often disregard living relations as temporally flat when juxtaposed with the temporal rhythms of perpetual perishing (Bailey 1981, 1983; Wandsnider 2004a, 2004b; see discussion in Witmore 2007 and below). The abstraction necessary to maintain this image of the past that was becomes problematic when it is taken to exist apart from the conditions of its own making.

Is the past absent? To say yes doesn't quite account for how ancient Greeks, Franks, Venetians, and Ottoman Turks came to the aid of a motley force of Greek freedom fighters in 1822. So, then, the past cannot be wholly absent, because something of past achievements is nonetheless present. Then the past is present? Yes, the past is amassed, aggregated, enrolled, mixed up, recirculated, unforgotten, or torn out. It is the exchange with things that gather the "pasts" that is of importance and not an orientation with respect to a measured and passing temporality. *The past as it was is at all times the outcome of the gathering of previous pasts.*

Let's be clear. First, we do not seek to debunk chronology. Rather, we wish to separate our measures from an oversimplified image of time as a linear, passage temporality; of time as an external parameter (Shanks 1992; Olivier 2004). It goes without saying: *we need our measures.* But we must also recast metrology through material relations (Webmoor

5. These are often centered solely upon living beings whose proximate relations are played out within dramas of subjects among subjects (consider the work of Shennan 2006). Let it suffice to say, such forecloses on unanticipated connections because of the issue of measured distance is held to bar contact between living communities across distances that overshoot any human life span. Such a scheme either forgets the action of things or denies them altogether.

2012a, b). Second, we argue, it is the myriad engagements between heterogeneous and often humble entities, whether they are archaeological or otherwise, that make time. The excavating archaeologist encounters hybridized conditions, such as overlapping and compressed layers, superimposed structures, artifacts, and debris mixed together—in short, sites that strike against modernity and historicism's wished-for ideal of completeness, order, and purified time. Paraphrasing Bruno Latour, *it is not the time that makes the sorting, it is the sorting that makes the time* (1993, 76). Because time isn't necessarily unidirectional, because time doesn't simply pass, we are not obliged to sort out our fields of engagement into syntheses oriented along a timeline. To better understand the nature of multitemporal relations, we may learn to dance through time in a different way, with a freedom of movement that a linear temporality denies us. This movement may even hold the seeds of a truly archaeological synthesis (Witmore 2007).

Let us pursue these arguments through more empirical vignettes. Consider now some details of archaeological engagement with diverse elements associated with a citadel across the Argive Plain.

## 1899: FROM STATION TO CITADEL

Wednesday, April 12, 1899. Having traveled by train from Athens, Gertrude Bell arrives at Phikhtia station at noon (it is worth noting how such matters of synchronicity have been taken for granted; indeed, prior to the railroad, one could not be sure that noon in Phikhtia was the same as noon in Athens). After a basket lunch in the company of her dragoman, Constantine Icomenides and his cook, Themistocles, Bell travels to the citadel of Mycenae.[6]

The small village of Charváti is on the road to the citadel, about a mile and a half from Phikhtia. Petros Christópoulos, the custodian of Mycenaean antiquities, who shows visitors the ruins for a drachma or two, lives at the south end of Charváti, near a small museum, which also provides food and accommodations (Klein 1997, 252).[7]

Bell and her entourage take the (new) track over the "bare hill side" and stop first by the Treasury of Atreus. In her wonderment, like so

6. Gertrude Bell to her mother, April 14, 1899, Gertrude Bell Archive, www.gerty.ncl.ac.uk/letter_details.php?letter_id=1050 (accessed April 11, 2012).

7. Christópoulos is mentioned in both the 1889 and 1894 versions of Baedeker's *Greece* (*Greece: A Handbook for Travellers* 1889, 253, and 1894, 258).

many travelers before her, she notes the tremendous lintel and corbelled vaulting. From here, they move on to "Mrs. Schliemann's tomb," the so-called Treasury of Clytaemnestra, then up to the Citadel where, turning an angle of the wall, they behold the Lion Gate. Next, Bell notes "the holes of the tombs where all the gold was found" and they proceed "up to the Palace where [they] traced the foundations with difficulty." Of the vista, Bell remarks in a letter to her mother: "He had a fine view from his palace, Agamemnon, right across the fertile ["horse bearing" is a descriptor used elsewhere in her diary] Argolic plain, with the Acropolis of Argos sticking up in the distance and the sea beyond." In her diary she adds: "Orestes' view in the opening of the Electra."

"This happened here." Connecting event to place is a quintessential leitmotif of the archaeological imagination (Shanks 2012). It invokes further questions of how this event played out and what remains of it. If we divert our gaze from this past drama, another unfolds. Bell's pronouncement arises in a simultaneous exchange with, among other things, her recall of a tragedy composed in 413 B.C.E., open trenches left by Schliemann's two-decade-old excavation, nineteenth-century notions of the picturesque, and the manifold material features, many from the Bronze Age, some from the Hellenistic, encountered on the ground.

## A BRONZE AGE "DISCOVERED"

Whether in the eighteenth, nineteenth, or twentieth centuries, or today, the draw of Mycenae for persons, like Bell, steeped in the epics of Homer, the tales of the Orestia, the texts of ancient authors such as Pausanias has been the citadel of Agamemnon. In 1899, this was also the spot where Schliemann found all the gold.

The notion of discovery is a familiar modernist trope. To discover a *past* on one level presupposes degeneration, loss, and an absolute break. In assuming a purified past, material entities are revelatory of someone, something else, something more important (cf. Shanks and Tilley 1992). Thus, as vestiges, old things are regarded as the outcome of events. Yes, but they are many other things in addition. This assumption of a past as past deflects from many other ontological co-possibilities, and it is within such simultaneous exchanges that time's brewing occurs.

On another level, the notion of discovery places the archaeologist at center. Prior to Schliemann's excavations, what would come to be called "Grave Circle A" had not passed away. The materials situated within did not lie in wait for some privileged human access. They were constantly involved in other relations. All the gold, all the bits of wood, all the skeletal remains were involved in different sets of relation with other entities (providing fodder for microbes), with other bits of matter gaining and loosing molecules all along. With an archaeological intervention, they take on new and continually changing associations. These are not so much discovered; it would be more precise to characterize them as remixed and continually modified in new sets of relation.

## THE ROUTES FROM CHARVÁTI

Baedeker's *Greece: A Handbook for Travellers* of 1889, a popular tourist guide, states that there are two routes from the small village of Charváti to the citadel. The shorter exits the north end of town. It runs "to the Káto Pigadi, a much-frequented fountain, with remains of ancient masonry, and then ascends right to the top" of the Panagia hill where it meets the second road. The latter starts on the east end of Charváti. Skirting a ruined Turkish aqueduct, it offers a gentler grade to the chapel of Agios Georgios. Along this line, it also affords a view to the ravine of Gouvia, where the ruins of the Cyclopean bridge (now dubbed the Agios Georgios Bridge) are located. This road continues to follow the path of the aqueduct beyond the chapel and across the shoulder of the hill passing just east of a square structure (marked as E4:12 by the Mycenae survey) of Mycenaean date and along the eastern shoulder of Panagia to the saddle by the Treasury of Clytaemnestra, where it reconnects with the aqueduct. It then faithfully follows the line of this water conduit along the north wall of the citadel and beyond to the Perseia Spring.

Compare the maps of subsequent editions of Baedeker's *Greece* and one will note fluctuations in the path of the route on top of Panagia (fig. 7.3). In 1889, a side path breaks off from the main road at an elevation of 662 feet and descends the hill to the base of the Treasury of Atreus, where it terminates (*Greece: A Handbook for Travellers* 1889, 254). In 1894, this side path continues from the Treasury as a lower road along the eastern slope of Panagia and meets up with the aqueduct and upper route just above the Treasury of Clytaemnestra. In 1909, the upper road along the eastern shoulder of Panagia is no longer marked as connected, and all traffic follows what is now the main path along the lower route.

Compare these maps to the one compiled by Sir William Gell and published in his 1810 *Itinerary of Greece* (plate 3) and a yet different image emerges. The old route closely follows the line of a water conduit (this "Turkish" aqueduct supplied water to Charváti at the time of Gell's visit in 1804–5) to the shoulder of Panagia, where it appears to cease following the watercourse. Each road network is situated in different fields of relation. Each track places emphasis on different features. These shifting tracks have temporal ramifications.

Related to the aqueduct, the road mapped by Gell was necessary for the continued maintenance of the waterline (a portion of this is still visible in an aerial photograph published in the *Archaeological Atlas of Mycenae* [Iakovidis and French 2003]). In 1889, the aqueduct is derelict and the track integrates the two chapels (Panagia and Agios Georgios) with a trail down the embankment to the Treasury of Atreus. The side path turned main path offers a more direct route between the Treasury of Atreus and that of Clytaemnestra. By the early twentieth century, apart from farmers visiting their terraces, villagers visiting the Chapel of Panagia, or archaeologists rummaging over features on the hill, travel is focused along the low shoulder of the Panagia. The present road would eventually be paved along a line just down the hill from this track, which is no longer in use. The road also avoids the steeper grade of the old road altogether by following a low grade farther down the slope just below the chapel of Agios Georgios.

These sporadic fluctuations are produced by different networks of multitemporal relation. Of course, understanding these fluctuations, we cannot take the line of these roads as wholes. Today, an old dirt road, one transformed by truck and tractor traffic, continues over Panagia hill. A portion of it follows the angled terrace of the Turkish aqueduct mapped by Gell. Another strays across a terrace line maintained to this day. Another section follows a course bulldozed along the ridgeline within the past few years near the Chapel of Panagia. In each and every one of these cases, achievements of one time impact daily routines in another. Such sporadic fluctuations characterize the mixing of pasts on a hill near Mycenae. In this, the material past is enrolled, forgotten, plowed over, recycled, translated, and circulated. We might describe these pasts as highly pleated. These routes from Charváti to the citadel are illustrative of the pleating and gathering that hybridizes all temporalities (Olivier 2008; Olsen 2010). Let us consider this folding once again with respect to a timeline.

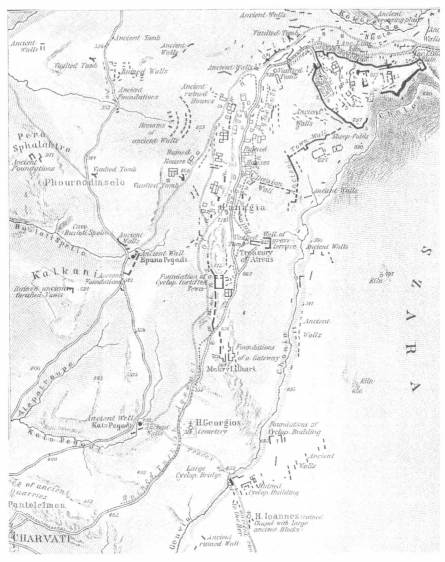

FIGURE 7.3. Juxtaposition of maps from Mycenae in Baedeker's *Greece: A Handbook for Travellers*, editions of 1889 *(above)* and 1894 *(opposite)*.

## MYCENAE 2007

In the summer of 2007 thousands of visitors, site guards, and guides walk paths and along walls laid out in a late Bronze Age architectural context. The approach to the Gate of the Lions, the Great Ramp, the walls of the

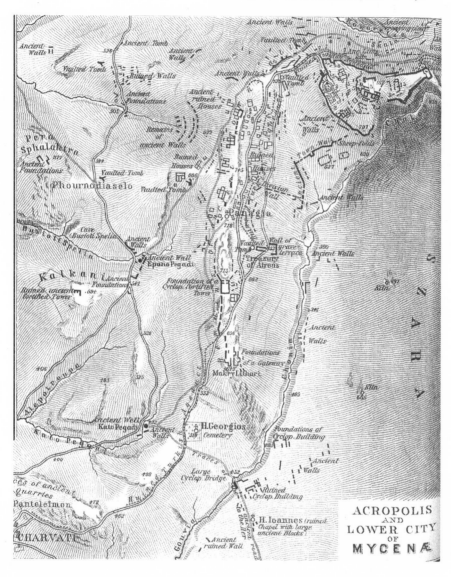

citadel, and key buildings continue to orient peripatetic interaction (Iakovidis and French 2003, 12). These modern engagements are to some
extent proximate to the spatial relationships of roughly 1200 B.C.E. in
the citadel. However, the nineteenth-century excavations of Schliemann
and Christos Tsountas and the subsequent work of Alan Wace and the

British School between 1920 and 1923 displaced an entire Hellenistic settlement and temple (along with earlier Geometric/Archaic remains), of which few visitors are aware (Klein 1997).

How does this connect to the image of a timeline? It perhaps seems more than trivial and, at this point, repetitive, to state that the Hellenistic comes after the Bronze Age. The Mycenaean phases of the citadel predate the Hellenistic period by up to a thousand years. Now envision this distance along a timeline on a flat sheet of paper in your hands. The summer of 2007 is over two millennia distant from the Hellenistic. The Hellenistic, again, is a millennium away from the late Bronze Age. These distances all seem straightforward. However, ball up this sheet of paper. 2007 and the thirteenth-century B.C.E., times distant with respect to the line, are now proximate and even touch each other. This similarly holds for other times, whether a Turkish aqueduct draws water from the very spring that once supplied the citadel or segments of Archaic, Hellenistic, or nineteenth-century paths follow portions of Mycenaean roads.

Tear out the Hellenistic and Geometric/Archaic periods and they become remote.[8] Because any physical engagement with the Hellenistic architectural fabric is no longer possible, these sets of relation are now more distant than the Bronze Age (see Klein 1997 for a discussion of excavation archives). This folded, wadded up, and torn diversity is indicative of Mycenae as it is.

PERCOLATING TIME

Time is paradoxical. Here it flows evenly. There it is turbulent, with countercurrents, eddies, and whirlpools. Here it is gathered. There it unfurls over the very long term. "Weather" and "time" are the same word in many languages: *le temps* in French; *o kairos* in Greek (Serres with Latour 1995, 60). Our aim in this chapter has been to suggest how time is much more complex than our archaeological traditions have allowed. Percolating time is a notion whereby time, no longer treated solely as an external parameter, arises out of the multifarious relations between entities of various pasts. In this, past and present are thoroughly blended. Indeed, it would not be an understatement to suggest that everything changes when we acknowledge the past to be no longer past. However, in clarifying our new role (which is really our old role shed of the burden

8. This image of the crumpled and wadded up timeline was inspired by Serres's lucid discussion of the handkerchief (Serres with Latour 1995, 60–61).

associated with an oversimplified empiricism) in relation to pasts understood as co-present, let us summarize some of the key arguments here.

A linear temporality lays out the drama in advance. In this sense, it is teleological. This is what we mean when we emphasize that time does not constitute the sorting. We must understand time as the other way round. Time arises out of the relations. We have everything to gain by understanding time in this way. The first payoff: the pasts live again. They are proximate. They have action. They matter in more ways than the detached glass case of modernism permits. If we can no longer seek to purify pasts from the present world in advance, then we can no longer do so when we build accounts of these pasts.

Second payoff, we recognize how at all times, the elements of group formation, of the making of humanity, involve multitemporal entities. A Bronze Age wall works in the formation of communities a thousand years later in Hellenistic Mycenae. Likewise, the ensemble of our practices simultaneously draws upon eighteenth-century modes of topographical survey, nineteenth-century geology, and twentieth-century physics. Throughout this chapter, these co-possibilities have been emphasized in numerous ways. They are worth revisiting.

Distributed memory: relations leave myriad traces. We would not be able to speak of the Battle of Champions or the siege of the Larissa in 1821 without a writer having left a few lines to describe them or marks where musket balls dislodged bits of stone. Whether they are delineated by different modes of wall construction at Mycenae or manifest as the diaries and letters of Gertrude Bell, the ability of mnemonic traces to persist despite subsequent transformations are what contributes to the depth and complexity of time. Of course, there are now some excellent works on memory in archaeology (e.g., Alcock 2002; Bradley 2002; Boric 2010; Jones 2007; Mills and Walker 2008; Olivier 2004, 2008; van Dyke and Alcock 2003; Yoffee 2007). With such work we are beginning to attend to such dynamics: what comes to be dubbed "Grave Circle A" serves as a mnemonic reference for what lies beneath the ground. Likewise, the imprint of the very bullet that killed the first prime minister of Greece is still to be seen in the door to the church of Agios Spyridon on the street in Nauplion that bears his name, Kapodistrias. Distributed memory is an issue of duration.

Duration: this notion, closely associated with the philosopher Henri Bergson, permeates our discussion of time (for an excellent discussion of duration in archaeology, see Olivier 2001, 2008). Duration denotes the extension of the past and the constant aggregation (or sedimentation) of this past in the present (Bergson 1998; also Deleuze 1991). Despite the radical changes at Argos over the past six thousand years, relations between mud, filler, and people forming and drying blocks have persevered over the very long term. They are to be found in the mud-brick wall of a nineteenth-century workshop at 24 Nauplion Street. Duration plays out through iterative and often plainly given relations.[9] Things, despite radical transformations, may continue to fill their role as delegates for subsequent generations. Wheels and axles continue to turn in generating the force necessary for movement or energy across the long term. Despite the advance of the coastline from its proximity to Tiryns, the noise of the sea is nonetheless recurrent near the water's edge.

Gathering: things gather achievements considered distant in a time ordered by a metrical geometry. Made, unmade, and remade, the composition of a wall may assemble actions from several different eras. A section of the Late Bronze Age circuit of Mycenae is razed by the Argives; Hellenistic occupants reconstruct a portion of wall and build a tower; an earthquake topples the ashlar above the Gate of the Lions; the Greek Archaeological Service repairs these sections: the walls of Mycenae are an aggregate mixture of multiple groups and multiple times. Pasts proliferate in the present.

Simultaneity: the Argolid is a polychronic ensemble, a palimpsest. Early mornings in the villages to the west of Argos, one regularly has to give right-of-way to donkeys laden with fodder. Roadways many centuries old, now paved over, direct movement between Argos and Nauplion in 2007. Channeling water from where the Kefalari exits underground caverns, the old Ottoman stone water leats, patched over with concrete, still spill forth into hollows that once held the horizontal wheel that turned grinding stones over salt and grain. These waters are routinely

9. Duration should not be confused with durability. Durability is partially a quality of distributed relations. And yet, to take an example, in no two cases can the durability of Mycenae's walls be regarded as equivalent. Their durable strength waxes or wanes with each case. Communities in the past maintained a wall that was delegated the task of protecting and maintaining the community. All along, the wall was only as hard or as soft as the whole of its associations with communities that fended off and fell in the face of various hordes. The walls of Mycenae are not only held together by the superb craftsmanship of the Mycenaeans (of the Bronze Age, Archaic, and Hellenistic periods), the angle of the joints, and the sheer weight of stone but also by site guards, protective fences, other measures of the archaeological service, the Greek police, and the authoritative stamp of UNESCO. Given this, how can we *pace* Geoff Bailey (1981, 1983, 2007; also Wandsnider 2004a, 2004b) assume a constant timescale for the whole of Mycenae's walls? And yet the wall endures.

released by Albanian immigrants to clean carpets in the hollows left by the derelict millhouses. A linear, successive historicism would regard these instances as remnants of archaism soon to be relegated to the past in the wake of modernism (Snodgrass 1987; Latour 1993), but simultaneity underlines how these pasts are spatially coextensive.

Percolation: all the preceding themes may be assembled under the banner of a percolating time. Time often vindicates that which has been forgotten or rendered outmoded and obsolete. Today a once forgotten theater again resonates with ancient dramas during summer festivals in Epidaurus. Yesterday a ruin above Argos once again became a defensive castle during a desperate battle. It is by being there that this so-called ruin is able to actualize a past that is otherwise forgotten. We hear of financial details related to Athena's treasury today. An Ottoman-era aqueduct once again drew water from the ancient spring that supplied Hellenistic Mycenae. Percolation is not limited to such localized material relations. Organic farming, sustainable design, alternative modes of movement, past practices might even return to the Argolid Plain. Archaeology in struggling against forgetting, adds to these reverse fluxes.[10]

The time we endeavor to articulate here hinges upon how we as archaeologists regard ourselves in these scenarios. However, if archaeology has never considered itself contemporary with the things it studies, how can it become so now? It can become so because, as we have emphasized throughout this book, archaeology has always been contemporary in terms of what we do. Despite the imbalance archaeology has long sought to maintain, the discipline does not stand apart from these relations. Excavators have always exchanged properties with floor surfaces in square holes or with recently exposed wall lines. Surveyors, using a host of instruments and techniques, have always bestowed temporalities upon bits of terrace wall, and these walls have given competency to these surveyors. Archaeology has always been a force in the percolation of times by remixing the past in the present. Such polychronic simultaneities generate a time of successions.

In this, the old Greek distinction between *kairos* and *chronos* is helpful. *Kairos* is simultaneous. *Chronos* is successive. *Kairos* is primary. *Chronos* is secondary. They are not oppositional. One is born of the

---

10. It has nonetheless has forgotten things. Our theories of continuity and change are so impoverished because they adhere to the rigidity of a line centered upon humans solely as living beings (see Shennan 2006). Here, we forget the importance of things in slowing the pace of our revolutions (Olsen 2010; Serres with Latour 1995, 87).

other. Primary times provide the grounds for secondary times. Primary times are relational. Secondary times are processual. Primary times are spatial, yet saturated with a ceaseless, liquid motion. Secondary times separate space and time.

## POSTSCRIPT: THE HERA OF POLYKLEITUS, OR, TIME'S TWO ARROWS

To sum up, allow us to provide yet one more example. No trace of the gold and ivory statue of Hera was found during the excavations of the Argive Heraion. Whether worn out by supplicant kisses of the faithful, dismantled by the irreverent, shattered by the iconoclasts, or left to rain, rot, and ruin, Polykleitus's celebrated statue had long since perished. For Strabo, it was the most beautiful of all such masterpieces (but Charles Waldstein [1901, 30] calls Strabo a less than discriminating art critic). According to Pausanias the statue "of Hera is seated and of colossal size. It is made of gold and ivory and is a work of Polykleitus. She wears a diadem worked with Graces and Seasons; in one hand she holds a scepter, in the other a pomegranate" (Pausanias 2.4). Imperial Roman coinage of Argos inscribes the enthroned goddess with Hebe and a peacock between them (the latter two also described by Pausanias). Other coins render the figure of Hera alone.

Even if Polykleitus's statue no longer exists, its manner or style persists through various stand-ins, and Waldstein enables us to visualize something of it. Strabo's accolade, Pausanias's brief *ekphrasis*, coins of Argos, Waldstein 1901, and potential copies in stone, articulations in other media, and subsequent engagements with them constitute negative entropic processes. Life, though always susceptible to death, nonetheless persists through extensions, distributions, and transformations. Entropy, the perpetual perishing, has won out over Polykleitus's goddess. Still, through information and life an image of this very goddess has been re-formed elsewhere (Serres 1982, 74). Matter/entropy and life/information are not opposed. They are mixed properties, and life/information allows for fluxes in negative entropy. This is the reverse arrow of time. These fluxes are born out of the commotion of simultaneous exchange, noise (for a detailed examination of these relations in late antiquarian practice as well as archaeology see Shanks 2012). In this, archaeology, through its co-production, staves off entropy, at least to some degree, and contributes to time's percolation.

# CHAPTER 8

# Making and the Design of Things

*Human Being and the Shape of History*

Previous chapters have explored the ways in which archaeology and cognate fields are best treated as active engagements with things. We have explained the proposition that archaeology is itself a mode of cultural production, a creative enterprise of authoring, delivering goods and artifacts, and involving material modes of production.

In this chapter, we turn to the history of human engagements with things, and to making and consuming in particular. Archaeological research occurs at the hinge between materiality and immateriality, culture and artifacts, people and things. Archaeology has a unique view because of its long-term, comparative perspective on these relationships, with archaeological sources being our sole access to most of the one-hundred-and-fifty-thousand-year history of our species. Our chapter connects things and humanity in addressing the broad question of the character of human *being*, raising some of the issues already introduced in chapter 2, particularly a radical separation between human and object worlds.

We frame the debate over what it is to be human by asking the question: What is the *subject* of history? Archaeological approaches to this question typically invoke three fields of agency:

- Society—involving different characterizations of social structure, system, social organization, and culture; a particular concern is the relationship between structure and the individual social agent, individual autonomy and agency, the duality of structure, and people's creative agency in social practice.

- Species—the evolutionary character of *Homo sapiens,* the relationships between biological and cultural evolution (coevolution), with debates about the driving forces of evolutionary change (adaptation, selection), species variability (particularly genetic; the relation of contemporary variability in DNA to evolutionary change).

- Environment—the role of humanity in ecological systems, questions of the relationship between environmental change, human agency, and social change, with, of course, particular attention being given to the economics of resource management, use, and consumption in subsistence, surplus distribution, and the production of goods and commodities.

We mention here again the current interest in connecting these different fields, cutting across the biological, behavioral, social and cultural, across the world of human and nonhuman materiality. Within archaeology, such work comes under the rubrics of material engagement theory (Boivin 2008, Renfrew 2004), material agency (Knappett and Malafouris 2008), cognitive evolution (Malafouris 2004, 2008; Renfrew, Frith, and Malafouris 2009; Renfrew and Malafouris 2010), phenomenology and posthuman phenomenology (Olsen 2007, 2010; Tilley 1994, 2004, 2008; Thomas 1993), behavioral archaeology (Skibo, Walker, and Nielsen 1995; Schiffer with Miller 1999), evolutionary archaeology (Shennan 2008), posthumanism and actor-network theory (Dolwick 2009; Shanks 2007; Webmoor 2007; Witmore 2007), and entanglement (Hodder 2011).

We also recognize synergistic developments with diverse and various disciplinary fields collectively contributing to what has been termed "the ontological turn."[1] We work within this current and begin to address the matter of human being with a question. Because humanity is typically defined by what it is not, by the nonhuman world of things and

---

1. Within anthropology (Descola 2005; Holbraad 2009; Viveiros de Castro 1996), ecology (De Jonge 2004), geography (Whatmore 2002), philosophy (Harman 2009b; Meillassoux 2008; Sloterdijk 2009), politics (Bennett 2010), and so on. This chapter also touches specifically upon debates within the "social shaping of technology" literature, its influential characterization of the essentialism of technology and society, and the character of the purported interrelationship (MacKenzie and Wajcman 1999; Bijker, Hughes, and Pinch 1989).

nonhuman species, we ask: How do we conceive of humans without things and nonhumans? Our answer is simple—we cannot. Emphatically, this is not to say that we cannot conceive of things and nonhumans without humans (Fowles 2010). Rather, as we have specified throughout the book, it is to deny any image of humans as pure, free-standing subjects. Considering human being must take account of our engagement with the world of things; human agency is inseparable from the world of things in practices of reflection upon, manipulation, and management of the material environment, in making and production, labor and work, in exchange, consumption, discard, and reuse. Key topics here are how human creativity and innovation always involve delegation and cooperation, a concerned exchange with things and their affordances. People make manifest their human being in labor and work, not as embodiment or as a transcendental drive to objectify or externalize, but as a symmetry of actions, a relational field. And in this we regard the human as a mingled assemblage, part *cyb*ernetic, part *organism*.

Here we find it useful to introduce a term and transdisciplinary practice (or praxis—defined as theoretically informed practice). Not normally associated with archaeology (although see Schiffer 2011), *design* has come to be a key contemporary field concerned with things. A set of practices (e.g., architecture and graphics), a pragmatics (management operating in business and the market), a way of thinking, and a key component of engineering and manufacture, design has considerable application. We are, however, less interested in tightly defining a concept of design than in recognizing this considerable contemporary currency, because it offers, we suggest, help in integrating the three fields of agency, mentioned above, at the heart of (archaeological) debates about human being.

Design is closely connected, ultimately, with the industrialization of production in eighteenth- and nineteenth-century Europe and the United States, when factory mass production, division of labor, and its organization through larger companies and corporations entailed the emergence of a production function concerned with managing the manufacture of goods for a modern market: this is *industrial design*. Design is best treated as a diverse and contested field with a ramified genealogy and sometimes contradictory, but cognate, components (Buchanan, Doordan, and Margolin 2010; Norman 2002). The term receives multidisciplinary, indeed transdisciplinary, application: from God's intelligent design to Giorgio Armani, from architecture to cybernetics, objects to intangible experiences, from jeans to your genes. Nevertheless, let us start by saying that, for our purposes here, design refers to processes of originating, conceptualizing, and manufacturing a product or system, material or immaterial. In archaeology, simply because of the character of its material sources, the remains of society, but also for strong analytical reasons regarding the nature of cultural systems, these processes are inseparable from the distribution, consumption, discarding, or abandonment of the product or system and its subsequent decay and ruin. Subsumed are matters of individual agency and intentionality—what people want to achieve with the outcomes of their making, and how making (and the management of) things is at the heart of the reproduction of society. In this, no *homo faber* myth will do—no form is simply forced upon amorphous matter (Ingold 2010). One should also acknowledge that to make something is not to guide it through its new configurations—things often move on to take on lives of their own. As Tim Ingold has recently put it, things arise through an intervention in "fields of force and flows of material" (2010, 2). We connect this with the work of Gilbert Simondon (1989 [1958]) by recognizing how makers coax forth metastable states that slumber in matter, and where materials play a role in their own self-formation.

Understanding how and why people and things are co-produced is intimately associated, of course, with the dynamics of social and cultural change, including invention and innovation. Rather than thinking of this as a unidirectional process by which a human idea is implanted into something raw and meaningless, we should think of design as also emerging from the materials and the practices themselves, in their intimate involvement with human ideas and intentions (see Lemonier 1992, 1993; Ingold 2000, 2007, 2010; Sennett 2008; Olsen 2010).[2] The qualities that slumber inherent in the material used, the equipment involved in the processing, the ready-to-hand knowledge of the human producer, the effective history of former things and their production, the current assemblage of associations, all affect the outcome, implicit in design practice (in archaeology, cf. Gosden 1994, 2005; Thomas 1996). The old style-function debate in archaeology attempted to deal with some of this, but failed to capture this distributed scope of design (Sackett 1982, 1985; Wiessner 1983; see also Boast 1996; Lucas 2001a, 86–90; Shanks and Tilley 1992, chap. 7).

The culmination of the chapter will be a presentation of nine archaeological theses on design. These are more than tentative hypotheses, but

2. See also extensive discussion at http://mshanks.com (accessed April 13, 2012).

fall short of an archaeological orthodoxy. Based upon current archaeological thinking, they are what we consider to be the rudiments of a relational perspective on design that takes us from things in themselves to processes of making and consuming at the heart of which are issues of human agency and creativity. In accordance with the arguments presented in the rest of the book, we continue to propose a fundamental symmetry between people and things, materiality and immateriality, natures and cultures, in understanding how making things is all about reweaving our social fabric. Specifically, we argue that any resolution of distinction between person and thing, natural and artificial, material and immateriality is a relative matter—local and historically contingent. Two slogans capture much of our argument: we have always been cyborgs, and making can belong to the most humble of things. No entity has a monopoly upon design.

We work these points through two archaeological examples. These case studies are offered as heuristic and not as definitive research statements on their subject matter. We take some liberties and risks, cutting through careful qualification and control of detail to get to the core of our concern here with the subject of history, design, and human being. This is not an excuse to ignore relevant work, which we cite where appropriate. We simply ask that it be noted that our fidelity is to these core matters of concern.

A PREHISTORIC BUILT ENVIRONMENT

The first farmers of northern Europe, 6000 and 5000 years ago, along the Atlantic fringe, built earthen barrows and stone tombs and monuments (fig. 8.1). Thousands of them are scattered across the landscape— barrows, dolmens, cromlechs, stone circles and alignments, megaliths, avenues, causewayed camps. These are, and these have been, some of the most conspicuous and evocative of prehistoric remains. No two are precisely alike. There is certainly a sense of design to these architectures in the recurrent features, in the sculptural forms. Antiquarians and archaeologists have long been fascinated by the question of why they were built, how the particular form they took can throw light on their makers.

Fussell's Lodge, an earthen long barrow on the edge of Salisbury Plain in England, not far from Stonehenge, looks unexceptional among the evidence—a low, long mound of earth, like the others. It was well excavated in 1957, and the published scientific report lists all the bones and remains found in what looked like a timber mortuary house buried in

FIGURE 8.1. Passage grave at Carlshögen, Sweden, studied by Shanks and Tilley 1982, 1987.

the mound (Ashbee 1966). This, the report, is unusual: until the 1970s and 1980s, British archaeologists rarely recorded such detail for this kind of site, assuming the human remains in such structures to be simply those of communal burial. The plans of the barrow and what it contained are excellent. There is a wealth of detail to explore just what was going on in these structures, investigating whether it was indeed just laying down the remains of the dead.

The usual explanation of the barrows, dolmens, and cromlechs has long been that they were tombs, containing communal inhumations—the remains of many generations mingled in stone chambers or under great mounds of earth (see Thomas 1999, 126–62). The usual piles of bones, some quite weathered, were found in the excavation of Fussell's Lodge. One body at the end of the mound looked like someone buried in a crouched position, lying on his or her side. On close inspection, it wasn't *a* body. It was the bones of at least two people, rearranged, and not very accurately, to look like a single complete body. It seemed to be lying in the entrance of the three-posted mortuary house that had been buried in the earthen barrow. But this was another deceiving appearance—the house may have been dismantled and then the remains laid in a row on the ground, as if within the ghost of the house. The barrow wasn't even a simple mound of earth—it had started as an enclosure.

The old established account of these times is of a wave of agricultural revolution that spread across Europe from the Near East, leaving communities of farmers, living an egalitarian and quite simple life, centered upon family and kin, in its wake. Some have envisaged megalithic missionaries spreading the cult of monumental mortuary practices (Renfrew 1973; Pluciennik 2005). Many archaeologists since the 1960s have considered that economic forces drive history—the need to feed and sustain such a community; links have been sought between farming practices and funerary monuments such as a long barrow.

A range of interesting accounts since the 1970s have connected the building of these monuments to land and territory (Barker and Webley 1978; Fleming 1971; Renfrew 1976; Tilley 1994). Farmers value land, and a community's attachment to its fields may be manifest in, among other things, the building of ancestral tombs, houses of past generations laying claim to a right to farm or even own the land (see also Whitley 2002; Parker-Pearson et al. 2006). Such explanations do not, however, account for the likes of the reconfigured body at Fussell's Lodge, the other bones in the mortuary house, and the particular sequence of enclosure, house, and earthen mound. Nor do they deal with the evocation of everyday experience far removed from our own.

In chapter 3, we discussed the development of infrastructures in an archaeological ecology of practices in the nineteenth century and after. Over a century of archaeological research has established the outlines of prehistory—when and where things happened, from the Stone through the Iron Ages, through a myriad of regional cultural forms. Schemes of cultural evolution have been used to make sense of these timetables, based upon the categorization and classification of vast quantities of archaeological finds in a coherent and consistent time-space systematics. Though it differs from region to region, the overall narrative behind the systematics is usually presented as one of progression from simple band societies, hunter-gatherers who dominate most of human history, on through clan- and kin-based communities, those established by what still gets called the agricultural revolution, to "big-man" societies, chiefdoms, and then to states and civilization, based upon economic intensification and agricultural surplus (Sahlins and Service 1960; Service 1962).

With the renovation of theories of cultural evolution in the 1960s and 1970s came a new emphasis upon cross-cultural social science (Binford 1962; Braidwood 1959; Harris 1979; Steward 1955; White 1959). This offered tremendous scope, a way of seeing the forest beyond the trees, a big picture. It also allowed something of a human face to be put on the past, as outlined in chapter 2. Under this perspective, then, at Fussell's Lodge, we are to see a kin-based community; later came big men and chiefs, drawing power from their effective intervention and manipulation of reciprocal transactions and control of redistributed resources like food and prestige goods and their claim to esoteric fields of knowledge, to organize grander projects like Stonehenge.

Nevertheless, processes of evolutionary change, rooted in a driving mechanism of the selective advantage of one economy over another, have been questioned. It is quite reductive to hold that these monuments were the expression of a stage in cultural evolution; again, much of the specificity of activity is left unexplained. Most important, of course, the notion of cultural evolution assumes that human nature possesses certain characteristics. The big picture of evolutionary stages driven by group adaptation and selective advantage begged the question of the connection between these social and environmental forces and the everyday life of people who make up societies (Shanks and Tilley 1987); it begged the question of the significance of belief, perception, and cognition. Were intentions, belief, and perception secondary to a community's adaptation to the local environment, its ecological niche; or were they themselves adaptive functions?

These old issues are the subject of sophisticated ongoing commentary and debate, and we do not wish here to resort to crude caricature that would dismiss the applicability of evolutionary modeling (see Shennan 2008, 2009). We simply raise the question of how such a paradigm can address that question of *design* raised at the beginning of this case study. Why were these structures built? How can the particular forms they took throw light on their makers?[3] The latter clearly found gratification in fiddling with the remains of the dead to judge from the remains of the feasting outside many monuments, from those rearranged bones at Fussell's Lodge, and from the probable inclusion of old ancestral

---

3. See Dennett 2004 for a discussion of the connection between evolutionary process, design, and agency.

remains in the deposition of fresh remains of the dead. There is, of course, a factor of scale—evolutionary change and causality on a broader, long-term scale, to be contrasted with the micro-scale experience of constructing and using a monument such as this earthen long barrow—the details of process and use. A cursory glance at the evidence of the likes of Fussell's Lodge also instantly raises questions of categorization, but one could also raise the question of metaphysical grounding, thus taking us back to David Clarke's insistence on questioning fundamental entities (1968; see Webmoor 2012a, 2012b; Witmore 2012b). The heterogeneous components of the process of building and using the monument, the enclosure turned into a timber structure, turned into a charnel house, turned into a barrow, and all the associated activities of deposition, visiting, arrangement of bones, burning and feasting are only subsumed in the concept of tomb or barrow with a loss of hold on the details of process and use that give insight into what the structure actually was or how it happened.

Address to such questions has benefited greatly since the 1960s from the application of quantitative and comparative analysis, from descriptive statistics to computer-based multivariate statistical processing of large amounts of data. Following a simple proposition that, if this was the collective burial of community members, the proportion of bones and body parts in the heaps of communal burial would be about the same as you find in a complete body, most bones would be the more numerous hand and foot bones, and there would be proportionately fewer skulls, for example. Differential preservation is important: some bones are tougher than others. Even factoring this in, however, comparative and quantitative analysis of the numbers and types of bones in monuments from the Neolithic in southwest England and southern Sweden (the sample size determined by publication) showed very clearly that all the expected body parts were not, on the whole, present (quantitative analysis presented in Shanks and Tilley 1982).

And more. There was a clear distinction being made between right and left body parts. Male and female, adult and child, were treated differently. Skulls and long bones were arranged in patterns, as well as to resemble a complete body, as at Fussell's Lodge. Many people never received burial—there simply were not enough monuments and remains to make up a viable community. An old observation that the design of chambered monuments and barrows resembles the long houses of central European farmers can be confirmed in statistical analysis of ten points of structural similarity (Hodder 1982, 1984, 1990; see also Bradley 1996,

1998; Sherratt 1990). Many so-called tombs had never contained any bodies. Human remains are not only found in tombs. They were also carefully deposited with the bones of animals, pots, and stone axes in the ditches of earthworks that enclosed great timber circles and roofed halls. And few traces of houses for people actually to live in have been identified.

So much for the story of a simple farming community burying its dead! Close scrutiny questions the simple category of "tomb," and indeed, as just mentioned, its ontology. What was actually going on? The dead were not simply buried in a communal tomb. Some human remains were left out to weather; they were buried and reburied, removed from chambered tombs and perhaps earthen barrows, organized, and sorted, circulated through their communities. This happened where people met, gathered, and held feasts, organized labor, and built great arrangements of stone, timber, and earth.

Recent work has questioned the long-term, continuous use of monuments like Fussell's Lodge, proposing instead constant and consistent use spanning only a few generations at most (Whittle and Bayliss 2007). This revised chronology does not invalidate the argument we are making about the purpose of design and use. On the contrary, it could be said to strengthen the focus upon design decisions as much as determinate social structures.

One culmination of this set of practices is Stonehenge—a great public monument set in a landscape of monuments, structures, and happenings, old and new. But the remains also ended up buried where few or any could go—as in the earth at Fussell's Lodge. The remains we find of feasts in the courtyards outside some monuments contrast starkly with the decayed, weathered remains placed in damp ditches or stone chambers— something here of a sharp contrast between living and dead. Signs of the careful design of activities and monuments abound, and include the famous astronomical alignments of Stonehenge and its landscape, oriented on the solar, and perhaps the lunar, calendar.

The connections, the articulations that run through the bones, bodies, and monuments arranged in the land mean that it makes only limited sense to talk of tombs and burial of the dead, or indeed of individuals and communities and their homes in the way we understand these aspects of life. This is one reason why "monument" or even "structure" is a better description than more specific terms like "tomb." The human body has been considered something of a historical and material constant that everyone shares (see also Harris and Robb forthcoming).

Consider, for example, how phenomenologists in archaeology have conceived of the body as a datum, as an analog—no, to be more precise, as a *homolog*—between eras (see, e.g., Tilley 1994, 2004). But in this world of prehistoric farmers, it was subject to quite different perceptions and experiences—the very experience of our human bodies has changed. Prehistoric farmers lived as different assemblages with polished stone adzes, wooden hoes, grooved-ware pots, gossip, marshes, cattle herds, caves, boars, oblique flint arrows, resin, trees, longhouses, hearths, ancestors, chalk, music, and bones. Whereas we living today are modified by new technological prosthetics—footwear, eyeglasses, MacBooks, automobiles, steel-and-concrete apartment buildings, even guide dogs. What we are attentive to in experience has also changed—we live with different ratios of senses (McLuhan 1994 [1964]; Witmore 2006). More will be said of this shortly. For now let it suffice to say that no body, living and material, understood as mingled and hybrid can act as a constant datum with these pasts. How "other" this Neolithic world was (Bailey, Whittle, and Cummings 2005)!

This need to coordinate category with process and use, and assess the variability inherent in any category such as "barrow" or "tomb," has profound implications for the way we understand design. As well as focusing on the attributes of an artifact, we should take account of process and use, the (cultural) work done by building and manipulating. Two structures that look quite similar may, of course, be quite different *things*.

In the 1980s, those archaeologists who started focusing in this way on how people looked at their world, on ideologies and cosmologies, systems underlying people's attitudes and beliefs, got called "coggies"— archaeologists practicing a new *cognitive archaeology* of the mind (Leone 1982; Renfrew 1993; Renfrew and Zubrow 1994; Hodder et al. 2007). The claim certainly is that archaeology can gain insight into past systems of belief, experience, and perception. But as we endeavor to indicate in our short examples in this chapter, a radical separation of mind and material world, or religious belief and economic or material necessity, of cognition and practice is hard to sustain (see Bradley 2005). We have treated this point more analytically in previous chapters. We uphold a materialist outlook—you don't have to talk to people to find out how they conceive of the world, because something of the way people operate, work, and do is wrapped up in their achievements. People are so involved with the world of material goods that we can put to one side the old split between mind and matter, beliefs and the material world that may leave traces for the archaeologist to work upon. These distinctions are real, but that is not to say that they are essential or a priori. They are *realized* as outcomes.

It is the strength of archaeology that we actually can identify the components of an underlying logic or story that makes sense of the rather strange (to us, at least) practices found at the likes of Fussell's Lodge. We can also reach beyond the relatively short local sequence of construction and use of Fussell's Lodge (again according to Whittle and Bayliss 2007) to comparative instances, to the broader and longer-term phenomena associated with early farming life in northwestern Europe. We can have confidence in such interpretation because of re-peated material associations elsewhere (bones, artifacts, worked stone, and earth found together in different ways, for example). Pattern and the routines of everyday life, such as a preference for particular treat-ment of certain parts of the body, as at Fussell's Lodge, can be securely identified.

Stepping back, what is the big picture of everyday life in this society of early farmers? To explain a particular design, it is important to look further than the single artifact. What are the articulations within which the building of this monument can be set?

Ironically, farming itself is hardly visible as a focus of the makers' energies. We can assume people grew crops and looked after their ani-mals, though it is clear that early farming is not to be pictured in stereo-typical terms of fields of ripening grain swaying in the breeze and herds of lowing cattle. It is much better understood as a more mixed affair—gardens of mixed plants and animals in clearings in the forest, clearings that only gradually grew into the great field systems of later prehistory. Being a farmer—although not necessarily in a very intensive way—involves transforming the ground, a direct engagement with the earth in terms of clearing—cutting trees and moving stones, turning/breaking up the soil surface for cultivation, weeding, keeping away voracious ani-mals, and so on. This emerging altering of the earth (Bradley 1993), the daily practices that are implied in being a farmer (in contrast—but not necessarily in opposition—to a hunter-gatherer) is closely related to the emerging "monumentalism." That is, the monuments and, literally, earth-work, may be seen as part of the bundled processes (see below) of the Neolithic assemblage and of the Neolithic engagement with the world.

These early gardeners and agriculturalists were expending consider-able energy on building monuments and on arranging associated cere-monies that dealt with bodies, feasting, and depositing the remains of the dead in the ground. There is a clear play on house design in some of the chambered monuments—they look like houses, houses of the dead, as it were. No individuals are singled out as special in the treatment of the dead, through rich graves goods, for example. Instead, there is emphasis on the performance of community—building great earthworks where people gathered, mingling bones, even reconstituting the bones of several people as one, as at Fussell's Lodge. This is a particular expression of temporality, with monuments built of the land itself giving expression to community, its members, and their connection with the past. These concerns are well established (Edmonds 1999; Parker-Pearson and Richards 1997; Thomas 1991, 1999).

The monuments themselves are arranged in what can for the first time be called a built environment. The trees were gradually being felled, clearings created for gardens and fields, and earthworks and stone structures mark out whole landscapes: there is much evidence of careful placing of monuments and structures. We should see the likes of Stonehenge and its landscape in this light. Its astronomical alignments are the incorporation of the community's efforts in the order of the universe; the seasonal routine upon which farming, of course, so depends, was marked out on the land itself. This prehistoric world of monuments built community into deep time and deep time into community. A designed landscape and cosmology goes with the manipulations of earth, stone, timber, and bone, through eating, through walking, moving, arranging, building, depositing.[4]

The selection and different treatment of particular parts of dead bodies is further clear evidence of organized cult. This is new—at least cult had never before received such material expression. But this is so much more than "religious" cult. These associations of physical community, different genders, different parts of the human frame, the ancestral dead, animals, land, heavenly order, and spectacular monumentality are embedded in the routines of everyday life—walking across the landscape to tend the garden, with animals to be slaughtered or animal parts to be consumed, tending to the remains of a family member, feasting and smashing domestic pots at a chambered tomb, observing the solar calendar, organizing a labor team to build a new stone circle. The routines of farming life, the iterations of cropping and breeding, are literally being grounded in routine, cult, and ritual.

4. For confirmation of such as designed built environment, see the latest work of the Stonehenge Riverside Project (Parker Pearson et al. 2006).

Causality? What role does the farming economy play in the design of these monuments? Our argument is that both agriculture and monumentalism formed part of and were enabled by these very same processes of entangled changes—the invention of cult, of architecture and the built environment, altering the landscape, the incorporation of other species, nature, and the heavens into everyday experience (Hodder 2011). Transforming and weaving one's self, one's community or shared group identities into the earth. New bodies of knowledge of what was right and proper, as well as the astronomical order lying behind the built environment, must spring forth to make sense of these new ecologies of practice. People were living with animals and plants, with the land itself in new ways, and they brought them into cultural understanding through clearing land and breaking soil, through ceremony and cult. Cohabitation with animal and plant species to create food, warmth, a roof above one's head, the ceremonies of feasting on these species associated with the dead, the mingling of both human and animal remains with the living groups of humans and animals in ways never experienced before makes it possible to call this a new kind of *intimacy*. Roast pork from a sow slaughtered at harvest, an old cup filled with beer brewed last week, talking with old friends and family, by the monument as old as the land itself and capturing in its design, in the performance of its very shape and setting, knowledge of eternal order . . . as thirteen decayed human femurs are passed around the fire (Edmonds 1999; Whittle 2003).

As a corollary, now consider the implications of this micro-focus on the social and thus also material context of the making and use of a monument such as Fussell's Lodge for understanding why people became farmers.

These changes in everyday life and the way people thought of the world predate the emergence of full agriculture in the sense of a highly managed system. And there were elements of this life before. People had long been profoundly knowledgeable about nature and followed annual circuits around sources of animal and plant food in the landscape. They did pay some attention to the dead, though not on the scale that comes in the fourth millennium B.C.E. There is evidence that they built some ceremonial timber monuments. These set the scene for the changes.

*Questions of invention and innovation.* Why the switch from the old ways? Why become a farmer and start building monuments? It was not sudden, but we have to look in more detail at previous ways of life, and the seeds of change they contain, for the reasons: we need what Friedman and Rowlands (1977) call an epigenetic model of change, one that, in other terms, connects tradition and innovation through a genealogical perspective. An inexorable logic of material advantage and the undoubted higher productivity of wheat cultivation and domesticated animals cannot be taken as the origin of agriculture in these new archaeological accounts. The archaeological evidence is beginning to lead us to a provocative alternative—that what mattered to those prehistoric farmers was propagating everyday experiences such as those we have just traced (consider recent analysis of early agriculture—Bellwood et al. 2007; Bolender 2010). It is in the richness of these experiences, these heterogeneous assemblages of people and things, that the seeds of change grew.

## AN ANCIENT GREEK PERFUME JAR

Art and material culture have long been seen as direct evidence of the cultural miracle of ancient Greece. Corinth, on its isthmus in Greece, in the eighth and seventh centuries B.C.E., was one notable place in this time of urbanization, as *poleis,* a term conventionally, though controversially, translated as city-states, crystallized across the Mediterranean, and within only a few decades. Normative accounts place the Corinthians at the heart of this process of innovation. This has been seen as finding expression in material culture: the potters of Corinth produced high-quality goods for an export market (even if we question the existence then of a fully functioning international market, the fine wares do certainly travel far and wide). Corinthians have also been seen to be at the forefront of the developments in political economy, with their early centralized tyranny. And a vanguard in the fine arts: since the late eighteenth century C.E., ancient Greek ceramics had been treated as fine art. The Corinthians led the way with a resurgence of figurative design, drawing on Near Eastern forms and schemata (see Shanks 1999 for extensive bibliographies).

The design of ceramics has frequently been an archaeological lens through which to view what has been taken as a pivotal historical juncture—the beginnings of classical Greek art. By 750 B.C.E. the walls of a typical wine cup made in Corinth were eggshell thin, pale buff, and covered with ruled black lines, reserved spaces for triangles, outlined lozenges, schematic water birds lined in soldier files. It was a tight and terse visual vocabulary. The firing process, to effect dark on light surface, required careful manipulation of kiln atmosphere. With regulated techniques, expert kiln management, and using multiple brushes and a turntable, the potters had the making of ceramics well worked out—risk and experiment minimized in producing the finest wares of their time (see Cook 1972).

And then, within a generation, Corinthian potters did something radically new. First, they made miniatures a specialty, particularly the famous perfume jars (*aryballoi*) that were sent all over the Mediterranean to be dedicated as gifts to gods in temple sanctuaries, and to be laid down with the dead in so many colonial and provincial cemeteries (fig. 8.2). Second, they began painting polychrome figures freehand and with details incised through the paint. At risk of messing up the design with the slip of the super-fine brush dipped in clay slip, the potters made daring displays of technical facility in tiny scenes of animals, monsters, men fighting, stylized flowers. In David Pye's terms (1969), they shifted from a workmanship of certainty to one of risk.

This is conventionally termed Protocorinthian pottery. The ubiquity of the Protocorinthian perfume jar, the aryballos, makes it a type fossil and chronological index for much of the Mediterranean in the mid first millennium B.C.E. (Shanks 1999). Find an aryballos and its distinctive style will give you the date of the find spot.

Virtually all the study of these artifacts has been within an art historical tradition, with Protocorinthian positioned in the developmental sequence of Greek art as an inception of figurative design. Most of this work has aimed to identify chronological sequence through the comparison of stylistic traits. Protocorinthian is thus phased as early, middle, and late, and has a special position in the traditional ancient Greek design sequence of geometric, orientalizing, archaic, and classical; geometric receives external inspiration on the way to classical florescence. The figurative scenes have attracted iconographic interpretation—attempts to identify characters and narratives, especially from Greek myth, through comparative examples. This has assumed a separation of iconography and decoration, certain scenes bearing meaning, others, especially floral and geometric patterns, treated as devoid of meaning—as "decorative." Following paradigms of nineteenth-century connoisseurship, attempts have also been made to relate the stylistic sequence to individual artists; the orthodox art historical narrative here is one of the genius of Greek artists reconfiguring the stylistic vocabularies of the Near East (Burkert 1992).

Unfortunately, many of the fine chronologies are based upon the interpretation of stylistic attributes alone and are thereby suspect due to a

FIGURE 8.2. An aryballos in the Boston Museum of Fine Arts (#95.12), recorded as from Corinth, with detail of its main frieze. Catherine Page Perkins Collection.

lack of independent stratigraphical substantiation (a problem of context; Shanks 1999, 41–42), and because the phasing depends upon a presupposition of stylistic development (early, mature, late) handed down from the kind of eighteenth-century art history popularized by Winckelmann and others. Understanding design in orthodox archaeological treatment of classical ceramics is also dependent upon iconology and a model of art workshops commonly associated with post-Renaissance art history, as well as John D. Beazley's classical archaeological connoisseurship in the tradition of Giovanni Morelli. The conventional categorization of Protocorinthian, the regular accounts of workshops and stylistic change, what we identify as a discursive infrastructure in archaeology's ecology of practices (chapter 3), should be recognized as useful but narrow. Another qualification of classical art history concerns the limitations of the distinction between meaningful iconography and meaningless decoration—is meaning only to be found in attribution of narrative and character, when we can identify a narrative subject? Is meaning all that mattered?

Archaeological approaches to understanding style and design, in the project of what has come to be called social archaeology, have long stressed the importance of context and quantification. There have been several such treatments of archaic Greek material culture (Morris 1987; Morgan and Whitelaw 2001; Shanks 1994, 1999; Whitley 1987). We shall follow the components of such analysis and interpretation. Contextual treatment addresses processes of origination, manufacture, distribution, consumption, discard, and reuse in these times of the development of the city-state. Another way of describing this is the tracking of the life cycles of these pots, from manufacture to discard, connecting particularly with political economy, the consolidation of a citizen body of yeoman farmers (Shanks 1992, 1995).

The questions of design include the following. Were the great changes in Greek society responsible for the changes in the production of Corinthian pottery? If so, how? What were the motivations of the potters? What incentives lay behind the changes? Were the means of distribution a relevant factor in the design of the ceramics? How attuned to patterns of consumption were the potters? And yes—was it down to the genius of the Greeks to invent both the city-state and the wonders of figurative Greek art? Are we encountering a manifestation of an archaic Greek *Kunstwollen* (a cultural impulse or will to artistic expression)? These are the questions associated with the topic of this chapter—the character of making and its relationship to the shape and forces of history.

One context for the design and production of these pots is a narrative of the development of a particular polity form, the Corinthian polis. A systemic model of design in such an early state form can connect the motivations of producers and consumers to class culture, with ceramics produced in a reshaping of class definitions, ideologies, and identities. The miniature jars can be related to their use in new kinds of sanctuaries and for the dead. They display scenes from the ideological world of the new state. These are the classic concerns of what has been termed a social archaeology (Shanks 1996, chaps. 5 and 6). There is also something to be said about craftsmanship, skill, manipulation, and the negotiations that transpire within processes of co-emergence forming pots and potters, decorated vessels and painters, scented oils and perfumers.

The typical categories in this argument, of rank, wealth and resources, trade, state formation, urbanization, market, and manufacture (see, e.g., Renfrew and Cherry 1986) are tightly associated with long-standing tendencies to emplot archaeological material in standardized *metanarratives* (here, of the expansion of certain kinds of polity associated with the city-state and as a component of an ancient Mediterranean ecology; Morris 1995; Dyson 1998; Hamilakis 2006; even Bernal 1991). These interpretive and analytical categories for understanding the context of production of items such as Corinthian aryballoi are broad and blunt (see Shanks and Tilley 1987 on narrative and explanation in social archaeology). This connects with another old tendency to subsume histories of material culture beneath those established by textual sources, features of the context of production being defined by textual sources. Archaeology has often been seen as "the handmaiden of history," and this period of history is dominated by narratives developed by the nineteenth-century historiography normally labeled *Altertumswissenschaft* or classical studies.

There is even a sense of *overdramatization* in these accounts of everyday items, however accomplished their craft may be: the overdetermining narrative of the birth of classical Greece, witnessed in the rise of the Greek polis, the invention of democracy, and that birth being ancestral to the civilized West. Such accounts press upon big explanations of what are seen as the critical transitions in the evolution of complex societies, such as the "invention of the notion of the autonomous human being" (Forrest 1966, 66) or the birth of democracy (cf. essays in Raaflaub, Ober, and Wallace 2007). Such accounts extend ideological questions and set out the character and configuration of events in advance in an a priori schema. They are often teleological, with an end that is implicit in the beginning and that, whether implicit or overt, signals a kind of transcendence. And many often seek to provide more parsimonious explanations for the development of the Greek polis centered upon specific prime movers—population growth, agricultural intensification, developments in urban form, and so on.

To avoid such overdetermination, another more humble path is simply to start in medias res with a vessel and follow the lines of investigation arising from its particular life cycle. And as much as treating the aryballos as a discrete artifact with separable attributes, we can focus on practice and process, opening, as it were, the black box that is an artifact to see what work is being performed, that is, what connections are established by its attributes and contexts of origination, manufacture, distribution, and consumption. We can let the pot lead us into its world, by following networks of empirical, statistical, metaphorical, narrative, conceptual, causal, and systemic association (for specifications, see Shanks 1999, chap. 2). This can be described as a methodological process of rearticulation.

It goes like this. A scene on a pot of monsters (combined animal, bird, and human parts), a lion, and soldier-citizen (hoplite) raises themes of the partible body (monstrously recombined), and, through an opposed figure of a second hoplite, a contrast with the armored body, one encased in metal. Animal metaphors of experience are also a topic—the hero seen as lion, for example. The probability that this was a jar of perfumed oil (somewhat substantiated by trace element analysis of other aryballoi), and the deposition of aryballoi in graves, leads to further questions of the material body in the early city-state, its grooming, trauma, and decay, in relation to the citizen male and the experience of fighting as an individual or a member of the citizen body in phalanx formation. Floral decoration, stylized designs from the east, introduce themes of cultural affiliation with other states and class groups.

So, in addition to a model of household production and changing definitions of class identity, empirical attention to the material can lead into a quite different, but clearly complementary, story of animals, corporeality, violence, potters' wheels, and brushes used in the miniature work, physical and imagined mobility, flowers, food and consumption, sanctuary dining rooms, sovereignty, gender, ships, clothing.

Let us give a flavor of this *assemblage* (for full documentation, please see again Shanks 1999).

*Dining and the sanctuary.* To be a sovereign member of the community of the city-state of Corinth, a citizen, was to take the boat across the gulf to the sanctuary of the goddess Hera at Perachora for the annual festival. There to eat in style—dining was a principal cult activity—and, perhaps, to leave a perfume jar painted with eastern designs and images of the soldier-citizen as gift for the divinity.

*The soldier-citizen and the hoplite body.* To be a member of the community was to bear arms for the body politic as a hoplite soldier-citizen—carrying eighty pounds, more or less, of bronze, iron, and leather. A cuirass was often molded as torso; it accompanied shield, stabbing spear, helmet. Beaten from a single sheet of bronze, the Corinthian helmet is a remarkable achievement of the metalworkers' craft. Many have attachments for crests of display. Encasing the head, the helmet gives protection at the expense of hearing and visibility. The face becomes a system of holes and slits. Cheek pieces frame the noseguard between the eyes, cut out from the sheet metal. Illustrations of this new form of fighting first appear on these pots. Hoplites, anonymous in helmets, apart from shield devices, sometimes lined up in phalanx formation, fight one another, as well as monsters and animals; there are also birds and flowers, robed figures. There are virtually no women painted on the pots.

Fellow citizen hoplites lined up in the standardized equipment all look alike on the summer field chosen for battle. They stare at one another over the rims of shields: the experience of fighting is focused upon this gaze—the only mark of the individual, apart from shield devices and things done that mark out the doer as special. To fight effectively on the open field many must move as one, in the phalanx where the sense of touch, the sense of balance—*equilibrioception*—and the sense of extension and occupying one's mixed, hoplite body—*proprioception*—are all amplified. There is pushing and jostling; the spears come over or below the shields. Typical wounds are to the neck, face, and groin. And afterward, bodies could lie for hours or even days in the sun before they were recovered. Disfigured by the wounds to the face and with bloated bodies cooked in the cuirass, there were always problems of identification.

*The importance of the eyes.* Faces are modeled on some aryballoi and are painted on shields. A late eighth-century B.C.E. grave in Argos excavated in 1971 contained a bronze helmet with two extra eyes embossed upon the forehead.

*Proxemics and the body.* A miniature jar is suitable for transport. Containing oil for dressing the body, it makes a suitable gift for divinity or for the dead. Displaying figures in tiny scenes, a fraction of an inch high, of grand events, the pot is designed to be held and scrutinized in the palm of your hand.

*Sites of innovation.* The new shield is called Argive, the new helmet Corinthian. It has long been clear that the cites of Argos and Corinth in the northeastern Peloponnese were at the center of innovation in warfare in these times. But it is more than just warfare.

In a scene upon a perfume jar found at Perachora, a sanctuary across the gulf from Corinth, soldiers fight to the accompaniment of a piper. The Spartan poet Alkman writes: "counterbalanced against the iron of the spear is sweet lyre-playing" (Davies 1991, 41). Archilochus, a traveling mercenary in the seventh century B.C.E., connects his life with the way one should eat and drink: "By spear is kneaded the bread I eat, by spear my Ismaric wine is won, which I drink, leaning upon my spear" (West 1992, 2). The word he uses for leaning (upon his spear) is the same as that used for reclining (on a couch to eat). He says: "I would as soon fight with you as drink when I'm thirsty" (125). War is his lifestyle. For a man to bear arms is to claim civic representation, to have the right of participation in cult, to eat and drink in the way one should.

Wine cups carried such pictures too. And at about this time, it became the style to recline on couches to eat, an eastern custom.

The deportment of the leisured citizen: to walk and stand in public. They showed it in the scenes upon the pots. In about 650 B.C.E., there is a broad change of fashion when the sword disappears as an item of civilian dress. A new type of cloak, the *himation,* appears, men carry spears, and swords are reserved for battle. The *himation* is not pinned and requires constant attention, hitching it up and holding it in place. It is an item that prevents much activity—except watching, listening, talking, and making decisions. The cloak enforces and proclaims leisure—you are not a slave or artisan, but a landowning soldier-citizen.

*Perfumed, embalmed bodies.* A few aryballoi, with heads modeled upon the top, distinctively reference through their design canopic jars made in Middle and New Kingdom Egypt and after, which were meant to contain the intestines and inner organs of the deceased. Liquidity, perfumed oil, and fluid intestines are constitutive of the design, as much as bodily ergonomics. The modeled hairstyles too are eastern, seen also on some of the paintings—a coiffure that German scholars have called *Etagenperücke,* or layered wigs. We know from contemporary poetry that there was something of a style war between those who flaunted their wealth with eastern flair and perfumed hair, and those who saw such *habrosunē* (an aesthete's fondness for fine goods) as decadent and superficial (Kurke 1992, 1993).

*The topology of design.* The making and illustration harks backward and forward, folded into the life of forms and processes. Notoriously, it literally prefigures the achievements of classical Greek figurative art. But the iconography has an ancient genealogy. Iconographic elements (lions, geometrics, lotus, palmette) can be traced back for centuries and even millennia through the Near East (Payne 1931, 1933; Amyx 1988). The slip and oxide paint combined with skilled manipulation of kiln atmosphere (alternating reducing, and oxidizing) was also an ancient process. This is how we use the term "topology" with respect to artifacts (see below; and see Mol and Law 1994). It emphasizes the percolation of forms and techniques, rather than their linear development.

These are just indications of the kinds of association and translation running through the artifact and configured in this rhizomatic method (Shanks 1992). Connect them with the city of Corinth at its beginnings in the eighth and seventh centuries B.C.E. and we have the components of a materialist narrative:

- New spaces of assembly and monuments are built: large stone architecture, public and figurative imagery, public areas, processional ways, spaces for gatherings and displays, places to watch and listen.

- Formally designated and sacred places—springs, temple sanctuaries—appear, which coexist with spaces of public assembly.

- Language is pooled through media and this helps to stabilize politics: inscriptions and writing walls provide the evanescent word with a spatial presence.

- Reworkings of personal and public space create new ways to dress, walk, and talk: citizens are strengthened through eating, the use of perfumed oil and unguents, scrutinizing tiny pictures upon a perfume jar held close, hitching up a cloak, bearing arms, wearing armor in the summer sun.

- New axes are made through the community's territory: city walls, roads for goods and boats (the *diolkos* for transporting ships over the isthmus of Corinth), views across the gulf, from the heights.

- Goods and people are on the move: pots containing oil and other things are exported far from the city, to new settlements in northern Greece and Sicily, conventionally called colonies.

- New lifestyles: clothes, ornamentation (or not), hair style, the cultivation of skills of hunting, riding, athletics, music, poetry at a drinking party, speaking, drinking, eating, violence, sexuality, how to behave. And not everyone agreed on what was proper.

- Myths and legends of personal and collective sovereignty, real and ideal, are retold, written, and pictured. This involves an explicit reworking of relationships with the past.

Many centuries of achievement, manifest as architectures, spaces of assembly, monuments, laws, writing, trade, pots, oils, agricultural fields, olive groves, roads, walls, merchant ships, and so on co-emerge with and contribute to the group formations of bodies politic taking place in early Corinth (Rothaus 2000; Salmon 1984; Williams 1982; Wiseman 1978).

Tracking and rearticulating this distributed networking, following the connections suggests that it is not enough to conceive of the design of an aryballos as *representing* something else, such as a change in economy, in ways of fighting, or of legends and myths. Nor can the design be simply understood as a relay carrying a message from potter to buyer, or between consumers. Such views treat the aryballos as a secondary representation or expression of something more primary, or real, or material, a point we elaborated in chapters 2 and 5 in relation to the notion of "an expressive fallacy." Instead, we can treat the design of an aryballos as located within the work of potter, acts of exchange and consumption, rituals of death and dedication. The design is a material part of what it may be showing us: it forms an *assemblage*. Our understanding of this notion intersects with Manuel DeLanda's realist theory of assemblage (2006) to which we shall return in the next section. Archaic Corinthian society, its ideologies, and the aspirations of its potters or citizens are not experienced directly and in themselves, for what would that reality be? They appear sphinx-like in the riddles of the object seen as a bundle of such processes. These are its design.

This assemblage is precisely homologous with the work of archaeology as described in previous chapters.

## THE ASSEMBLAGE AND LIMITS OF DESIGN

There is no end to the process of research we have just sketched, no determinate destination, only detours in an ongoing process of making. We can say that in tracking these associations, the aryballos appears in multiple guises, or, more strongly, is a motley, heterogeneous thing. We call it heterogeneous because tracking the acts of making and use, the manufacture and consumption, of an aryballos combines achievements, goods, experiences, materials and psycho-political commitments, which are often treated as quite different and even incomparable (Law 1994). This makes the aryballos a multiplicity.

This notion of thing as distributed through these connections, these *internal* relations that make it what it is, may well justify designating the thing as *res* (Heidegger 1971; Shanks and Tilley 1987; and Shanks 1992 on internal relations). Property, entities, things, the physical world, deeds, exploits, a matter of speech, a concern, a matter at hand, an event; the Latin term *res* contains a range of associations.

We connect this mode of existence, this ontology, with Manuel De-Landa's reworking of the Deleuzian notion of assemblage (2006). The aryballos is both more and less than the sum of its parts. More, because it moves on to new adventures far beyond the roles originally delegated to it; and it cannot be reduced to any of its parts or to the society that produced it. Less, because the aryballos can never encapsulate any, much less all, of what it draws together. The aryballos is irreducible to any economic, juridical, moral, aesthetic, religious, or mythological associations. All kinds of institutions—religious, legal, moral, and economic—find simultaneous expression in it as an assemblage. Their meaning can therefore only be grasped if they are viewed as a complex concrete reality. As a polyvalent assemblage, the aryballos *draws together* all the components of the archaic Corinthian state, along with all its ramified associations.[5] This is the significance of the concept of assemblage.

Cognate design issues emerge from such archaeological experience. In earlier chapters, we have pointed to the wonderful richness of archaeological research. It may be difficult for someone not familiar with it to appreciate the vast quantities of detritus encountered in fieldwork—the myriads of potsherds, flint flakes, broken oyster shells, the matrix of building rubble, sand, and silt. Most has simply to be discarded; against

---

5. Assemblages are multilayered; every constituent is itself an assemblage, and this regresses infinitely. Assemblages are made of assemblages and everything is equally real, but this doesn't mean that they are equal.

a background of incidental and ephemeral details that are the remains of past experiences of making and consuming, the archaeologist seeks the significant, seeks to distinguish signal from background noise, figure from ground. But the two are inseparable; noise constitutes signal, and they may even change places as what was overlooked steps into significance under a new viewpoint or purpose (Witmore 2009). Some significant association of temple building with an imported artifact that may lead to a new understanding of a site only makes sense against a background of sameness, regular patterning against which an anomalous significant item may stand out. We would have no understanding of the site without the ambient noise, the mundanity of texture, the iterations of the everyday that, of necessity, usually go unspoken, remain unremarkable (see chapter 6).

To put it another way: so much is ultimately not open to explanation and interpretation. Interpretation always risks overly reducing the richness of historical and archaeological detail to plot, account, cause, effect. The aryballos becomes simply "a perfume jar." This reduction is part of what we describe as a fallacy of representation or expression. In the face of the heaps of ruin, a response of archaeology has always been to stop short of interpretation and explanation and instead to present and make manifest, through display, illustration, listing, annotation. Archaeologists have frequently pioneered new media in the illustrated book, architectural drawing, photography, museum display, or 3D reconstruction, as well as in transformations of artifacts and sites into various textual forms (see discussion above in chapter 5). Therefore, in dealing with the multiplicities encountered in exploring the design of an assemblage, to analysis, explanation, and interpretation, we suggest we add *manifestation* as a key component of methodology, involving ways of revealing the heterogeneity, different forms of translation and mediation, text, and graphics, an empirics that lets the artifact manifest itself.

It is important to note that we are not talking about distinguishing the essential from the inessential, random, or inconsequential. This notion of design makes of any artifact a multiplicity, because the thing, the aryballos, is dispersed through processes of manufacture and use that may be summarized in the notion of its life cycle. Figure and ground (or signal and noise) are intimately woven; each strand the fabric of the other.

There is no determinate end to the exploration of the aryballos, but there is a message. It is this. The Greek city-state was more about the way the bodily experiences and pleasures of different male subcultures were remodeled in new architectures and urban spaces than it was an evolutionary trend, or a function of economic growth, or Greek cultural genius inventing European civilization, though all these have been made to make sense with hindsight. The innovation of the Greek body politic, including democratic forms, was about the way different groups of men defined themselves through the way they ate, walked down the street, fought together on a field outside the city on a summer afternoon, talked in political assembly, held a perfume jar and scrutinized its painted scenes, deposited that same aryballos with a dead companion or in a sacred enclosure. The city-state of Corinth did not exist somehow outside of these practices, expressing itself in them; these spaces, things, practices and experiences were the city-state. It is not that the Greek city-state engendered new kinds of ceramic and figurative design; the pursuit of particular designs engendered the state. Those micro-articulations hinged on the agency of the potters, traders, users—that is, how their actions created the world they lived. These perfume jars were not only produced by the early Corinthian city-state; making the pots made the city-state.

## CONTEMPORARY ARCHAEOLOGICAL INTERESTS IN MAKING AND DESIGN

Let us now ground some of the themes of these case studies in archaeology since the 1960s. Culture history, a dominant archaeological paradigm since the early twentieth century, continues to hold sway in those archaeologies primarily interested in regional sequences of change in material culture, associating style of goods and architectures with cultural identity, tracking innovations and their diffusion, plotting the movements of cultures, peaceful and aggressive, through their supposed stylistic traits.

Another traditional interest remains—in the history of technology. Materials science has an important role in contemporary archaeology, helping us understand raw material extraction, processing, and manufacture, though, arguably, its relationship with interest in the sociology and culture of technology is weak. Noteworthy in this context is the well-established field of experimental archaeology, where archaeologists seek to replicate processes of manufacture, use, and discard, whether it be the making of a flint blade or the way a pot fractures (cf. Schiffer 1987; though see González-Ruibal, Hernando, and Politis 2011). We note how the focus on tacit knowledge or know-how in this epistemic field is a crucial component of the emphasis we are placing upon the indeterminacy of the processes of making and design at the heart of human being.

Cultural evolution is probably the most prevalent set of approaches in contemporary archaeology. Distinct variants include those influenced ultimately by Marxian social evolution, and those derived from evolutionary anthropologies like those of Lewis Henry Morgan (1818–81) and Sir Edward Burnett Tylor (1832–1917, revitalized in the anthropological turn of the 1960s and 1970s, often labeled processual archaeology (Binford 1962; Braidwood 1959; Harris 1979; Steward 1960; White 1959). Schemes of sociocultural types, such as band societies, chiefdoms, and states, or modes of production, provide a broad analytical and historical context within which archaeologists interpret material sources. Attention is primarily given to human-environment relationships, mediated, of course, by social and cultural forms, including material culture—artifacts. Typically, the analytic apparatus of cultural evolution involves concepts such as selection and adaptation to explain the way forms of (material) culture act to extend the adaptive possibilities of human populations. Modeling sociocultural processes involves key variables of resource extraction, control, and distribution, the exchange of goods, and social ranking (horizontal and social divisions in society). Understanding the design of goods involves, in the last resort, associating artifact traits with the exigencies of a society's adaptive requirements in a particular environment, more generally with processes of selection operating upon materials. Methodologically, this means that the archaeologist looks for patterning comprised of vestiges and remains in the archaeological record and treats this patterning, for example in the range of elite goods manufactured, or in the types of housing and storage, as an expression of social process, such as a redistributive economy in a chiefdom.

However powerful a paradigm this archaeology remains, it has undergone considerable criticism from traditional and new perspectives, and from within, since the 1980s. This criticism can be summarized as broad dissatisfaction with the narrow focus on social and cultural evolution and adaptation to the environment, and upon a certain kind of political economy as the driving causality behind human history. That a limited range of simple and adaptive sociocultural forms might hold the key to understanding the wealth of human making can seem overly reductive.

As alternatives, postprocessual, cognitive, and interpretive archaeologies draw on a wide range of disciplines in the humanities and social sciences in offering more nuanced interpretations of systems of meaning lying behind the style and function of goods. There are strong alliances with semiotics, and with structuralist anthropology and after, with artifacts treated as a textual system, grammar-based and embroiled in networks of strategized manipulation, material cultures constituted by communicative practices and performances (Hodder 1982; Shanks and Tilley 1987). Key factors, apart from communication, are agency—the role of actors in reproducing social structure, identity, gender, and locality—the site specifics of cultural experience.

Though not so often explicitly acknowledged in archaeology, there are strong alliances here with art historical fields of iconographic interpretation—relating imagery to systems of meanings. There is another more anthropological component too—focus upon the materiality of human engagement with the world. This has involved an archaeological variant of phenomenological interpretation, particularly of prehistoric landscapes. In this, mention has already been made above of how the human body is taken as something of a historical constant, a homolog, that offers a direct route into understanding how ancient populations encountered their built environment: walk where they did and the archaeologist may, with appropriate methodological sensitivity, gain some idea of their experience of place (e.g., Tilley 1994).

Acknowledgement that archaeology is much more than the study of the past has been growing over the past thirty years. The anthropological turn in the 1970s involved the displacement, for some, of historiography as a defining feature of archaeology in favor of generalization about features of human society. Under the banner of modern material culture and later "the archaeology of us," the subtitle of a book edited by Richard Gould and Michael Schiffer (1981), William Rathje pioneered garbology, the application of archaeological method to a neglected aspect of contemporary material culture—discard and garbage (Rathje 1989; Rathje and Murphy 1992). Material culture studies developed in two variants, one in the United States and the other in the United Kingdom, drawing on both anthropology and British cultural studies, taking as its subject the artifacts of everyday life.

We take encouragement from these initiatives to showcase the "material" of culture (see chapter 2). Nonetheless, their general outcomes are unsatisfactory in several respects. One reason is the widely shared assumption that the main significance of things always lies in their symbolic and representative functions, while their habitual everyday uses are trivial and of interest only to old-fashioned "folk" studies. But habitual use is anything but "trivial." With habitual use comes tacit knowledge, care, and respect for what objects are in their own being. The significance of an aryballos is not primarily a function of the symbolic role it potentially may serve by acting as an embodied sign of power or by communicating individual or group identity. What seems forgotten in the vast majority of material culture studies is that an aryballos is also significant for what it *is*—that is, a container for perfume. It is significant because of the knowledge and skill it assembles, the capacities it possesses in terms of the closed containment of liquid, controlled pouring, or its fit within a hand. In a similar way, an ax is significant due to its ax qualities, and a reindeer due to its reindeer qualities. Whatever symbolic roles they may play are basically residues of the primary significance of their own being (Olsen 2010).

There is another, closely related, asymmetry written into these numerous texts: the focus is almost entirely on how things are creatively used by people for their various purposes. Thus, in most debates about things' "meaning," the material qualities of the objects in question actually seem rather irrelevant to this meaning or to their own "cultural construction." As with the "readerly" text (after Barthes 1977), the transformation is always supposed to involve a hierarchical and unidirectional move from signified to signifier, from content to form, and from idea to expression. Beyond being a concrete and visible medium for inscription and embodiment, things' integrity has been sacrificed or subsumed to the dominant social and humanist trope in which their role is always to represent something else, something extramaterial.

Throughout this chapter we make no distinction between material properties and what Michael Schiffer calls artifact performance characteristics. These characteristics are "defined relationally, for they refer to the capabilities of one interactor in its engagement with another in a specific real-world, not laboratory, interaction," and they should not be confused with properties "intrinsic to an interactor, such as shape, size, surface texture, chemical composition, molecular structure, cellular structure and organization, color weight, and density" (Schiffer and Miller 1999, 19). This distinction reiterates the separation of primary and secondary qualities, what Whitehead referred to as the bifurcation of nature, where the definitive attributes of a pot, a canvas, or an arm are placed on one side and what is supposedly added to this reality through an interaction is placed on the other. Relations, as alleged secondary qualities, are merely derivative of the deeper substance of entities (see Webmoor 2012a, 2012b; Witmore 2012a, 2012b). And yet those properties that can be measured have as much to do with relations, whether they are with a microscope, a theodolite, or perspective space, as they do with the definitive attributes of an artifact. Neither the brown of the soil nor the chemical composition of its organic materials is a matter of choice (Whitehead 2006 [1920], 44; in archaeology, see, e.g., Tilley 2004, 10–12; Webmoor 2005; Witmore 2006). William James stated the point as follows: "the parts of experience hold together from next to next by relations that are themselves parts of experience" (James 1978 [1907], 173).

We need to pay far more attention to the questions of why and how things are significant. What difference do *they* make in making the world meaningful?

## ARCHAEOLOGICAL DEBATES ABOUT DESIGN

What was driving people to make things the way they did? There are a number of ongoing debates in archaeology pertinent to this question.

*Material culture and association.* One debate concerns the relation of groups of associated artifacts or design traits with categories and experiences relating to identity. How do packages of goods relate to gender, class, rank, and ethnicity? How should the classification of artifacts proceed with respect to such important variables?

*Style and function.* Is the function of an artifact distinguishable from the style of its making, form, and appearance? Is a materialist perspective that emphasizes the primacy of function in understanding design (perhaps as an adaptive response to environment) appropriate? Again—how is style to be distinguished from function in the description and classification of artifacts, if at all?

*Symbol and meaning.* Can material culture be treated as text? To what extent do grammars of design lie behind making and consumption? To what extent are artifacts determined by systems of meaning?

*Agency and structure.* How do the actions of the maker and the consumer, and the affordances and flux of materials, relate to social structures and cultural constraints? To what extent are the artist's or maker's intentionality and design determined by the context of tradition, social structure and prevailing cultural values?

*Embodiment and materiality.* What are the significances of materiality, both of artifacts and the human body itself? Factors here include duration and temporality, and the way materialities can confront us as independent others. To what extent is it possible to distinguish an immaterial component of kinetic experience? Certainly, much design is focused upon intangibles. Or is there a tautology implicit in the notion of material culture? Because all culture necessarily takes a material form.

All these debates reference classic long-standing tensions in the arts, humanities, and social sciences. Many revolve around the nature of the subject and creative agency (cf. Sennett 2009). What is happening when someone makes something? What is the constraining or enabling role of tradition, accumulated knowledge, norms and expectations, the intentionality of the maker, and his or her relationship with the materials, strategizing, and future orientation upon the realization of goals?

Some things are clear in these debates. Reductive and simple causality rarely, if ever, explains artifact design and change in a rich way. The prime mover arguments of such reductive explanation have included the following: invention followed by the diffusion of a good idea; environmental change or economic need prompting a specific response; artistic genius or an individual's intentionality generating artworks and artifacts; religious ideas bringing about certain material manifestations. Two centuries and more of the accumulation of archaeological evidence indicates that it has never been this simple and that things could always have been done differently. So too, many of the assumed dimensions of human experience are difficult to uphold as constant, a priori or defining and essential characteristics of what it is to be human and engage with the world. This is not to argue that the natural and the artificial, person and thing, immaterial and material are indistinguishable, but rather that they exist as local, temporarily stabilized mixtures that can shift and take very different particular forms.

NINE ARCHAEOLOGICAL THESES ON DESIGN

We conclude this chapter with nine theses that summarize some key trends in archaeological research into design. This is not a statement of any current orthodoxy in the discipline; it is our personal assessment of a state of thinking about human being, making, and design, the shape of history, hosts of material things, and how we might approach an understanding of these things.

## 1. The Fallacy of Expression

Does an artifact *express* its maker's intentions or the context of its origin? We argue it does not, or often does so only minimally. Things are not well explained by referring them to some outside agency or force, such as an artist's will or economic necessity. While there may indeed be strong connections between maker and artifact, artifact and contexts of manufacture and use, these are not well understood as relationships of expression, because this subordinates materiality to the will of a maker or the strength of social structure, leaving unanswered questions of the nature of raw materiality, of mediation, of the force behind the expression, of what drives the imposition of form upon raw matter, of how things get made (Ingold 2010). And whatever the force seeking expression, it could always be made manifest differently. In our example of the aryballos, it is very reductive to argue that such pots were expressing social structure, or that they were representing Greek myth or an appropriation of eastern design, even though there are connections with the organization of society, with narrative, and eastern iconography. Quite simply in such accounts, so many of the specifics of making remain obscure.

The anthropologist Maurice Bloch (1995) gives an illustration of this point from his fieldwork in Madagascar. Topic: the meaning of architectural decoration. Asked what the significance of a carving he was cutting into the structural beam of a house was, the carpenter replied that it had no meaning; it was simply that this was what it was proper to carve. A weak thesis here is that the carver was simply not aware of the signification of his work, or couldn't put it into words (though he didn't see the point of trying). In contrast, the interpretive work of the anthropologist is sometimes seen as one of establishing what aspects of person and society are expressed in material culture (as discussed above). A strong thesis is that it may not be appropriate to look for this kind of expression, but that the significance of artifacts is better sought in the *processes* of their making (thesis 5 below).

We dealt with the secondary status of things in chapter 2—the way that particularly academic study has consistently privileged the human and cultural over the material thing-world, supposedly contradictory. We are arguing for a symmetrical treatment of maker and material in the processes of making.

## 2. *The Fallacy of Context*

To understand an artifact's design, it is crucial to look beyond the thing itself. But how is this context to be characterized? If we predefine "context" as involving components such as economic relations, raw material extraction, cultural values, and political ideologies, we invoke two problems. First, we assume the essential character of context, that it involves components such as these listed, and again we risk overlooking heterogeneity. We risk prejudging and neglecting crucial specifics and details that don't fit our definitions and categorization of context. Second, this establishes, again a priori, separation of the artifact from its context or location and situation, something that interpretation and explanation then have to overcome.

Better, we suggest and have illustrated above, is to begin in medias res, with a specific artifact and specific practices and processes (thesis 5) and trace the connections, rather than separating a perfume jar, say, from what is conventionally conceived of as its context—manufacture from raw clay, luted shaped form, working surface, kiln, risk, figurative design, perfume, merchants, tombs. The context of the prehistoric barrow in our example is better identified by studying how it was built and used, and how it related to other aspects of contemporary experience. We call this a heretical empirics, because it does not assume certain categories that organize society and experience, but looks to define such categories in the process of empirical investigation and so to generate potentially unorthodox and heterodox characterizations of an artifact (theses 6 and 7).

## 3. *The Fallacy of Invention*

Many approaches to understanding the design of an artifact give primacy to origin and invention and seek to understand how and why certain inventions occurred (see, e.g., Hughes 1983). But it is increasingly clear that invention is by no means an uncommon phenomenon. All the basic components of the farming of managed domesticated species, for example, existed for millennia before the widespread adoption of agriculture in several independent parts of the world. The ontogenesis of a Leica M9 camera only minimally involves the inventive genius of the engineers who designed it. The long-term background of the history of design is one of constant human creativity, innovation, and achievement. With Kristian Kristiansen (2006), we suggest that invention should be distinguished from innovation, and that the key question is not what led to an invention, a question of origin, but rather what prompted the adoption of certain assemblages of artifacts and practices. This is a question of genealogy (thesis 8) and accords with the topological understanding of human temporality outlined in chapter 7. That tradition and cultural stability are an active state of hindering the adoption of new designs and solutions is a corollary that applies in much of human history.

So, the manufacture and use of archaic Corinthian aryballoi were rooted in age-old techniques and traditions in ceramic and figurative design. The world of the early city-state was one of profound innovation, but not based upon new invention or discovery. What was new about the earthen long barrow at Fussell's Lodge was the particular articulation of the deposited remains of human and nonhuman species, of architectural forms built of earth and timber, in experiences that involved the domestication of certain animals and plants, in what became highly designed landscapes or built environments, and in the performances of passing through such spaces.

The fallacies stated above as theses 1 to 3 can all be sidestepped by recognizing humbler entities as interlocutors.

### 4. We Have Always Been Cyborgs

This proposition is rooted in the argument and evidence for the coevolution of culture and biology, that for as long as we have been our human species, and probably before that, (material) culture and biology have been part of the same evolutionary process. Given also the way a practice such as making is distributed through social and material structures, past and future, people have always been embroiled in mixtures of material and immaterial forms and systems. With respect therefore to both people and things, we should adopt a relational, distributed ontology. Connections, internal relations, make an artifact or person what they are; we find ourselves in others. People have always been prosthetic beings, sharing their agency with others, with things and processes beyond them. People are more than just living beings. We have always been cyborgs—human-machine hybrids.

### 5. Creativity Is More Than Human Inspiration

Understanding the design of an artifact is best done by looking at it as a network of connections among processes, uses, techniques, and performances, rather than treating it primarily as a discrete bundle of attributes or qualities. We would do well to look at what work is being done by such networks, which for present purposes include Fussell's Lodge, Neolithic herders, human femurs, the taste of beer, sows, stone axes, aryballoi, perfumes, phalanxes, Corinthian helmets, the need to reciprocate, and the psycho-political commitment of ancient Greek citizens. It is useful to think of these assemblages as machines, with a machine defined as an interconnected set of resistant parts and functions, of whatever nature, that performs work.

Designing and making are thus much more than simply producing a discrete form. They are enabled by a preexisting ecology of entities and relations, under which fall structures, values, forms, expectations, knowledge, and resources available to the maker. Simultaneously, design and making reconfigure these entities and relations into machinic (re)articulations, reweaving the threads of the social fabric. Making can belong to the most humble of things; no entity has a monopoly on design.

## 6. The Artifact as Scenario

An artifact is much more than a list of defining attributes. Think less of discrete things and more of the thing as *res,* as a gathering, forging heterogeneous connections in its making and use (Law 1994). We call these heterogeneous because all kinds of different things and experiences might be connected: consider again the examples of Fussell's Lodge and the aryballos and how they brought together extraordinary associations of know-how and ideologies, past and present. Again, we can treat these gatherings as scenarios: models or outlines of contexts and sequences of possible events. Every act of design and making relates to constraints and possibilities, sketching utopias, and containing the possibility of unimagined and unwanted consequences.

Is Fussell's Lodge an earthen long barrow? Yes, but it is also much more. It acted as a node of articulation, gathering all kinds of practices and experiences, real and imagined, past and future. The "monument's" attributes are only the beginning of its story.

## 7. The Heterogeneity of Value

Any artifact is an irreducible multiplicity. Our designation *res* is intended to signal this multiplicity that is also a temporal folding, a collocation or topology (thesis 8). What an artifact *is* depends upon how the connections that run through its origination, manufacture, distribution, use, and discard are traced.

Value is a key component of any understanding of design. It is implicit in all choices made in this life cycle: one material or manufacturing process over another, the value of one aryballos assessed against another by visitors to a sanctuary. With a perspective of design and artifacts as dispersed and heterogeneous, systems of value or worth are similarly heterogeneous. The value of one aryballos over another intended as a gift to divinity depended upon a local assessment of the *fit* of one aryballos over another.

This is something different from saying that such systems of value are culturally relative and so incomparable. It means we should look to specific contexts of use, technique, performance, and engagement to understand how makers and users assess worth, and how we, as design researchers, should assess the worth of a particular design solution. These may well be comparable across different times and cultures.

## 8. Temporal Topology

Seeking origins and invention in an attempt to understand the design of an artifact implies a linear chronology of discovery and adoption. Viewing design as process and assemblage implies a complementary folded temporality, a topology that can juxtapose old and new with the prospect of yet unrealized futures. An aryballos contained age-old technologies, techniques, forms, and iconographies reworked into a radically new assemblage suited to the emerging states of the Mediterranean. A Leica digital camera, the M9, for example, is an item of apparent extreme modernity; it enfolds relationships of observer and observed that have an ancient, deep genealogy and that involve several well-worn design paths and dependencies. The temporality of an aryballos or camera is thus multiple, including, yes, its date of manufacture and consumption, but also the genealogy of its constituent components (see chapter 7). These topological foldings of time can be highly significant in some experiences: for example, in urban planning, where a walk down a street can be a percolating ferment of past traces and remains tied to material embodiments of utopian futures. Landscapes, as built environments, can be similarly rich examples, juxtaposing ancient features, routes and ways, place-names of forgotten origin, recent plantings that may last only a season, building projects intended to last a millennium. This point is now being well explored in some cultural geographies and landscape archaeologies. Consider, for example, Rebecca Solnit's extraordinary deep map of San Franscisco, *Infinite City* (2010; also see Latour and Hermant 1998; in archaeology, see Alcock 2002; Fleming 2007, 2010; Olivier 2008).

Understanding the temporality of an artifact can be likened to tracing a genealogy, in that the present, the state of an artifact, is unthinkable without an ancestral past of multiple lineages. But these relationships imply no teleology of necessity, no necessary or unavoidable line of descent from past to present, no necessary coherent narrative, because each generation reworks its past and can, in its historical agency, change direction.

## 9. The Unspoken Life of Things and the Noise of Life

Looking at processes as well as discrete objects leads us to manifold connections and trajectories. In the heterogeneous networking that is the engineering of a thing, there is no end to ramification. An artifact disperses through its scenarios, networks, and genealogies of origination, manufacture, distribution, use, and discard. Sustaining any particular arrangement of an artifact, which takes on new configurations and is never reducible to the action of its maker, requires great effort and coordination.

Interpretation, as rearticulation, can track certain affiliations or lines of connection, as we have sketched in the case of the aryballos. There is always more that remains unsaid, unacknowledged, unseen, because interpretation may not go down a particular track. This is all too evident in archaeological fieldwork, or indeed in any scientific research, where there is always a choice to be made of what matters to the research interest. What is left behind, ignored, or discarded is the background noise of history and experience. This is far from inconsequential. First, because something important may have been overlooked—science constantly takes a second look at things and finds something that was missed. Second, because things stand out as significant against this background; without it there could be no story, no message, no understanding. Third, because this is the noise of the ambient everyday work that makes society what it is; it is the noise of the life of things constantly reweaving our social fabric.

## BEING HUMAN AND HUMAN BEING

In accounting for the integral relations of the myriad entities behind what was once glossed as social structure and seeking a view that resists teleology (grand, often overdramatized narratives taken to constitute history), we see the subject of history, not as an entity with a narrative or a set of systemic components that we define a priori, but as an indeterminate field of relations constantly reproduced through collective practices, that is, an ontogenetic and genealogical field. While we accept that our representations of the past need to be selective, focusing and reducing to intelligible order and sense, employing social and cultural modeling, we nevertheless need to witness the heterogeneity of the past, the ultimate irreducibility of things, the noise and contingency, the grounds for those creative acts of articulation that are the core of cultural work.

We have proposed using the term *res*—the thing as a gathering, assemblage, folding—for the (archaeological) subject of history. This immediately evokes the *res publica*—the body politic as an assemblage of people and objects. In approaching this *res,* it is appropriate to begin in medias res, and to be flexible and pragmatic, sensitive to contingencies and heterogeneity. Previous chapters have identified the outlines of such pragmatic understanding of archaeology; in this chapter, we have attempted to sketch what it looks like in specific archaeological case studies. In exploring where things come from, why they were designed the way they are, what Michel Serres terms *pragmatogony,* we alternately follow lines of extension out and then focus back on the thing, extending and compressing the folds that are an artifact's topology like a concertina.

In such a perspective, human being is not just being "human"; human being is being-for and being-by others, where others refers to heterogeneous alterity—other things, other species, as well as other people. This is the heteronomy of "humanity." Being is a collective state of affairs. The qualities of these articulations demand an ethics as we attend to *how* we get on with others, *the ways and means.* It is to such ethics and politics that we turn in our final chapter.

# CHAPTER 9

# Getting on with Things

## A Material Metaphysics of Care

Throughout this book we have made the case that we are more than ever merged with our material pasts, and that the things of those pasts push back. As we have often repeated, the reason why—and how—they push back cannot be reduced to this imbrication itself. Things are not merely "enslaved in some wider system of differential meaning" (Harman 2002, 280). They possess their own capacities, inhabit their own compartments; in short, they have at least partial autonomy.

As a discipline concerned with things, archaeology helps one realize that objects cannot simply be sorted into the easy categories of "flatland philosophies" (Harman 2005, 231). Neither exhausted by their relations with other objects and people nor islands of unalloyed integrity, things blend both their inherent qualities and their alliances. This is why we have made the analogy to isotopic elements: real and enduring, while nonetheless shifting states of compositional stability. This holds whether we speak of Acrocorinth, Fussell's Lodge, or a map of Teotihuacan. Archaeology's intimacy with things and the processes that involve them in human affairs over the long term sheds light on the irreducibility of things in their bewildering differences and ambiguities.

The irreducible paradox of things as fields in which we are immersed, while they simultaneously retain individuality and integrity, is not solely an issue of ontological or metaphysical concern. It also has wide-ranging ethical implications, which extend far beyond any disciplinary boundaries, archaeological or otherwise. However, the suggestion that humans have neither generalized autonomy nor particular hegemony, that we reside among other entities in a differentiated, but not oppositional, world is countered with the expected, predictable, charge of reification. That is to say, putting humans on the same ontological footing as nonhumans inevitably evokes the modernist and humanist horror scenario of making people into things. Let's not rush to cast out our Frankenstein's Monsters, however. The radical ethical implication of our approach is to refit humanism's tradition of attentiveness and care for people to embrace things and nonhumans as well, and in no small measure (so subtly worked out in Mary Shelley's original). Also taking into consideration the current debates on environmental issues and the accelerated exhaustion of Earth's bounty, such an inclusive ethics does not seem untimely, if even belated.

In this chapter we conclude the book with an appeal for "collective care," specifically, symmetrical care for people and things (and all nonhumans), and the rapports between things, a care that is more responsive to the "wicked problems" characterizing the complexly interdependent circumstances of our contemporaneity. Furthermore, we urge archaeologists to practice their discipline with trust and confidence. What is needed today is an archaeology that looks back at its own past with neither embarrassment nor contempt, but with wonderment combined with the will to revitalize its important legacy.

## ARCHAEOLOGICAL ETHICS

Ethics have become a serious concern in archaeology. Indeed, surveying the literature one can find a number of ethical theories and positions (among many others, for example, see Green 1984; Hamilakis and Duke 2007; Karlsson 2004; Lynott and Wylie 1995; Scarre and Scarre 2006; Zimmerman, Vitelli, and Hollowell-Zimmer 2003). By the 1970s and into the 1980s, questions of how to act and issues of accountability increasingly became an outspoken agenda for archaeologists. During this period, normative issues as to how archaeologists conducted their work were debated and eventually codified into professional codes and ethical protocols. The adoption of its code of ethics by the Society for American Archaeology (SAA),[1] the largest professional archaeological

---

1. See www.saa.org/AbouttheSociety/PrinciplesofArchaeologicalEthics/tabid/203 /Default.aspx (accessed April 13, 2012).

society in the world, was an indicator of the widespread urgency about taking normative issues seriously. What caused this turn?

Alison Wylie, a primary participant in the formulation of the SAA's Principles of Archaeological Ethics, suggests that the accelerating destruction of archaeological resources in the wake of increased land development and trade in illegal antiquities, coupled with the professionalization of cultural resource management (CRM) made the formalization of archaeology's conservation ethic a necessary countermeasure (Lynott and Wylie 1995; Wylie 1996; 2006, 15). This move prompted a number of professional bodies to follow suit and establish codes for their members. For instance, the Register of Professional Archaeologists (RPA; formerly the Society of Professional Archaeologists [SOPA]) and the Archaeological Institute of America (AIA) developed principles of good practice. Both not only established codes of ethics, but also, uniquely, provided for tribunals for punitive enforcement of its agreed-to statutes (RPA 2002 [1998]; AIA 2004; cf. Smith and Burke 2003, 192). And in 1997, the European Association of Archaeologists (EAA) adopted codes similar to that of the SAA (Hamilakis and Duke 2007, 26).

An increased concern for indigenous people further fueled these developments. Such interests were, at least in part, aroused by representatives of various indigenous/ethnic minority groups, who increasingly asserted their presence in archaeological discourses and practices. Very important in this respect was the establishment of the World Archaeological Congress (WAC) in 1986 (Ucko 1987). The codes of ethics adopted by this organization, such as the Vermillion Accord (1989), the First Code of Ethics (1990), and the Tamaki Makau-rau Accord (2006), were all implemented in response to the appeals of indigenous peoples regarding their own heritage, including access to sacred sites and objects and the treatment of human remains. Indigenous rights to heritage also became legally recognized in a number of countries, such as Norway, where since 1978, the National Cultural Heritage Act has provided automatic protection to Sámi monuments and sites over one hundred years old. In 1990, the Native American Graves Protection and Repatriation Act (NAGPRA) was passed as a U.S. federal law. This demanded, among other things, the repatriation of culturally significant Native American material (human remains, sacred objects, etc.) from federal agencies and institutions (Thomas 2000; Fine-Dare 2002). The whirlwind of archaeological activity surrounding these native, normative, and legal initiatives leaves no doubt that archaeologists took ethical issues seriously and responded thoughtfully to changes and discourses in contemporary society. Some opted for a "political ethic" and judged archeological activity as a tool for social and political justice (see Hamilakis 2007, 35; Shanks and Tilley 1987; McGuire 2008).

As outlined above, ethical issues in archaeology have frequently been raised in relation to what suggestively is known as *cultural* heritage. Loss of heritage is seen as a loss of identity and self, and provides a major rationale for its protection (Rowlands 2002; Brattli 2009). The development of this ethics has also clearly been motivated by groups reclaiming heritage and history from Western possession. No one can therefore deny a sincere concern with how archaeology has been involved in depriving people of their heritage on the part of practitioners (Trigger 2006 [1989]). However, at the same time, the question of possessing a past as a foundation for identity is also related to an effective tradition of historicist and nationalist ideologies (Olsen 2001). Moreover, one finds less discussion about how these discourses and positions, as also reflected in international laws and conventions, are grounded in liberal ideals of human rights and autonomy, and increasingly twinned with neoliberal definitions of identity linked to possession and property. Proprietary relations and the attribution of ownership with respect to archaeological materials have been a vocal component of the ethical debates in archaeology and heritages studies over the past thirty years (Shanks 2008). In their book *The Ethics of Archaeology* (2006), Christopher and Geoffrey Scarre demonstrate how the enfolding of archaeological materials within notions of property has led to a politicized ethics. They define ethics as "the relations between *archaeologists' goals* and the morally significant *interests of those whom* their activities affect" (Scarre and Scarre 2006, 4; emphasis added).

Established ethical principles in archaeology are undoubtedly reflecting a willingness to see heritage as a matter of concern both to the interested public and to science. It is also true that the relative importance of the outlined social and political concerns has increased in relation to matters of pure scholarly interest. Nevertheless, despite all good intentions to purge potentially unethical behavior from archaeology and to protect heritage from destruction, there has been a conspicuous and increasing elision of things themselves in these concerns. While at least marginally present at the beginning of the debates about normative behavior, the focus upon archaeological politics, upon justice and just engagement with the world, has displaced a care for things.

The primacy of notions of property and rights of access and ownership in concern over the illicit trade in antiquities and artworks serves to focus attention on *human* rights and responsibilities. While raising awareness of the scale of the damage done by robbers and hobbyists wielding metal detectors, who destroy ancient sites in search of loot and collectibles, does indeed express care for the protection of heritage, we are often caught in the contradictory bind that we have been at pains to challenge in this book. That is, the push for things themselves all too easily deflects to the register of non-things: meaning, informational context, identity construction, and so forth. Consider, for example, how protecting cultural heritage for its rightful owners is identified with retaining the proper contexts for things. Contexts make the human past more readable, help us access the Indian behind the artifact; plundered artifacts sold on the art and antiquities market without context and provenance/provenience become supposedly "mere things," commodities detached from what gives them meaning and significance as expressions of creative *human* achievement.

Advocacy for such a human-centered archaeological practice in the service of social justice is succinctly expressed by Randall McGuire, who in his foreword to Hamilakis and Duke 2007 repeatedly asks: "archaeology for *whom?*" (McGuire 2007, 10). By slow degrees, the discipline of things has veered toward a discipline for "people," that is, a discipline for a purified image of human beings separate from things whose performance of the visible is merely a derivative aspect of their social compacts. Throughout this book, we have explored how this dislocation and anthropocentrism have been an ambiguous part of the archaeological project, especially, and increasingly, articulated in its theoretical formulations, its working assumptions of key concepts, and indeed its notion of what it is to be human. It is, however, in the disciplinary arms of public outreach, in cultural heritage and ethics, where care for things is most clearly spurned.

## HERITAGE, THINGS, AND THE QUEST FOR MEANING

The major imperative accepted today for protecting and preserving things and monuments is that they are of concern to people. So the argument often goes that they are of importance for cultural identity and well-being, and/or for serving as a resource, for science and society, for psycho-politics and the economy. Without such human attachment and utility, sites such as Stonehenge, Machu Picchu, and Pompeii are hardly more than bundles of inanimate materials, devoid of any need for ethical concern. Reading through heritage conventions, rationales for stewardship of heritage, and the ever more abundant literature in heritage studies, it is hard to find any statement expressing any explicit concern with things in their own being (*qua* things). "While places, sites, objects, and localities may exist as identifiable places of heritage . . . these places are not *inherently* valuable, nor do they carry a freight of innate meaning. Stonehenge, for instance, is basically a collection of rocks in a field," Laurajane Smith asserts. What makes these things and places valuable and meaningful, and thus turns them into heritage, according to her, "are the present-day cultural processes and activities that are undertaken at and around them, and of which they become a part. It is these processes that identify them as physically symbolic of particular cultural and social events, and thus give them value and meaning" (Smith 2006, 3; see Solli 2011 for critical discussion).

While it is indisputable that many people are concerned with the things of the past, and that many do feel a strong attachment to sites and monuments, it is less evident that this attachment is just an asymmetrical product of emotive narratives and cultural habits. Actually, it may as well be the case that "significant" sites evoke *their own* importance. Things—monuments, topographic features, landscapes—may stand out as significant because of their unique, conspicuous qualities. Stonehenge after all *is* different from other collections of rocks in the field (fig. 9.1). Not just any collection of rocks is the focal point for the accretion of numerous landscape features over the millennia. Not just any collection of rocks has a parking lot, museum, and hundreds of texts written about it that are easily found on most library shelves. Not just any collection of rocks draws paying crowds by the hundreds of thousands annually. And not just any collection of rocks is listed as a UNESCO world heritage site. Stonehenge's inherent, exposed difference has played a major role in making it unique as heritage.

In less conspicuous cases, things such as abandoned mining shafts, derelict ironworks, and 1913 Coca-Cola bottles also facilitate *their own* construction as heritage (or anti-heritage) through their intrinsic qualities. There is a reason why things are more suited to be heritage than spoken words and passing thoughts (Shanks 2012). An ethics that embraces things also involves acknowledging the humble principle of symmetry that they themselves may be the source of their signification (Benso 2000, xxvii). Our approach to things as outlined is this book is grounded in the recognition that things make a difference, that they play a role in

FIGURE 9.1. A sixty-ton crane, one of only two of its kind in the United Kingdom, sets the eighteen-ton lintel as part of the reconstructed trilithon during restoration work at Stonehenge ca. 1950. Three Lions, Getty Images #3332900.

their own formation, and that their ability to affect and act on us cannot be reduced to our inescapable entanglement with them (Hodder 2011). The way things affect us—and each other—is also a product of their own specific qualities, of the fact that they are "capable of an effect" (Harman 2002, 21). These should not be conflated with human-like qualities, which implicitly become the case when according things qualities and significance through association with humanity. This would be (again) to deflect attention away from things, to commit ontological ventriloquism.

One radical implication of this proposal is the need for an ethics embracing things in their own being, recognizing that things are valuable in and of themselves. Again, this is not a question of anthropomorphizing things, treating them as humans, but rather of respecting their otherness and integrity (Benso 2000; Olsen 2012). It implies adopting a more humble attitude of knowledge, care, and esteem for what things are in their own being. Needless to say, such an attempt is fraught with difficulties. The dominant approach so far in archaeology, heritage, and material culture studies has been isomorphic, subjecting things to sameness. Things are little more than things-for-us, reduced to what Heidegger termed *Bestand* (stock, inventory), by which only their manipulative being as a "standing reserve" for us remains (Heidegger 1993; cf. Introna 2009; Olsen 2010, 82). Through processes of embodiment, things are claimed to have been made social and meaningful, advanced from inanimate to animate beings and charged with sociality and personality (Appadurai 1986; Meskell and Joyce 2003). However, their own "voices" are silenced, their destiny is "always to live out the social life of men" (Pinney 2005, 259), clinging to them as private labels. And if these things speak, it is only our own voices that are heard (Andersson 2001, 30–36; Benjamin 2003, 255–56).

Being attentive to and respecting the integrity and otherness of things includes their right *not* to be meaningful in the dominant interpretative sense (to be the background noise of history of which we spoke in chapter 6). In the latter conception, meaning has always been confused with representative, symbolic, or metaphorical meaning, whereby the only possible significant role of things is to serve as a window onto cultural or cognitive realms; to provide a means by which to reach something else, something more important (the fallacy of expression or representation, outlined above in chapters 5 and 8). An ethics encompassing things also involves their liberation from this imperative of intellectualization; such an ethics impels one to be attentive to the significance of their own being (Olsen 2010, 84–87, 152–53; 2012). The significance of a boat, for example, is not primarily a function of the symbolic role it potentially may serve in transitional rituals, by acting as an embodied sign of power or by communicating individual or group identity. What seems forgotten in the vast majority of material culture studies is that the thing is mostly significant for what it *is*—that is, as boat, ax, house, laptop, drum, birch tree, and so forth. Whatever symbolic roles they may play, these are mostly residues of the primary significance of their own being.

## AN ARCHAEOLOGY OF CARE

However, in all this, we should not forget that archaeology also has another face, though one that has been stigmatized and bricked up behind the humanist imperative to be "concerned with people rather than things" (Leach 1973, 768). This face of archaeology, as practiced by archaeologists and museum curators and technicians alike, is characterized by a devotion to things. This attitude, this passionate interest is rarely seriously discussed and brought to attention, and if on rare occasions it is acknowledged, it has mostly been subsumed by the rationale provided by William Lipe in his influential conservation ethic, which has been embraced to the point of having become something of a credo for the profession (Lipe 1974; cf. Shanks and Tilley 1992, 27–28). Lipe's ethic centers on the recognition of archaeological material as a nonrenewable resource, a record that may be destroyed only if justified by the benefit to research (Lipe 1974, 243). Though a concern for things is apparent, the conservation ethic nonetheless views archaeological resources as valuable primarily for information extraction. Since such material is the "base" and justification for the profession, this ethic aims at the self-perpetuation and legitimation of the discipline. The stuff of the past is valuable to the discipline to the extent that it is able to extract it efficiently for the information economy.

Notwithstanding its rationale—scientific, political, interpretative—the categorical imperative to care for things that is primarily voiced has been that they are a resource and thus valuable for us. To care for or to study "just things" has long been a source of disciplinary embarrassment, equated with a mindless antiquarianism surviving in dusty museum spaces. Still, despite all criticism and contempt, and despite the lack of expressed and codified justification, this face of archaeology has stubbornly survived. It represents a kind of altruistic attitude that has become rare and even ridiculed in more theoretically oriented archaeology and material culture studies where dirty hands do not feature too prominently anymore and things are permitted importance only insofar as they reveal something about people (Ingold 2007). The painstaking toil of cleaning, examining, describing, drawing, photographing, conserving, and storing artifacts by technicians and curators reflects a concern with what things are in their own thingness, their quiddity (whatness) and haecceity (thisness); it denotes a respect for their allure; it expresses an attentive care for their well-being. In this way the archaeologist, the curator, is more akin to Walter Benjamin's collector than to his counterpart theoretician. The collector's lot, according to Benjamin, is the Sisyphean task of emancipating things from their use-value and commodity character, which is associated with a desire for a better world "in which things are freed from the drudgery of being useful" (Benjamin 2002, 39).

We suggest "care" as an alternative mode of getting on with things. Health care provides some interesting parallels. As practiced in the secondary sciences of nursing, physical therapy, or nutrition, the feeling and logic of care is to be attentive, responsive, and nondiscriminatory. As Annemarie Mol argues in her ethnography of health care, the more mundane aspects of healing are often seen as supplemental, as incidental or subsidiary to the supposed real activities of medicine, intervention and invasive procedures, surgically excising, manipulating, adjusting, and suturing, what might be called "the logic of cure" (Mol 2008, 1). There is more than just a metaphorical resemblance to archaeological interventions here. The political economy, institutional power relations, and operational procedures that undergird such a denigration of care are not that dissimilar from the factors that facilitate and frame archaeology's attentiveness to the past. As with archaeological sites that are transformed into rubbish dumps, exposed wall remains left to collapse, and so on, care regularly becomes visible only when it is lacking.

We have already discussed many of these facets of archaeological professionalization (chapter 3). Here we are not arguing that current frameworks for attending to the past are deluded, misguided, or, worse, detrimental. Instead, rather like the good intentions of medical professionals who advocate patient choice and holistic methods for curing ills, we suggest that within archaeology "good care is often silently incorporated into practices and does not speak for itself" (Mol 2008, 2). We therefore ally archaeology's skilled attentiveness to mundane objects with the good care of the secondary health sciences (Star 2009). For Mol, the humility of care in the health sciences results in the misattribution of healing to the heroic efforts of doctors and specialists; this at the expense of the many minute and seemingly inconsequential interactions between patients, care providers, and the material integument of healing practices (Mol 2002; 2008, 2; Mol, Moser, and Pols 2010, 14).

Similar to the structuring logic of cure that Mol describes, archaeology has misattributed good professional practice to ethical conduct. Not just any ethical conduct, for, like Mol, we are not arguing against established methodologies for caring for the past. Rather, we argue that the development of archaeological professional principles has mistakenly incorporated a care for things into a framing or logic of human-centered ethics. Indeed, it is here that our contemporary ethics resides, because this morality is rooted in a modernist humanism crafted to maintain the autonomy and sovereignty of the human subject (Verbeek 2009; Sloterdijk 2009; Latour 2002). Thus, it is not that we are seeking to extend ethics but that they need to be reformed, rearticulated, augmented, and transformed. This is a subtle distinction that deserves reemphasizing.

Care as an alternative mode of getting on with things clearly triggers a number of other critical questions. Should we extend our care to a pair of Nike shoes produced at factories using child labor? And what about nuclear weapons, concentration camps, or run-down factories polluting our environment (fig. 9.2)? If things themselves are capable of an effect, have agency, do things that do bad things deserve our care? Should we judge them consequential, deontological, or as reflecting their own virtue? If things have intrinsic capacities, a relative autonomy, does this also imply that they are moral agents to be judged by the virtue of their affordances? Although this raises important questions, which need to be carefully debated, one should nonetheless acknowledge that the problems created by "bad entities" are not an issue reserved for things or nonhumans. Just as little as we can exclude our species from attentive care because of the shortcomings of individuals, we cannot a priori dismiss things per se from any ethical concern because of the destructive potential of some things.

Care is symmetrical in its mode of being-with-others. Archaeology has taken part in an epistemological tradition "happily equating our understanding with an active elimination of everything about 'us' that cannot be aligned with a so-called 'scientific' conception of matter" (Stengers 2011, 368). "Bad" matter, matter out of place, awkward or abject things have too readily been excised away from the "us" of humanity. Technoscience writers placed the unseemly figure of the cyborg at the center of modern and future existence (Haraway 1990). In this book, we have shown how we have always been inseparable from our nonhuman "selves" (chapter 8). Mess, disorder, and other "impurities" in Mary Douglas's (1966) sense, noise and interference as opposed to clean signal, have always been a part of our being. Indeed, we might say that this state of mess increases, that the real mark of the contemporary age is not purifying ourselves from the stuff of the past, but instead the mounting weight of accumulating pasts (Olsen 2010). So rather than something to be explained away through categorical thinking, messiness must be recognized as the normal state of affairs (Law 2004, 6). With

FIGURE 9.2. Chemical waste from a broken vial, surrounded by animal tracks, discarded documents, wiring, and other materials, on a floor in the abandoned biological station at Dalniye Zelentsy, inside the Arctic Circle on the Kola Peninsula, Murmansk Oblast, Russia, July 2011. Photo by þóra Pétursdottir.

Isabelle Stengers (2011), we affirm that care often involves wondering *with* things rather than reducing them to intellectually assimilable scenarios (Webmoor 2012b).

Care and concern, both from the Latin root *cura,* imply devotion, nurturing, and thoughtfulness directed toward something. Care is "an affective state, a material vital doing, and an ethico-political obligation" (Puig de la Bellacassa 2011, 89). It is transitive in the sense of *to care.* As such, care invokes intimacy: an intimacy with things and animal species and other nonhumans that is impartial in term of epistemic and ontological discriminations. Care moves us on from the eliminativist and reductionist tendencies in the natural sciences that Isabelle Stengers bemoans (2011). Caring is immanent. It does not view the world in terms of transcendent reasoning and ethical principles that, however well-meaning, restrict us to human fraternity. Rather than for breaks, divides, and disjuncture, it looks for the connections among objects, environments, people, and animals, all of which share membership in the dwelt-in world (cf. Merleau-Ponty 1968). Things care for themselves, each other, and other entities too. It is this broader, more inclusive "self"-interest that we advocate (cf. Bennett 2010).

## CONCLUSION: ARCHAEOLOGY AS ARCHAEOLOGY

The advent of the new or processual approach in the 1960s initiated a development that gradually turned archaeology into a theoretically more reflexive and mature discipline. In his fin de siècle celebration of this achievement, Ian Hodder wrote with confidence that "[t]here is in the years around 2000 an undoubted diversity of archaeological theory, and an undoubted vigour in theoretical debates. . . . Archaeologists . . . are more than ever aware of the theoretical underpinnings of all data recovery, description and sequencing, and . . . they are more than ever aware of the diversity of theoretical approaches being explored" (Hodder 2002, 77). What is not as explicitly expressed or celebrated is that this "diversity of theoretical approaches" almost exclusively originates from other disciplinary domains where things hold little dignity. Despite the optimism expressed by Lewis Binford and others on behalf of the potentials of the archaeological project, archaeologists were increasingly made consumers of theories produced by forerunner disciplines. Archaeology was no longer a place to look for theoretical inspiration. It is perhaps symptomatic that theorizing in archaeology was almost consistently paired with denunciation of our own disciplinary past.

Indeed, there is nothing negative about being familiar with philosophies and social theories, quite the contrary, the new and unrestricted transdisciplinary outlook was clearly needed and refreshing, and also well in accordance with the nineteenth-century roots of the profession itself. However, and contrary to the symmetry characterizing the interdisciplinary toil of our forebears, the new eagerness to look to other disciplines somehow made us lose sight of our larger loyalty to things by subsuming them under these discourses. Theories largely ignorant of things were parasitically adopted without recognizing how this actually contributed to a devaluation of our own subject matter (e.g. Webmoor 2012b on science and technology studies and archaeology).[2] Without this concern for things, the distinctiveness of the archaeological project is lost. In fact, archaeology's tools, concepts, and vocabularies arise from and are best adapted to things, and this is precisely where the bricoleur thrives (cf. Olsen 2010).

Archaeology's past was never entirely innocent, but in writing this book, we have confronted its extraordinary history with wonderment

---

2. This is not to say that these theories were not transformed and granted different nuance by being brought into a new habitat such as archaeology.

and reaffirmed our trust in our discipline's ability to confront any situation presented by things in our engagements with the material past. Ironically, archaeology's most significant theoretical asset has been its name, which has become a popular catchphrase among philosophers, psychologists, social scientists, and literary critics. Even if few of those attracted by its metaphorical payoff have bothered to think seriously about what an archaeological contribution to the topics they address might actually look like, the fascination with the term still points to something genuinely and intellectually appealing about the archaeological project. However, to reveal its potential it is necessary to repatriate archaeology from its intellectual staging as a convenient but semantically obligation-free metaphor in social and cultural theory.

This book is an attempt to achieve this by exposing the archaeological project as a distinct, content-filled, and intellectually rewarding undertaking. Archaeology is first and foremost a concern with things and inasmuch as *things* are once again the subject per se of social and cultural discourses, archaeologists, arguably their most dedicated students, should naturally make their voices heard. Our long-held concern with things constitutes an intellectual skill that is clearly highly relevant to these debates. Moreover, given our concern with things, it is appropriate that writing and reading theory from an archaeological point of view should make a difference. Our theorizing, although in part dedicated to common materials, objects, and things, and the processing of similar philosophies, should be distinguishable—at least to some extent—from other theoretical discourses. Archaeology's habitat is unique and rich.

# References

Achterhuis, Hans, ed. 2001. *American Philosophy of Technology: The Empirical Turn*. Translated by Robert P. Crease. Bloomington: Indiana University Press.

Adam, Hans C. 1990. Heinrich Schliemann und die Photographie. In *Das Land der Griechen mit der Seele suchen: Photographien des 19 und 20 Jahrhunderts*. Cologne: Agfa Foto-Historama.

AIA. *See* Archaeological Institute of America.

Alberti, Benjamin, and Tamra L. Bray, eds. 2009. *Animating Archaeology: Of Subjects, Objects and Alternative Ontologies*. Special section of the *Cambridge Archaeological Journal* 19(3): 337–441.

Alberti, Benjamin, Severin Fowles, Martin Holbraad, Yvonne Marshall, and Christopher Witmore. 2011. Worlds Otherwise: Archaeology, Anthropology and Ontological Difference. *Current Anthropology* 52(6): 896–912.

Alcock, Susan E. 2002. *Archaeologies of the Greek Past: Landscape, Monuments, and Memories*. Cambridge: Cambridge University Press.

Alcock, Susan E., and John F. Cherry, eds. 2004. *Side-by-Side Survey: Comparative Regional Studies in the Mediterranean World*. Oxford: Oxbow Books.

Alexander, J. 1970. *The Directing of Archaeological Excavations*. London: John Baker.

Alpers, Svetlana. 1983. *The Art of Describing: Dutch Art in the Seventeenth Century*. Chicago: University of Chicago Press.

Amann, K., and Karen Knorr Cetina. 1990. The Fixation of (Visual) Evidence. In *Representation in Scientific Practice*, ed. Michael Lynch and Steve Woolgar. Cambridge, MA: MIT Press.

Amyx, D.A. 1988. *Corinthian Vase Painting in the Archaic Period*. 3 vols. Berkeley: University of California Press.

Andersson, Dag. 2001. *Tingenes Taushet, Tingenes Tale*. Oslo: Solum Forlag.

212 | References

Andreassen, Elin, Hein B. Njerck, and Bjørnar Olsen. 2010. *Persistent Memories: Pyramiden—a Soviet Mining Town in the High Arctic*. Trondheim: Tapir Forlag.

Andrews, Gill, John C. Barrett, and John S. C. Lewis. 2000. Interpretation Not Record. The Practice of Archaeology. *Antiquity* 74: 525–30.

Andrews, Kevin. 2006 [1953]. *Castles of the Morea*. Princeton, NJ: American School of Classical Studies at Athens.

Andrews, Malcolm. 1999. *Landscape and Western Art*. Oxford: Oxford University Press.

Appadurai, Arjun. 1986. *The Social Life of Things: Commodities in Cultural Perspective*. Cambridge: Cambridge University Press.

Archaeological Institute of America. 2004. Code of Ethics. December 29, 1997. www.archaeological.org/news/advocacy/130 (accessed March 31, 2012). Cited as AIA.

Ashbee, Paul. 1966. *The Fussell's Lodge Long Barrow Excavations 1957*. London: Society of Antiquaries.

Atkinson, Richard John Copland. 1953. *Field Archaeology*. London: Methuen.

Authier, M. 1995. "Refraction and Cartesian 'forgetfulness.';" In *A History of Scientific Thought*, ed. M. Serres, 315–43. Oxford: Blackwell .

Bailey, Douglass, Alasdair Whittle, and Vicki Cummings. 2005. *(Un)Settling the Neolithic*. Oxford: Oxbow Books.

Bailey, Geoff N. 1981. Concepts, Time Scales and Explanation in Economic Prehistory. In *Economic Archaeology*, ed. A. Sheridan and G.N. Bailey, 97–117. Oxford: British Archaeological Reports .

———. 1983. Concepts of Time in Quaternary Prehistory. *Annual Review of Anthropology* 12: 165–92.

———. 1987. Breaking the Time Barrier. *Archaeological Review from Cambridge* 6: 5–20.

———. 2007. Time Perspectives, Palimpsests and the Archaeology of Time. *Journal Anthropological Archaeology* 26(2): 198–223.

Baird, Davis. 2004. *Thing Knowledge: A Philosophy of Scientific Instruments*. Berkeley: University of California Press.

Bandaranayke, Senake. 1977. *Arkeologi och imperialism*. Stockholm: Ordfront

Banning, Edward B. 2002. *Archaeological Survey*. Manuals in Archaeological Methods, Theory, and Technique Series. New York: Plenum.

Baker, Karen, and Geoffrey Bowker. 2007. Information Ecology: Open System Environment for Data, Memories, and Knowing. *Journal of Intelligent Information Systems* 29: 127–44.

Bapty, Ian, and Timothy Yates, eds. 1990. *Archaeology after Structuralism: Post-structuralism and the Practice of Archaeology*. London: Routledge.

Barad, Karen. 2007. *Meeting the Universe Halfway: Quantum Physics and the Entanglement of Matter*. Durham, NC: Duke University Press.

Barker, Graeme, and Derrick Webley. 1978. Causewayed Camps and Early Neolithic Economies in Central Southern England. *Proceedings of the Prehistoric Society London* 44: 161–86.

Barker, Philip. 1982. *Techniques of Archaeological Excavation*. 2nd ed. New York: Universe Books.

Barrett, John. 1988. Fields of Discourse. Reconstituting a Social Archaeology? *Critique of Anthropology* 7: 5–16.

Barthes, Roland. 1977. Rhetoric of the Image. In id., *Image-Music-Text*. London: Fontana.

Bassalla, George. 1988. *The Evolution of Technology*. Cambridge: Cambridge University Press.

Beek, Gosewijn van. 1989. The Object as Subject: New Routes to Material Culture Studies. Review of *Material Culture and Mass Consumption*, by Daniel Miller. *Critique of Anthropology* 9(3): 91–99.

Bellwood, Peter, Clive Gamble, Steven A. LeBlanc, Mark Pluciennik, Martin Richards, and John Edward Terrell. 2007. Review Feature. *Cambridge Archaeological Journal* 17(1): 87–109.

Bender, Barbara, Susan Hamilton, and Christopher Tilley. 2007. *Stone Worlds: Narrative and Reflexivity in Landscape Archaeology*. Walnut Creek, CA: Left Coast Press.

Benjamin, Walter. 1996. *Selected Writings*, vol. 1: *1913–1926*. Cambridge, MA: Belknap Press.

———. 1999a. *Selected Writings*, vol. 2: *1927–1934*. Cambridge, MA: Belknap Press.

———. 1999b. *The Arcades Project*. Cambridge, MA: Belknap Press.

———. 2002. *Selected Writings*, vol. 3: *1935–1938*. Cambridge, MA: Belknap Press.

———. 2003. *Selected Writings*, vol. 4: *1938–1940*. Cambridge, MA: Belknap Press.

Bennett, Jane. 2010. *Vibrant Matter: A Political Ecology of Things*. Durham, NC: Duke University Press.

Benso, Silvia. 2000. *The Face of Things: A Different Side of Ethics*. Albany: State University of New York Press.

Benson, Elizabeth, ed. 1981. *Mesoamerican Sites and World-Views*. Washington, DC: Dumbarton Oaks.

Berger, John. 1984. *Ways of Seeing*. London: BBC.

Berggren, Åsa, and Mats Burström. 2002. Reflexiv fältarkeologi?: återsken från ett seminarium. Stockholm: Riksantikvarieämbetet; Malmö: Malmö Kulturmiljö.

Berggren, Åsa, and Ian Hodder. 2003. Social Practice, Method and Some Problems of Field Archaeology. *American Antiquity* 68: 421–34.

Bergson, Henri. 1998 [1907]. *Creative Evolution*. New York: Dover.

Berlo, Janet, ed. 1992. *Art, Ideology, and the City of Teotihuacán*. Washington, DC: Dumbarton Oaks Research Library and Collection.

Bernal, Martin. 1991. *Black Athena*. Vol. 1. New Brunswick, NJ: Rutgers University Press.

Bijker, Wiebe, Thomas Hughes, and Trevor Pinch. 1989. *The Social Construction of Technological Systems: New Directions in the Sociology and History of Technology*. Cambridge, MA: MIT Press.

Binford, Lewis. 1962. Archaeology as Anthropology. *American Antiquity* 28(2): 217–25.

———. 1964. A Consideration of Archaeological Research Design. *American Antiquity* 29: 425–44.

————. 1977. General Introduction. In *For Theory Building in Archaeology*, ed. Lewis Binford, 1–10. New York: Academic Press.

————. 1981. Archaeology and the "Pompeii Premise." *Journal of Anthropological Research* 37(3): 195–208.

————. 1989. *Debating Archaeology.* New York: Academic Press.

Bjørklund, Ivar, and Johan Albert Kalstad. 1997. *Noaidier og trommer: Samiske religiøse tradisjoner fra vår nære fortid.* Ottar no. 217. Tromsø, Norway: Tromsø Museum.

Black, R.M. 1983. *The History of Electric Wires and Cables.* London: Peter Peregrinus.

Bloch, Maurice. 1995. Questions Not to Ask of Malagasy Carvings. In *Interpreting Archaeology: Finding Meaning in the Past*, ed. Ian Hodder et al. London: Routledge.

Boast, R. 1996. A Small Company of Actors: A Critique of Style. *Journal of Material Culture* 2(2): 173–98.

Bohrer, Frederick N. 2003. *Orientalism and Visual Culture: Imagining Mesopotamia in Nineteenth-Century Europe.* Cambridge: Cambridge University Press.

Boivin, Nicole. 2008. *Material Cultures, Material Minds: The Impact of Things on Human Thought, Society, and Evolution.* Cambridge: Cambridge University Press.

Bolender, Douglas J., ed. 2010. *Eventful Archaeologies: New Approaches to Social Transformation in the Archaeological Record.* Albany: State University of New York Press.

Boric, Dusan, ed. 2010. *Archaeology and Memory.* Oxford: Oxbow Books.

Bouquet, Mary. 1991. Images of Artefacts: Photographic Essay. *Critique of Anthropology* 11: 333–56.

Bowker, Geoffrey. 2000. Biodiversity Datadiversity. *Social Studies of Science* 30(5): 643–83.

————. 2005. *Memory Practices in the Sciences.* Cambridge, MA: MIT Press.

Bowker, Geoffrey, and Susan Leigh Star. 1999. *Sorting Things Out: Classification and Its Consequences.* Cambridge, MA: MIT Press.

Bradley, Richard. 1983. Archaeology, Evolution and the Public Good: The Intellectual Development of General Pitt Rivers. *Archaeological Journal* 140: 1–9

————. 1993. *Altering the Earth.* Edinburgh: Society of Antiquaries of Scotland.

————. 1996. Long Houses, Long Mounds and Neolithic Enclosures. *Journal of Material Culture* 1(2): 239–56.

————. 1998. *The Significance of Monuments: On the Shaping of Human Experience in Neolithic and Bronze Age Europe.* London: Routledge.

————. 2002. *The Past in Prehistoric Societies.* London: Routledge.

————. 2003. Seeing Things: Perception, Experience and the Constraints of Excavation. *Journal of Social Archaeology* 3(2): 151–68.

————. 2005. *Ritual and Domestic Life in Prehistoric Europe.* London: Routledge.

Braidwood, Robert J. 1958. Vere Gordon Childe, 1892–1957. *American Anthropologist*, n.s., 60(4): 733–36.

————. 1959. Archeology and the Evolutionary Theory. In *Evolution and Anthropology: A Centennial Appraisal*, ed. Betty J. Meggers, 76–89. Washington, DC: Anthropological Society of Washington.

Brattli, Terje. 2009. Managing the Archaeological World Cultural Heritage: Consensus or Rhetoric? *Norwegian Archaeological Review* 42(1): 24–39.

Brooker, Peter. 1999. *A Concise Glossary of Cultural Theory*. London: Arnold.

Brown, Bill. 2003. *A Sense of Things: The Object Matter of American Literature*. Chicago: University of Chicago Press.

Brown, Linda A., and William H. Walker. 2008. Archaeology, Animism, and Non-Human Agents. Special issue of the *Journal of Archaeological Method and Theory* 15(4): 297–99.

Brück, Joanna. 2005. Experiencing the Past? The Development of a Phenomenological Archaeology in British Prehistory. *Archaeological Dialogues* 12(1): 45–72.

Bryant, Levi. 2010. The Ontic Principle: Outline of an Object-oriented Philosophy. In *The Speculative Turn: Continental Materialism and Realism*, ed. Levi Bryant, Nick Srnicek, and Graham Harman, 261–78. Melbourne: re.press.

Bryant, Levi, Nick Srnicek, and Graham Harman, eds. 2010. *The Speculative Turn: Continental Materialism and Realism*. Melbourne: re.press.

Buchanan, Richard, Dennis Doordan, and Victor Margolin. 2010. *The Designed World: Images, Objects, Environments*. Oxford: Berg.

Buck-Morss, Susan. 1999. *The Dialectics of Seeing: Walter Benjamin and the Arcades Project*. Cambridge, MA: MIT Press.

Burkert, Walter. 1992. *The Orientalizing Revolution: Near Eastern Influence on Greek Culture in the Early Archaic Age*. Cambridge MA: Harvard University Press.

Butler, Judith. 1993. *Bodies That Matter: On the Discursive Limits of Sex*. London: Routledge.

Callon, Michel. 1986. Some Elements of a Sociology of Translation: Domestication of the Scallops and the Fishermen of St. Brieuc Bay. In *Power, Action and Belief: A New Sociology of Knowledge?* ed. John Law. London: Routledge.

————. 1999. Actor-Network-Theory—The Market Test. *Sociological Review* 46: 181–95.

Callon, Michel, and John Law. 1997. After the Individual in Society: Lessons on Collectivity from Science, Technology and Society. *Canadian Journal of Sociology* 22(2): 165–82.

Candea, Matei. 2010. *The Social after Gabriel Tarde: Debates and Assessments*. London: Routledge.

Carandini, Andrea. 1991. *Storie dalla terra. Manuale di scavo archeologico*. Turin: G. Einaudi.

Carne, Peter. 2010. On Archaeology, Teaching and Excavation Practice: An Interview with Peter Carne. Archaeolog. http://traumwerk.stanford.edu/archaeolog/2010/09/notes_on_archaeology_teaching.html (accessed March 31, 2012).

Carpenter, Rhys, and Antoine Bon. 1936. *The Defenses of Acrocorinth and the Lower Town*. Cambridge, MA: Harvard University Press.

Carusi, Annamaria, Aud Sissel Hoel, and Timothy Webmoor. 2012. *Computational Picturing*. Special issue of *Interdisciplinary Science Reviews* 37(1).

Carusi, Annamaria, Aud Sissel Hoel, Timothy Webmoor, and Steve Woolgar, eds. In press. *Visualization in the Age of Computerization*. London: Routledge.

Carver, Martin. 2009. *Archaeological Investigation*. London: Routledge.

Carver, Geoff. 2011. Reflections on the Archaeology of Archaeological Excavation. *Archaeological Dialogues* 18(1): 18–26.

Certeau, Michel de. 1984. *The Practice of Everyday Life*. Berkeley: University of California Press.

Chadha, Ashish. 2002. Visions of a Discipline: Sir Mortimer Wheeler and the Archaeological Method in India (1944–1948). *Journal of Social Archaeology* 2(3): 378–401.

Chadwick, Adrian. 2003. Post-processualism, Professionalization and Archaeological Methodologies. Towards Reflective and Radical Practice. *Archaeological Dialogues* 10(1): 97–117.

Cherry, John F. 1983. Frogs around the Pond. Perspectives on Current Archaeological Survey Projects in the Mediterranean Region. In *Archaeological Survey in the Mediterranean Area*, ed. Donald R. Keller and David W. Rupp, 375–416. Oxford: British Archaeological Reports 155.

———. 2011. Still Not Digging, Much. *Archaeological Dialogues* 18(1): 10–17.

Christensen, Christa L. 1993. Tingenes tidsalder. Kitsch, camp og fetichisme. In *Omgang med tingene. Ti essays om tingenes tilstand*, ed. Christa L. Christensen and Carsten Thau. Åarhus: Åarhus University Press.

Christenson, Andrew, ed. 1989. *Tracing Archaeology's Past: The Historiography of Archaeology*. Carbondale: Southern Illinois University Press.

Clack, Timothy, and Marcus Brittain. 2007. *Archaeology and the Media*. Walnut Creek, CA: Left Coast Press.

Clark, Andy. 2003. *Natural-Born Cyborgs: Minds, Technologies, and the Future of Human Intelligence*. Oxford: Oxford University Press.

Clarke, David. 1968. *Analytical Archaeology*. London: Methuen.

———. 1973. Archaeology: The Loss of Innocence. *Antiquity* 47: 6–18.

Cnattingius, Lars, and Nanna Cnattingius. 2007. *Ruiner. Historia, öden och vård*. Stockholm: Carlsson Bokförlag.

Cook, R.M. 1972. *Greek Painted Pottery*. 2nd ed. London: Methuen.

Cookson, Maurice B. 1954. *Photography for Archaeologists*. London: Max Parrish.

Cooper, Malcolm A., Antony Firth, John Carman, and David Wheatley, eds. 1995. *Managing Archaeology*. London: Routledge.

Coopmans, Catelijne, and Steve Woolgar. 2007. Virtual Witnessing in a Virtual Age: A Prospectus for Social Studies of E-science. In *New Infrastructures for Knowledge Production: Understanding E-science*, ed. Christine Hine. London: Information Science Publishing.

Coopmans, Catelijine, Michael Lynch, Janet Vertesi, and Steve Woolgar, eds. Forthcoming. *New Representations in Scienctific Practice*. Cambridge, MA: MIT Press.

Cowgill, George. 1970. Some Sampling and Reliability Problems in Archaeology. In *Archéologie et calculateurs: Problèmes sémiologiques et mathéma-*

*tiques, Marseille, 7–12 avril 1969,* ed. J.C. Gardin, 161–72. Paris: Centre national de la recherche scientifique.

———. 1983. Rulership and the Ciudadela: Political Inferences from Teotihuacán Architecture. In *Civilization in the Ancient Americas: Essays in Honor of Gordon R. Willey,* ed. Richard M. Leventhal and Alan L. Kolata. Albuquerque: University of New Mexico Press.

Daniel, Glyn E. 1950. *A Hundred Years of Archaeology.* London: Duckworth.

———. 1967. *The Origins and Growth of Archaeology.* Penguin Books.

———. 1976. *A Hundred and Fifty Years of Archaeology.* Cambridge, MA: Harvard University Press.

Daston, Lorraine. 1992. Objectivity and the Escape from Perspective. *Social Studies of Science* 22(4): 597–618.

Daston, Lorraine, and Peter Galison. 2007. *Objectivity.* New York: Zone Books.

Davies, Malcolm. 1991. *Poetarum Melicorum Graecorum Fragmenta,* vol. 1: *Alcman Stesichorus Ibycus.* Oxford: Oxford University Press.

De Jonge, Eccy. 2004. *Spinoza and Deep Ecology: Challenging Traditional Approaches to Environmentalism.* Burlington, VT: Ashgate.

DeLanda, Manuel. 2006. *A New Philosophy of Society* London: Continuum.

Deleuze, Gilles. 1997. *Bergsonism.* New York: Zone Books.

Delgado, Jaime. 2005. ¿Que es el patrimonio cultural? Paper presented at the Centro de Estudios Teotihuacanos, Teotihuacán, Mexico, April 2005.

Demant-Hatt, Emilie. 1913. *Med lapperne i høyfjeldet.* Stockholm: Nordiska bokhandelen.

DeMarrais, Elizabeth, Chris Gosden, and Colin Renfrew. 2004. *Rethinking Materiality: The Engagement of the Mind with the Material World.* Cambridge: McDonald Institute for Archaeological Research.

Dennett, Daniel C. 2004. *Freedom Evolves.* New York: Penguin Books.

Derrida, Jacques. 1976. *Of Grammatology.* Translated by Gayatri Chakravorty Spivak. Baltimore: Johns Hopkins University Press.

Descola, Philippe. 2005. *Par-delà nature et culture.* Paris: Gallimard.

Deuel, Leo. 1977. *Memoirs of Heinrich Schliemann: A Documentary Portrait Drawn from His Autobiographical Writings, Letters, and Excavation Reports.* New York: Harper & Row.

DeVore, Irven. 1968. Comments. In *New Perspectives in Archaeology.* ed. Sally Binford and Lewis Binford. Chicago: Aldine.

Dewey, John. 1980. *Art as Experience.* New York: Perigee Books.

Diaz-Andreu, Margarita. 2007. *A World History of Nineteenth-Century Archaeology: Nationalism, Colonialism, and the Past.* Oxford: Oxford University Press.

Dincauze, Dena F. 2000. *Environmental Archaeology: Principles and Practice.* Cambridge: Cambridge University Press.

Dion, Mark, and Alex Coles, eds. 1999. *Mark Dion: Archaeology.* [London]: Black Dog.

Dolwick, Jim. 2009. The Social and Beyond: Introducing Actor-Network Theory. *Journal of Maritime Archaeology* 4(1): 21–49.

Domanska, Ewa. 2006a. The Return to Things. *Archaeologia Polona* 44: 171–85.

———. 2006b. The Material Presence of the Past. *History and Theory* 45: 337–48.

Douglas, Mary. 1966. *Purity and Danger*. London: Penguin Books.

Dowdall, Katherine M., and Otis O. Parrish. 2003. A Meaningful Disturbance of the Earth. *Journal of Social Archaeology* 3(1): 99–133.

Downing, Eric. 2006. *After Images: Photography, Archaeology and Psychoanalysis and the Tradition of Bildung*. Detroit: Wayne State University Press

Driver, Felix. 2001. *Geography Militant: On Cultures of Exploration and Empire*. Oxford: Whiley-Blackwell.

Dunnell, Robert C. 1986. Methodological Issues in Americanist Artifact Classification. *Advances in Archaeological Method and Theory* 9: 149–207.

Durand, Jean-Nicolas-Louis. 2000. *Précis of the Lectures on Architecture*. Translated by David Britt. Los Angeles: Getty Research Institute.

Dyson, Stephen. 1998. *Ancient Marbles to American Shores: Classical Archaeology in the United States*. Philadelphia: University of Pennsylvania Press.

———. 2006. *In Pursuit of Ancient Pasts: A History of Classical Archaeology in the Nineteenth and Twentieth Centuries*. New Haven, CT: Yale University Press.

Edgeworth, Matt, ed. 2006. *Ethnographies of Archaeological Practice: Cultural Encounters, Material Transformations*. Lanham, MD: AltaMira Press.

———. 2011a. Excavation as a Ground of Archaeological Knowledge. *Archaeological Dialogues* 18(1): 44–46.

———. 2011b. *Fluid Pasts: Archaeology of Flow (Debates in Archaeology)*. London: Bristol Classical Press.

Edmonds, Mark. 1999. *Ancestral Geographies of the Neolithic*. London Routledge.

Enwezor, Okwui. 2008. *Archive Fever: Uses of the Document in Contemporary Art*. New York: Steidl.

Evans, Joan. 1956. *History of the Society of Antiquaries*. Oxford: Society of Antiquaries.

Fijn, Natasha. 2011. *Living with Herds: Human-Animal Co-existence in Mongolia*. Cambridge: Cambridge University Press.

Filippucci, Paola. 2010. Archaeology and the Anthropology of Recent Memory: Takes on the Recent Past. In *Anthropology and Archaeology*, ed. D. Garrow and T. Yarrow. Oxford: Oxbow.

Fine-Dare, Kathleen S. 2002. *Grave Injustice: The American Indian Repatriation Movement and NAGPRA*. Lincoln: University of Nebraska Press.

Finlay, George. 1877. *A History of Greece from Its Conquest by the Romans to the Present Time, B.C. 146 to A.D. 1864*. Vol. 6: *The Greek Revolution*. Part I. Oxford: Clarendon Press.

Fish, Suzanne K., and Stephen A. Kowalewski, eds. 1990. *The Archaeology of Regions: A Case for Full-Coverage Survey*. Washington, DC: Smithsonian Institution Press.

Fjellström, Pehr. 1981 [1755]. *Kort berättelse om Lapparnas björna-fänge samt deras der wid brukade widskeppelser*. Umeå, Sweden: Två Förläggare Bokförlag.

Flannery, Kent. 1982. The Golden Marshalltown: A Parable for the Archaeology of the 1980s. *American Anthropologist* 84(2): 265–78.

Fleming, Andrew. 1971. Agriculture on the Marginal Lands of North-East Yorkshire. *Agricultural History Review* 19(1): 1–24.

———. 1972. Vision and Design: Approaches to Ceremonial Monument Typology. *Man*, n.s., 7(1): 57–73.

———. 2007. *The Dartmoor Reaves: Investigating Prehistoric Land Divisions.* 2nd rev. ed. Oxford: Windgather Press.

———. 2010. *Swaledale: Valley of the Wild River.* Oxford: Oxbow Books.

Floridi, Luciano, ed. 2004. *The Blackwell Guide to the Philosophy of Computing and Information.* Malden, MA: Blackwell.

Forte, Maurizio, and Alberto Siliotti, eds. 1997. *Virtual Archaeology: Recreating Ancient Worlds.* New York: Abrams

Forty, Adrian, and Sussane Kuchler, eds. 2001. *The Art of Forgetting.* Oxford: Berg.

Forrest, William G. 1966 [1961]. *The Emergence of Greek Democracy: The Character of Greek Politics, 800–400 BC.* New York: McGraw-Hill.

Foster, Hal. 1996. *The Return of the Real: The Avant-Garde at the End of the Century.* Cambridge, MA: MIT Press.

Foucault, Michel. 1972. *The Archaeology of Knowledge: The Discourse on Language.* New York: Pantheon Books.

———. 1973. *The Order of Things: An Archaeology of the Human Sciences.* New York: Vintage Books.

———. 1977. *Discipline and Punish: The Birth of the Prison.* New York: Pantheon Books.

———. 1984. Nietzsche, Genealogy, History. In *The Foucault Reader,* ed. Paul Rabinow. New York: Pantheon Books.

———. 2003. *Society Must Be Defended: Lectures at the Collège de France, 1975–76.* Edited by M. Bertani and A. Fontana. New York: Picador.

Fowles, Severin. 2010. People without Things. In *An Anthropology of Absence: Materializations of Transcendence and Loss,* ed. Mikkel Bille, Frida Hastrup, and Tim Flohr Soerensen, 23–41. New York: Springer.

French, Charles. 2002. *Geoarchaeology in Action: Studies in Soil Micromorphology and Landscape Evolution.* London: Routledge.

Friedell, Egon. 1937. *Kulturhistorie 3. Kulturstrømninger fra den sorte død til verdenskrigen.* Copenhagen: Berlingske Forlag. Originally published as *Kulturgeschichte der Neuzeit: Die Krisis der europäischen Seele von der schwarzen Pest bis zum Ersten Weltkrieg,* vol. 3: *Romantik und Liberalismus. Imperialismus und Impressionismus* (Munich: Beck, 1931).

Friedman, Jonathan, and Michael Rowlands, eds. 1977. *The Evolution of Social Systems.* London: Duckworth.

Frieling, Rudolf. 2008. *The Art of Participation: 1950—Now.* New York: Thames & Hudson.

Frischer, Bernard, and Anastasia Dakouri-Hild, eds. 2008. *Beyond Illustration: 2d and 3d Digital Technologies as Tools for Discovery in Archaeology.* Oxford: BAR International Series 1805.

Fritz, John M., and Fred T. Plog. 1970. The Nature of Archaeological Explanation. *American Antiquity* 35(4): 405–12.

Galison, Peter. 1997. *Image and Logic: The Material Culture of Twentieth-Century Physics*. Chicago: University of Chicago Press.

Galtung, Johan. 1974. After Camelot. In *The Rise and Fall of Project Camelot*, ed. Irving Louis Horowitz. Cambridge, MA: MIT Press.

Garrow, Duncan, and Thomas Yarrow, eds. 2010. *Archaeology and Anthropology: Understanding Similarity, Exploring Difference*. Oxford: Oxbow.

Gell, Sir William. 1810. *The Itinerary of Greece: With a commentary on Pausanias and Strabo and an account of the monuments of antiquity at present existing in that country*. London: T. Payne.

Gernsheim, Helmut. 1969. *The History of Photography from the Camera Obscura to the Beginning of the Modern Era*. New York: Thames & Hudson.

Gero, Joan. 1985. Socio-Politics and the Woman-at-Home Ideology. *American Antiquity* 50(2): 342–50.

———. 1996. Archaeological Practice and Gendered Encounters with Field Data. In *Gender and Archaeology*, ed. R.P. Wright, 251–80. Philadelphia: University of Pennsylvania Press.

Gero, Joan, and Meg Conkey. 1991. *Engendering Archaeology: Women and Prehistory*. Cambridge: Blackwell.

Gero, Joan, and Doris Root. 1990. Public Presentation and Private Concerns: Archaeology in the Pages of *National Geographic*. In *The Politics of the Past*, ed. Peter Gathercole and David Lowenthal, 342–50. London: Routledge.

Giannacchi, Gabriella, Nick Kaye, and Michael Shanks, eds. 2012. *Archaeologies of Performance*. New York: Routledge.

Gibson, James. 1986. *The Ecological Approach to Visual Perception*. New York: Psychology Press.

Gibson, Kathleen. 1991. Tools, Language, and Intelligence: Evolutionary Implications. *Man* 26: 255–64.

Giebelhausen, Michaela. 2011. Museum Architecture: A Brief History. In *A Companion to Museum Studies*, ed. Sharon MacDonald, 223–44. Oxford: Blackwell.

Ginouvès, René. 1972. *Le Théâtrôn à gradins droits et l'Odéon d'Argos*. Paris: Vrin.

Godelier, Maurice. 1977. *Perspectives in Marxist Anthropology*. Cambridge: Cambridge University Press.

Gombrich, Ernst H. 1960. *Art and Illusion*. New York: Pantheon Books.

González-Ruibal, Alfredo. 2007. Arqueología simétrica: Un giro teórico sin revolución paradigmática [with commentary]. *Complutum* 18: 283–319.

———. 2008. Time to Destroy. An Archaeology of Supermodernity. *Current Anthropology* 49(2): 247–79. With comments by Tim Edensor, Pedro Paulo A. Funari, Martin Hall, Cornelius Holtorf, Mark P. Leone, Lynn Meskell, Laurent Olivier, Nicholas J. Saunders, John Schofield, and Andrés Zarankin.

González-Ruibal, Alfredo, Almudena Hernando, and Gustavo Politis. 2011. Ontology of the Self and Material Culture: Arrow-making among the Awá Hunter-Gatherers (Brazil). *Journal of Anthropological Archaeology* 30(1): 1–16.

Gordon, Alexander. 1726. *Itinerarium Septentrionale: Or, A Journey Thro' Most of the Counties of Scotland, and Those in the North of England*. London: Printed for the author.

Gosden, Chris. 1994. *Social Being and Time*. Oxford: Blackwell.

———. 1999. *Anthropology and Archaeology: A Changing Relationship*. London: Routledge.

———. 2005. What Do Objects Want? *Journal of Archaeological Method and Theory* 12(3): 193–211.

Gould, Richard A., and Michael B. Schiffer, eds. 1981. *Modern Material Culture: The Archaeology of Us*. New York: Academic Press.

Grant, Jim, Sam Gorin, and Neil Flemming. 2008. *The Archaeology Coursebook: An Introduction to Themes, Sites, Methods and Skills*. 3rd ed. London: Routledge.

Graves-Brown, Paul M., ed. 2000. *Matter, Materiality and Modern Culture*. London: Routledge.

Great Britain. Department of the Environment. Committee for Rescue Archaeology. Ancient Monuments Board for England. 1975. *Principles of Publication in Rescue Archaeology: A Report*. London: Department of the Environment.

*Greece: A Handbook for Travellers*. 1889, 1894, 1909. Leipzig: Karl Baedeker.

Green, Ernestine L. 1984. *Ethics and Values in Archaeology*. New York: Free Press.

Gross, Alan G. 1990. *The Rhetoric of Science*. Cambridge, MA: Harvard University Press.

Grosz, Elizabeth. 2002. *Architecture from the Outside: Essays on Virtual and Real Space*. Cambridge, MA: MIT Press.

Gupta, Akhil, and James Ferguson. 1997. *Anthropological Locations: Boundaries and Grounds of a Field Science*. Berkeley: University of California Press.

Haber, Alejandro. 2007. Reframing Social Equality within an Intercultural Archaeology. *World Archaeology* 39(2): 281–97.

Habermas, Jürgen. 1971. *Borgerlig offentlighet*. Oslo: Gyldendal.

Hacking, Ian. 1983. *Representing and Intervening:Introductory Topics in the Philosophy of Science*. Cambridge: Cambridge University Press.

———. 2001. *The Social Construction of What?* Cambridge, MA: Harvard University Press.

Hallowell, A. Irving. 1960. Ojibwa Ontology, Behaviour, and World View. In *Culture in History: Essays in Honor of Paul Radin*, ed. Stanley Diamond. New York: Octagon Books.

Hamilakis, Yannis. 2006. *The Nation and Its Ruins: Antiquity, Archaeology, and National Imagination in Greece*. Oxford: Oxford University Press.

Hamilakis, Yannis, and Phillip Duke. 2007. *Archaeology and Capitalism: From Ethics to Politics*. Walnut Creek, CA: Left Coast Press.

Hamilton, Sue, Chris Tilley, and Barbara Bender. 2006. *Stone Worlds: Narrative and Reflexive in Landscape Archaeology*. London: UCL Press.

Hankins, Thomas, and Robert Silverman. 1995. *Instruments of the Imagination*. Princeton, NJ: Princeton University Press.

Hansen, Mark. 2004. *New Philosophy for New Media*. Cambridge, MA: MIT Press.

Hansen, Lars Ivar, and Bjørnar Olsen. 2004. *Samenes historie fram til 1750*. Oslo: Cappelen.

Haraway, Donna. 1990. *Simians, Cyborgs, and Women: The Reinvention of Nature*. London: Routledge.

———. 1997. *Modest_Witness@Second_Millennium FemaleMan_Meets_Onco Mouse*. London: Routledge.

———. 2003a. *The Companion Species Manifesto: Dogs, People, and Significant Otherness*. Chicago: Prickly Paradigm Press.

———. 2003b. Cyborgs to Companion Species: Reconfiguring Kinship in Technoscience. In *Chasing Technoscience: Matrix for Materiality*, ed. Don Idhe and Evan Selinger, 58–82. Bloomington: Indiana University Press.

———. 2007. *When Species Meet*. Minneapolis: University of Minnesota Press.

Harman, Graham. 2002. *Tool-Being: Heidegger and the Metaphysics of Objects*. Chicago: Open Court.

———. 2005. *Guerrilla Metaphysics: Phenomenology and the Carpentry of Things*. Open Court.

———. 2005. Heidegger on Objects and Things. In *Making Things Public: Atmospheres of Democracy*, ed. Bruno Latour and Peter Weibal, 268–71 . Cambridge, MA: MIT Press .

———. 2009a. *Prince of Networks: Bruno Latour and Metaphysics*. Melbourne: re.press.

———. 2009b. Dwelling with the Fourfold. *Space and Culture* 12(3): 292–302.

———. 2010. *Towards Speculative Realism: Essays and Lectures*. Zero Books.

———. 2011. *The Quadruple Object*. Zero Books.

Harris, Edward C. 1979. *Principles of Archaeological Stratigraphy*. New York: Academic Press.

Harris, Marvin. 1979. *Cultural Materialism: The Struggle for a Science of Culture*. New York: Random House.

Harris, Oliver, and John Robb. Forthcoming. *Ontologies and the Material World: The Problem of the Body in History*.

Harrison, Rodney. 2011. Surface Assemblages: Towards an archaeology *in* and *of* the Present. *Archaeological Dialogues* 18(2): 141–61.

Harrison, Rodney, and John Schofield. 2010. *After Modernity: Archaeological Approaches to the Contemporary Past*. Oxford: Oxford University Press.

Hawkes, Christopher. 1954. Archaeological Theory and Method: Some Suggestions from the Old World. *American Anthropologist* 56: 155–68.

Hayles, N. Katherine. 1999. *How We Became Posthuman: Virtual Bodies in Cybernetics, Literature, and Informatics*. Chicago: University of Chicago Press.

Heidegger, Martin. 1962. *Being and Time*. New York: Harper & Row.

———. 1971. *Poetry, Language, Thought*. Translated by Albert Hofstadter. New York: Harper & Row.

———. 1993. The Question Concerning Technology. In *Martin Heidegger: Basic Writings*, ed. D. Farell Krell. San Francisco: Harper Collins.

———. 1994. Einblick in das was ist. In id., *Bremer und Freiburger Vorträge*. Frankfurt: Klostermann. Translated as Insight Into That Which Is: Bremen Lectures 1949, in *Bremen and Freiburg Lectures: Insight into That Which Is and Basic Principles of Thinking*. Bloomington: Indiana University Press.

Heizer, Robert, and John Graham. 1967. *A Guide to Field Methods in Archaeology: Approaches to the Anthropology of the Dead.* Palo Alto, CA: National Press.

Held, David. 1980. *Introduction to Critical Theory: Horkheimer to Habermas.* London: Hutchinson.

Henare, Amiria, Martin Holbraad, and Sari Wastell, eds. 2007. *Thinking through Things: Theorising Artefacts Ethnographically.* London: Routledge.

Hickman, Larry. 2001. *Philosophical Tools for Technological Culture: Putting Pragmatism to Work.* Bloomington: Indiana University Press.

Hicks, Dan, and Mary Beaudry, eds. 2010. *The Oxford Handbook of Material Culture Studies.* Oxford: Oxford University Press.

Hildebrand, Hans. 1873. *Den vetenskapliga fornforskingen, hennes uppgift, behof och rätt.* Stockholm.

Hine, Christine, ed. 2006. *New Infrastructures for Knowledge Production: Understanding E-science.* London: Information Science Publishing.

Hodder, Ian. 1982. *Symbols in Action: Ethnoarchaeological Studies of Material Culture.* Cambridge: Cambridge University Press.

———. 1984. Burials, Houses, Women and Men in the European Neolithic. In *Ideology, Power and Prehistory*, ed. Daniel Miller and Christopher Tilley, 51–68. Cambridge: Cambridge University Press .

———. 1990. *The Domestication of Europe.* Oxford: Blackwell.

———. 1993. The Narrative and Rhetoric of Material Culture Sequences. *World Archaeology* 25(2): 268–82.

———. 1997. Always, Momentary, Fluid and Flexible: Towards a Self-reflexive Excavation Methodology. *Antiquity* 71: 691–700.

———. 1999. *The Archaeological Process: An Introduction.* Oxford: Blackwell.

———, ed. 2000. *Towards Reflexive Method in Archaeology: The Example at Çatalhöyük.* Cambridge, MA: McDonald Institute for Archaeological Research.

———. 2002. Archaeological Theory. In *Archaeology: The Widening Debate*, ed. Barry Cunliffe, Wendy Davies, and Colin Renfrew, 77–90. Oxford: Oxford University Press.

———. 2003. Archaeological Reflexivity and the "Local" Voice. *Anthropological Quarterly* 76(1): 55–69.

———. 2011. Human-Thing Entanglement: Towards an Integrated Archaeological Perspective. *Journal of the Royal Anthropological Institute.* 17: 154–77.

Hodder, Ian, and Scott Hudson. 2003. *Reading the Past: Current Approaches to Interpretation in Archaeology.* 3rd ed. Cambridge: Cambridge University Press.

Hodder, Ian, Mark P. Leone, Reinhard Bernbeck, Michael Shanks, Silvia Tomášková, Patricia A. McAnany, Stephen Shennan, and Colin Renfrew. 2007. Review Feature: Revolution Fulfilled? *Symbolic and Structural Archaeology*, a Generation On. *Cambridge Archaeological Journal* 17(2): 199–228.

Holbraad, Martin. 2009. Ontology, Ethnography, Archaeology: An Afterword on the Ontology of Things. *Cambridge Archaeological Journal* 19(3): 431–41.

Holford-Strevens, L. 2005. *The History of Time: A Very Short Introduction.* Oxford: Oxford University Press.

Holtorf, Cornelius. 2005. *From Stonehenge to Las Vegas: Archaeology as Popular Culture.* Walnut Creek: Alta Mira Press.

———. 2007. *Archaeology Is a Brand!* Walnut Creek, CA: Left Coast Press.

Hope Simpson, Richard, and D.K. Hagel. 2006. *Mycenaean Fortifications, Highways, Dams, and Canals.* Sävedalen, Sweden: Paul Åströms Förlag.

Hughes, Thomas. 1983. *Networks of Power: Electrification in Western Society, 1880–1930.* Baltimore: Johns Hopkins University Press.

Hutchins, Edwin. 1995. *Cognition in the Wild.* Cambridge, MA: MIT Press.

Iakovidis, Spyros, and Elizabeth B. French. 2003. *Archaeological Atlas of Mycenae.* Athens: Library of the Athens Archaeological Society.

Ihde, Don. 1986. *Consequences of Phenomenology.* Albany, NY: State University of New York.

———. 1991. *Instrumental Realism: The Interface Between Philosophy of Science and Philosophy of Technology.* Bloomington: Indiana University Press.

Ihde, Don, and Evan Selinger, eds. 2003. *Chasing Technoscience: Matrix for Materiality.* Bloomington: Indiana University Press.

Ingold, Timothy. 1986. Tools and "Homo faber": Construction and the Authorship of Design. In *The Appropriation of Nature: Essays on Human Ecology and Social Relations,* ed. T. Ingold. Manchester: Manchester University Press.

———. 1988. Tools, Minds and Machines: An Excursion in the Philosophy of Technology. *Techniques et culture* 12: 151–76.

———. 1993. The Temporality of Landscape. *World Archaeology* 25(2): 152–74.

———. 2000. *The Perception of the Environment.* London: Routledge.

———. 2007. *Lines: A Brief History.* London: Routledge.

———. 2010. The Textility of Making. *Cambridge Journal of Economics.* 43: 91–102.

Introna, Lucas. 2009. Ethics and the Speaking of Things. *Theory, Culture & Society* 26(4): 25–46.

Ivins, William M. 1938. *On the Rationalization of Sight; with an Examination of Three Renaissance Texts on Perspective.* New York: Metropolitan Museum of Art.

———. 1953. *Prints and Visual Communication.* Cambridge, MA: The MIT Press.

James, William. 1925. *The Philosophy of William James.* New York: Random House.

———. 1978 [1907]. *Pragmatism and the Meaning of Truth.* Cambridge, MA: Harvard University Press.

Jameson, Michael H., Curtis N. Runnels, and Tjeerd H. van Andel. 1994. *A Greek Countryside: The Southern Argolid from Prehistory to the Present Day.* Stanford, CA: Stanford University Press.

Jenkins, Henry. 2006. *Convergence Culture: Where Old and New Media Collide.* New York: New York University Press.

Jenkins, Ian. 2001. *Cleaning and Controversy: The Parthenon Sculptures, 1811–1939.* London: Trustees of the British Museum.

Jensen, Casper Bruun. 2003. Latour and Pickering: Post-human Perspectives on Science, Becoming, and Normativity. In *Chasing Technoscience: Matrix for Materiality*, ed. Don Ihde and Evan Selinger, 225–40. Bloomington, IN: Indiana University Press.

Jensen, Jørgen. 1992. *Thomsens Museum: Historien om Nationalmuseet*. Copenhagen: Gyldendal.

Jones, Andrew. 2007. *Memory and Material Culture*. Cambridge: Cambridge University Press.

Joukowsky, Martha. 1980. *A Complete Manual of Field Archaeology: Tools and Techniques of Field Work for Archaeologists*. Englewood Cliffs, NJ: Prentice-Hall.

Joyce, Rosemary (with Robert Preucel and Jeanne Lopiparo). 2002. *The Languages of Archaeology: Dialogue, Narrative, and Writing*. Oxford: Blackwell.

Kant, Immanuel. 2001 [1783]. *Prolegomena to Any Future Metaphysics*. Indianapolis: Hackett.

Karlsson, Hakan, ed. 2001. *It's About Time: The Concept of Time in Archaeology*. Göteborg, Sweden: Bricoleur Press.

———, ed. 2004. *Swedish Archaeologists on Ethics*. Lindome, Sweden: Bricoleur Press

Kaye, Nick. 2000. *Site-Specific Art: Performance, Place and Documentation*. London: Routledge.

Kehoe, Alice, and Mary Beth Emmerichs, eds. 2000. *Assembling the Past: Studies in the Professionalization of Archaeology*. Albuquerque: University of New Mexico Press.

Kehoe, Elizabeth. 2004. Working Hard at Giving It Away: Lord Duveen, the British Museum and the Elgin marbles. *Historical Research* 77(198): 503–19.

Kelly, Thomas. 1976. *A History of Argos to 500 B.C.* Minneapolis: University of Minnesota Press.

Kintigh, Keith. 2006. The Promise and Challenge of Archaeological Data Integration. *American Antiquity* 71(3): 567–78.

Klein, Nancy L. 1997. Excavation of the Greek Temples at Mycenae by the British School at Athens. *Annual of the British School at Athens* 92: 247–322.

Klindt-Jensen, Ole. 1975. *A History of Scandinavian Archaeology*. London: Thames & Hudson.

Knappett, Carl. 2005. *Thinking through Material Culture: An Interdisciplinary Perspective*. Philadelphia: University of Pennsylvania Press.

Knappett, Carl, and Lambros Malaforis, eds. 2008. *Material Agency: Towards a Non-Anthropocentric Approach*. New York: Springer.

Kristeva, Julia. 1982. *The Power of Horror: An Essay in Abjection*. Oxford: Blackwell.

Kristiansen, Kristian. 2006. Cosmology, Economy and Long-term Change in the Bronze Age of Northern Europe. In *Ecology and Economy in Stone Age and Bronze Age Scania*, ed. Karl-Göran Sjögren. Lund, Sweden: Riksantikvarieämbetes förlag.

Kohl, Philip L. 1981. Materialist Approaches in Prehistory. *Annual Review of Anthropology* 10: 89–118.

Kroeber, Alfred L., and Clyde Kluckhohn. 1952. *Culture: A Critical Review of Concepts and Definitions*. New York: Vintage Books.

Kuchler, Susanne. 1987. Malangan: Art and Memory in a Melanesian Society. *Man* 22(2), 238–55.

Kuper, Adam. 1978. *Anthropologists and Anthropology: The British School, 1922–72*. Harmondsworth, UK: Penguin Books.

Kurke, Leslie. 1992. The Politics of *habrosune* in Archaic Greece. *Classical Antiquity* 11: 91–120.

———. 1993. The Economy of *kudos*. In *Cultural Politics in Archaic Greece*, ed. Carol Dougherty and Leslie Kurke, 131–62. Cambridge: Cambridge University Press .

Lampland, Martha, and Susan Leigh Star, eds. 2009. *Standards and Their Stories: How Quantifying, Classifying, and Formalizing Practices Shape Everyday Life*. Ithaca, NY: Cornell University Press.

Larsen, Jens-Eirik, Bjørnar Olsen, Anders Hesjedal, and Inger Storli. 1993. *Camera archaeologica: Rapport fra et feltarbeid*. Tromsø Museums Skrifter, 23. Tromsø, Norway: Tromsø Museum.

Latour, Bruno. 1986. Visualization and Cognition: Thinking with Eyes and Hands. *Knowledge and Society: Studies in the Sociology of Culture Past and Present* 6 (ed. Henrika Kuklick and Elizabeth Long): 1–40.

———. 1987. *Science in Action: How to Follow Scientists and Engineers through Society*. Cambridge, MA: Harvard University Press.

———. 1993. *We Have Never Been Modern*. Translated by Catherine Porter. Cambridge, MA: Harvard University Press.

———. 1999. *Pandora's Hope: Essays on the Reality of Science Studies*. Cambridge, MA: Harvard University Press.

———. 2002. Morality and Technology: The End of Means. *Theory, Culture & Society* 19(5–6).

———. 2003. Is Re-modernization Occurring? *Theory, Culture and Society* 20(2): 35–48.

———. 2004. *Politics of Nature: How to Bring the Sciences into Democracy*. Cambridge, MA: Harvard University Press.

———. 2005. *Reassembling the Social: An Introduction to Actor-Network-Theory*. Oxford: Oxford University Press.

———. 2010. An Attempt at Writing a "Compositionist Manifesto." *New Literary History*. 41: 471–90.

Latour, Bruno, and Emile Hermant. 1998. *Paris ville invisible*. Paris: La Découverte–Les Empêcheurs de penser en rond.

Latour, Bruno, and Adam Lowe. 2011. The Migration of the Aura, or How to Explore the Original through Its Facsimiles. In *Switching Codes: Thinking through Digital Technology in the Humanities and the Arts*, ed. Thomas Bartscherer and Roderick Coover, 275–98. Chicago: University of Chicago Press.

Latour, Bruno, and Peter Weibel, eds. 2005. *Making Things Public: Atmospheres of Democracy*. Cambridge, MA: MIT Press.

Latour, Bruno, and Steve Woolgar. 1986 [1979]. *Laboratory Life: The Construction of Scientific Facts*. 2nd ed. Princeton, NJ: Princeton University Press.

Latour, Bruno, and Albena Yaneva. 2008. Give Me a Gun and I Will Make All Buildings Move: An ANT's View of Architecture. In *Explorations in Architecture: Teaching, Design, Research*, ed. Reto Geiser, 80–89. Basel: Birkhäuser.

Law, John. 1987. Technology and Heterogeneous Engineering: The Case of Portuguese Expansion. In *The Social Construction of Technological Systems: New Directions in the Sociology and History of Technology*, ed. Wiebe E. Bijker, Thomas P. Hughes, and Trevor J. Pinch. Cambridge, MA: MIT Press.

———. 1994. *Organizing Modernity*. Oxford: Blackwell.

———. 2004. *After Method: Mess in Social Science Research*. London: Routledge.

Law, John, and J. Hassard. 1999. *Actor Network Theory and After*. Oxford: Blackwell.

Leach, Edmund. 1973. Concluding Address. In *The Explanation of Culture Change: Models in Prehistory*, ed. Colin Renfrew. Pittsburgh: University of Pittsburgh Press.

Leake, William Martin. 1830. *Travels in the Morea*. 3 vols. London: John Murray.

Lefebvre, Henri. 1987. The Everyday and Everydayness. *Yale French Studies* 73 (Fall): 7–77.

Lemonnier, Pierre. 1992. *Elements for an Anthropology of Technology*. Ann Arbor: University of Michigan Press.

———, ed. 1993. *Technical Choices: Transformations in Material Cultures since the Neolithic*. New York: Routledge.

Lenoir, Timothy. 1998. *Inscribing Science: Scientific Texts and the Materiality of Communication*. Stanford, CA: Stanford University Press.

Leone, Mark. 1982. Some Opinions about Recovering Mind. *American Antiquity* 47(4): 742–60.

———. 2007. Beginning for a Postmodern Archaeology. *Cambridge Archaeological Journal* 17(2), 203–7.

Leroi-Gourhan, André. 1993[1964]. *Gesture and Speech*. Translated by A.B. Berger. Cambridge, MA: MIT Press.

Lessig, Lawrence. 2008. *Remix: Making Art and Commerce Thrive in the Hybrid Economy*. London: Bloomsbury Academic.

Lipe, William. 1974. A Conservation Model for American Archaeology. *Kiva* 39(3–4): 213–45.

Lolos, Yannis A. 1997. The Hadrianic Aqueduct of Corinth. *Hesperia* 66(2), 271–314.

López Luján, Leonardo, Hector Neff, and Saburo Sugiyama. 2000. A Classic Thin Orange Vessel Found at Tenochtitlan. In *Mesoamerica's Classic Heritage. From Teotihuacan to the Aztecs*, eds. D. Carrasco, L. Jones, and S. Sessions, 219–49. Boulder: University Press of Colorado.

Lowenthal, David. 1996. *Possessed by the Past: The Heritage Crusade and the Spoils of History*. New York: Free Press.

Lucas, Gavin. 2001a. *Critical Approaches to Fieldwork. Contemporary and Historical Archaeological Practice*. London: Routledge.

———. 2001b. Destruction and the Rhetoric of Excavation. *Norwegian Archaeology Review* 34(1): 35–46.

———. 2005. *The Archaeology of Time*. London: Routledge.

———. 2010. Fieldwork and Collecting. In *The Oxford Handbook of Material Culture Studies*, ed. Dan Hicks and Mary Beaudry. Oxford: Oxford University Press.

———. 2012. Understanding *the Archaeological Record*. Cambridge: Cambridge University Press.

Lynch, Michael. 1990. The Externalized Retina: Selection and Mathematization in the Visual Documentation of Objects in the Life Sciences. In*Representation in Scientific Practice*, ed. Michael Lynch and Steve Woolgar. Cambridge, MA: MIT Press.

Lynch, Michael, and Samuel Edgerton. 1988. Aesthetics and Digital Image Processing: Representational Craft in Contemporary Astronomy. In*Picturing Power: Visual Depiction and Social Relations*, ed. Gordon Fyfe and John Law. London: Routledge.

Lynch, Michael, and Steve Woolgar. 1990. *Representation and Scientific Practice*. Cambridge, MA: MIT Press.

Lynnot, Mark, and Alison Wylie. 1995. *Ethics in American Archaeology: Challenges for the 1990's*. Washington, DC: Society for American Archaeology.

Lyons, Claire. 2000. Cleaning the Parthenon Sculptures. British Museum, London, England (November 30–December 1). *International Journal of Cultural Property* 9(1): 180–84.

Macfarlane, Alan, and Gerry Martin. 2002. *Glass: A World History*. Chicago: University of Chicago Press.

MacKay, Pierre. 1968. Acrocorinth in 1668, a Turkish Account. *Hesperia* 37(4): 386–97.

MacKenzie, Donald, and Judy Wajcman, eds. 1999. *The Social Shaping of Technology*. Milton Keynes, UK: Open University Press.

Madsen, Andreas P., Sophus Müller, Carl Neergaard, Carl George J. Petersen, Emil Rostrup, Knud Johannes V. Steenstrup, and Herluf Winge. 1900. *Affaldsdvnger fra Stenalderen i Danmark undersøgte for Nationalmuseet*. Copenhagen: C.A. Reitzel.

Makarius, Michel. 2004. *Ruines*. Paris: Flammarion.

Malafouris, Lambros. 2004. The Cognitive Basis of Mind with Material World. In *Rethinking Materiality: The Engagement of Mind with the Material World*, ed. Elizabeth DeMarrais, Chris Gosden and Colin Renfrew, 53–62. Cambridge: McDonald Institute for Archaeological Research.

———. 2008. "At the Potter's Wheel: An Argument *for* Material Agency." In *Material Agency: Towards a Non-Anthropocentric Approach*, ed. Carl Knappett and Lambros Malaforis, 19–36. New York: Springer.

Malafouris, Lambros, and Colin Renfrew, eds. 2010. *The Cognitive Life of Things: Recasting the Boundaries of the Mind*. Cambridge: McDonald Institute for Archaeological Research.

Malinowski, Bronislaw. 1935. *Coral Gardens and Their Magic*. London: Routledge.

———. 2002 [1922]. *Argonauts of the Western Pacific*. London: Routledge.

Manovich, Lev. 2001. *The Language of New Media*. Cambridge, MA: MIT Press.

Marx, Karl. 1975. *Early Writings*. Harmondsworth, UK: Penguin Books.

Maschner, Herbert, and Christopher Chippindale. 2005. *Handbook of Archaeological Methods*. 2 vols. Lanham, MD: Alta Mira Press.

Matos Moctezuma, Eduardo. 1990. *Teotihuacán: The City of Gods*. New York: Rizzoli International Publications.

Matthews, E. 2002. *The Philosophy of Merleau-Ponty*. Montreal: McGill-Queen's University Press.

Matzaridis, Prodromos. 1996. Συνοπτικό Ιστορικό των Ελληνικών Σιδηροδρόμων [Concise History of the Greek Railways]. 2nd ed. Athens: Greek State Railways.

McDonald, William A., and George R. Rapp. 1972. *The Minnesota Messenia Expedition. Reconstructing a Bronze Age Regional Environment*. Minneapolis: University of Minnesota Press.

McGlade, James. 1999. The Times of History: Archaeology, Narrative and Non-linear Causality. In *Time and Archaeology*, ed. Tim Murray 139–63. London: Routledge.

McGlade, James, and Sander E. van der Leeuw, eds. 1997. *Time, Process and Structured Transformation in Archaeology*. London: Routledge.

McGuire, Randall. 2007. Foreword. In *Archaeology and Capitalism. From Ethics to Politics*, ed. Yannis Hamilakis and Philip Duke. Walnut Creek, CA: Left Coast Press.

———. 2008. *Archaeology as Political Action*. Berkeley: University of California Press.

McLuhan, Marshall. 1994 [1964]. *Understanding Media: The Extensions of Man*. Corte Madera, CA: Gingko Press.

Meillassoux, Quentin. 2008. *After Finitude: An Essay on the Necessity of Contingency*. Translated by Ray Brassier. London: Continuum.

Merleau-Ponty, Maurice. 1968. *The Visible and the Invisible*. Evanston, IL: Northwestern University Press.

Meskell, Lynn, ed. 2005. *Archaeologies of Materiality*. Oxford: Wiley-Blackwell.

Meskell, Lynn, and Rosemary Joyce. 2003. *Embodied Lives: Figuring Ancient Maya and Egyptian Experience*. London: Routledge.

Mihesuah, Devon, ed. 2000. *Repatriation Reader: Who owns American Indian Remains?* Lincoln: University of Nebraska Press.

Miller, Daniel. 1987. *Material Culture and Mass Consumption*. Oxford: Blackwell.

———. 2010. *Stuff*. Cambridge: Polity.

Miller, William. 1966. *The Ottoman Empire and Its Successors, 1801–1927*. New York: Octagon Books.

Millon, René. 1973. *The Teotihuacán Map, Volume 1, Part 1*. Austin: University of Texas Press.

———. 1993. The Place Where Time Began. An Archaeologist's Interpretation of What Happened in Teotihuacán History. In *Teotihuacan: Art from the City of the Gods*, ed. Kathleen Berrin and Esther Pasztory. San Francisco: Fine Arts Museums of San Francisco; London: Thames & Hudson.

Millon, René, Bruce Drewitt, and George Cowgill. 1973. *The Teotihuacán Map, Volume 1, Part 2*. Austin: University of Texas Press.

Mills, Barbara J., and William H. Walker. 2008. *Memory Work: Archaeologies of Material Practices*. Santa Fe, NM: School for Advanced Research Press.

Mol, Annemarie. 2002. *The Body Multiple: Ontology in Medical Practice*. Durham, NC: Duke University Press.

———. 2008. *The Logic of Care*. London: Routledge.

Mol, Annemarie, Ingunn Moser, and Jeannette Pols. 2010. *Care in Practice: On Tinkering in Clinics, Homes and Farms*. Bielefeld, Germany: Transcript Verlag.

Mol, Annemarie, and John Law. 1994. Regions, Networks and Fluids: Anaemia and Social Topology. *Social Studies of Science* 24(4): 641–71.

Molyneaux, Brian, ed. 1997. *The Cultural Life of Images: Visual Representation in Archaeology*. London: Routledge.

Momigliano, Arnaldo. 1950. Ancient History and the Antiquarian. *Journal of the Warburg and Courtauld Institutes* 13(3–4): 285–315.

Montelius, Oscar. 1900. Typologien eller utvecklingsläran tillämpad på det mänskliga arbetet. *Svenska Fornminnesföreningens Tidskrift*, 10: 237–68.

Morelos García, Noel. 1993. *Proceso de producción de espacios y estructuras en Teotihuacán: Conjunto Plaza Oeste y complejo Calle de los Muertos*. Mexico City: Instituto Nacional de Antropología e Historia.

Morgan, Catherine, and Todd Whitelaw. 2001. Pots and Politics: Ceramic Evidence of the Rise of the Argive State. *American Journal of Archaeology* 95(1): 79–108.

Morris, Ian. 1987. *Burial and Ancient Society: The Rise of the Greek City-State*. Cambridge: Cambridge University Press.

———. 1994. Archaeologies of Greece. In *Classical Greece: Ancient Histories and Modern Archaeologies*, ed. id., 3–47. Cambridge: Cambridge University Press.

Moser, Stephanie. 2001. Archaeological Representation: The Visual Conventions for Constructing Knowledge about the Past. In *Archaeological Theory Today*, ed. Ian Hodder, 262–83. Cambridge: Polity Press.

Murdoch, Jonathan. 1997a. Toward a Geography of Heterogeneous Associations. *Progress in Human Geography* 21(3): 321–37.

———. 1997b. Inhuman/Nonhuman/Human: Actor-network Theory and the Prospects for a Nondualistic and Symmetrical Perspective on Nature and Society. *Environment and Planning D: Society and Space* 15(6): 731–56.

Myrstad, R. 1996. *Bjørnegraver I Nord-Norge: Spor etter den samiske bjørnekulten*. Stensilserie B, historie/arkeologi, no. 46. Tromsø, Norway: University of Tromsø.

Neuhaus, Fabian, and Timothy Webmoor. 2012. Agile Ethics for Massified Research and Visualisation. *Information, Communication and Society* 15(1): 43–65.

Nichols, Deborah L., Rosemary A. Joyce, and Susan D. Gillespie. 2003. Is Archaeology Anthropology? In *Archeological Papers of the American Anthropological Association*, no. 13, special issue, *Archeology Is Anthropology*, ed. Susan D. Gillespie and Deborah L. Nichols, 3–13.

Nora, Pierre. 1984. Entre mémoire et histoire: La problématique des lieux. In *Les lieux de mémoire*, vol. 1: *La République*, ed. id. Paris: Gallimard.

Norman, Donald. 2002. *The Design of Everyday Things*. New York: Basic Books.

November, Valerie, Eduardo Camacho-Hubner, and Bruno Latour. 2010. Entering a Risky Territory: Space in the Age of Digital Navigation. *Environment, Planning and Design D* 28(4): 581–99.

O'Brien, Michael J., R. Lee Lyman, and Michael Brian Schiffer. 2005. *Archaeology as Process: Processualism and Its Progeny*. Salt Lake City: University of Utah Press.

O'Brien, Michael J., and Stephen J. Shennan, eds. 2009. *Innovation in Cultural Systems. Contributions from Evolutionary Anthropology*. Cambridge, MA: MIT Press.

Olivier, Laurent. 2001. Duration, Memory and the Nature of the Archaeological Record. In *It's About Time: The Concept of Time in Archaeology*, ed. Håkan Karlsson, 61–70. Göteborg, Sweden: Bricoleur Press.

———. 2004. The Past of the Present. Archaeological Memory and Time. *Archaeological Dialogues* 10(2): 204–13.

———. 2008. *Le sombre abîme du temps. Mémoire et archéologie*. Paris: Seuil.

Olsen, Bjørnar. 1991. Metropolises and satellites in archaeology: on power and asymmetry in global archaeological discourse. In *Processual and Postprocessual Archaeologies: Multiple Ways of Knowing the Past*, ed. Robert W. Preucel. Carbondale: University of Southern Illinois Press.

———. 2001. The end of history. Archaeology and the politics of identity in a globalized world. In *The Destruction and Conservation of Cultural Property*, ed. R. Layton, P. Stone, and J. Thomas. London: Routledge.

———. 2003. Material Culture after Text: Re-Membering Things. *Norwegian Archaeological Review* 36(2): 87–104.

———. 2005. Scenes from a Troubled Engagement. Post-structuralism and Material Culture Studies. In *Handbook of Material Culture*, ed. C. Tilley, W. Keane, S. Kuechler, M. Rowlands, and P. Spyer, 85–103. London: Sage.

———. 2007. Keeping Things at Arm's Length. A Genealogy of Asymmetry. *World Archaeology* 39(4): 579–88.

———. 2010. *In Defense of Things: Archaeology and the Ontology of Objects*. Lanham, MD: AltaMira Press.

———. 2012. Symmetrical Archaeology. In *Archaeological Theory Today*, ed. Ian Hodder. Cambridge: Polity Press.

Olsen, Bjørnar, and Asgeir Svestad 1994. Creating Prehistory. Archaeology Museums and the Discourse of Modernism. *Nordisk Museologi* 1: 3–20.

Palter, Robert M. 1970. *Whitehead's Philosophy of Science*. Chicago: University of Chicago Press.

Parker Pearson, Mike, and Colin Richards. 1999. *Architecture and Order. Approaches to Social Space*. London: Routledge.

Parker Pearson, Mike, Josh Pollard, Colin Richards, Julian Thomas, Christopher Tilley, Kate Welham, and Umberto Albarella. 2006. Materializing Stonehenge: The Stonehenge Riverside Project and New Discoveries. *Journal of Material Culture*. 11(1–2): 227–61.

Pasztory, Esther. 1997. *Teotihuacan: An Experiment in Living*. Norman, OK: University of Oklahoma Press.

Patrik, Linda. 1985. Is There an Archaeological Record? In *Advances in Archaeological Method and Theory*, ed. Michael Schiffer, 8: 27–62. New York: Academic Press.

Patterson, Thomas C. 1995. *Toward a Social History of Archaeology in the United States*. Fort Worth, TX: Harcourt Brace.

Payne, Humfry. 1931. *Necrocorinthia: A Study of Corinthian Art in the Archaic Period*. Oxford: Clarendon Press.

———. 1933. *Protokorinthische Vasenmalerei*. Berlin: Keller.

Pearson, Mike, and Michael Shanks. 2001. *Theatre/Archaeology*. London: Routledge.

Peirce, Charles Sanders. 1940. *Philosophical Writings of Peirce*. New York: Dover.

Pels, Peter. 1998. The Spirit of Matter: On Fetish, Rarity, Fact, and Fancy. In *Border Fetishisms. Material Objects in Unstable Spaces*, ed. P. Spyer. London: Routledge.

Perlès, Catherine. 2001. *The Early Neolithic in Greece*. Cambridge: Cambridge University Press.

Petersen, Julius, and Thomas Bartholin. 1898. *Bartholinerne og kredsen om dem*. Copenhagen: G. E. C. Gad.

Petrelli, Daniella, Elise van den Hoven, and Steve Whittaker. 2009. Making History: Intentional Capture of Future Memories. Proceedings of the 27th International Conference on Human Factors in Computing Systems. www.elisevandenhoven.com/publications/petrelli-chi09.pdf (accessed April 15, 2012).

Petrie, William Matthew Flinders. 1904. *Methods & Aims in Archaeology*. London: Macmillan.

Pfaffenberger, Bryan. 1992. Social Anthropology of Technology. *Annual Review of Anthropology* 21: 491–516.

Pickering, Andrew. 1995. *The Mangle of Practice: Time, Agency and Science*. Chicago: University of Chicago Press.

Piérart, Marcel, and Gilles Touchais. 1996. *Argos. Une ville grecque de 6000 ans*. Paris: Centre national de la recherche scientifique.

Piggott, Stuart. 1965. Archaeological Draughtsmanship. Principles and Practice, Part I: Principles and Retrospect. *Antiquity* 39, 165–78.

Pinney, Christopher. 2005. Things Happen. Or, From What Moment Does That Object Come? In *Materiality*, ed. Daniel Miller. Durham, NC: Duke University Press.

Plog, Stephen, ed. 1986. *Spatial Organization and Exchange: Archaeological Survey on Northern Black Mesa*. Carbondale: Southern Illinois University Press.

Pluciennik, Mark. 2005. *Social Evolution*. London: Duckworth.

Pomian, Krzysztof. 1990. *Collectors and Curiosities. Paris and Venice, 1500–1800*. Cambridge: Polity Press.

Pomian, Kryzsztof. 1998. Vision and Cognition. In *Picturing Science, Producing Art*, ed. C. Jones and P. Galison, 211–31. London: Routledge.

Popper, Karl R. 1972. *Objective Knowledge: An Evolutionary Approach*. Oxford: Clarendon Press.

Preda, Alex. 1999. The Turn to Things: Arguments for a Sociological Theory of Things. *Sociological Quarterly* 40(2): 347–66.

Price, Neil. 2002. *The Viking Way. Religion and War in Late Iron Age Scandinavia.* Uppsala, Sweden: Uppsala Department of Archaeology and Ancient History.

Prigogine, Ilya, and Isabelle Stengers. 1984. *Order Out of Chaos. Man's New Dialogue with Nature.* Toronto: Bantam Books.

Puig de la Bellacasa, Maria. 2011. Matters of Care in Technoscience: Assembling Neglected Things. *Social Studies of Science* 41(1): 85–106.

Putnam, Hilary. 1981. *Reason, Truth and History.* Cambridge: Cambridge University Press.

———. 1988. *Representation and Reality.* Cambridge, MA: MIT Press.

———. 2002. *Pragmatism and Realism.* London: Routledge.

Pye, David. 1968. *The Nature and Art of Workmanship.* Cambridge: Cambridge University Press.

Quirke, Stephen. 2010. *Hidden Hands: Egyptian Workforces in Petrie Excavation Archives.* London: Duckworth Publishers.

Raaflaub, Kurt A., Josiah Ober, and Robert Wallace, eds. 2007. *Origins of Democracy in Ancient Greece.* Berkeley: University of California Press.

Ramenofsky, Ann F. 1998. The Illusion of Time. In *Unit Issues in Archaeology: Measuring Time, Space and Material,* eds. Ann F. Ramenofsky and Anastasia Steffen, 74–86. Salt Lake City: University of Utah Press.

Raskin, Jef. 2002. *The Human Interface: New Directions for Designing Interactive Systems.* Reading, MA: Addison Wesley.

Rathje, William. 1989. Rubbish! *The Atlantic* 246(6): 99–109.

Rathje, William, and Cullen Murphy. 1992. *Rubbish! The Archaeology of Garbage.* New York: Harper Collins.

Read, Rob, and Graham Smith. 2009. Training the Undervalued and Unacknowledged: Specialist Training for Archaeological Illustrators in the UK. Presentation at the 2nd Visualisation in Archaeology Conference, Southampton, UK.

Redman, Charles L. 1973. Multistage Fieldwork and Analytical Techniques. *American Antiquity* 38: 61–79.

Register of Professional Archaeologists. 2002 [1998]. Code of Conduct. www .rpanet.org/displaycommon.cfm?an=1&subarticlenbr=3 (accessed 10 May 2012). Cited as RPA.

Renfrew, Colin. 1973. *The Explanation of Culture Change.* London: Duckworth.

———. 1976. Megaliths, Territories and Population. In *Acculturation and Continuity in Atlantic Europe,* ed. Sigfried de Laet, 198–220. Bruges: De Tempel.

———. 1993. Cognitive Archaeology: Some Thoughts on the Archaeology of Thought. *Cambridge Archaeological Journal* 3(2): 248–50.

———. 2003. *Figuring It Out. What Are We? Where Do We Come From? The Parallel Visions of Artists and Archaeologists.* London: Thames & Hudson.

———. 2004. Towards a Theory of Material Engagement. In*Rethinking Materiality: The Engagement of Mind with the Material World,* ed. E. DeMarrais, C. Gosden, and C. Renfrew, 23–31. McDonald Institute Monographs, Cambridge.

Renfrew, Colin, and John F. Cherry. 1986. *Peer Polity Interaction and Socio-Political Change*. Cambridge: Cambridge University Press.

Renfrew, Colin, and Ezra Zubrow, eds. 1994. *The Ancient Mind: Elements of Cognitive Archaeology*. Cambridge: Cambridge University Press.

Renfrew, Colin, and Paul Bahn. 1996. *Archaeology. Theories, Methods and Practice*. London: Thames & Hudson.

Renfrew, Colin, Chris Frith, and Lambros Malafouris, eds. 2009. *The Sapient Mind: Archaeology Meets Neuroscience*. Oxford: Oxford University Press.

Renfrew, Colin, and Lambros Malafouris. 2010. *The Cognitive Life of Things. Recasting the Boundaries of the Mind*. Cambridge: McDonald Institute for Archaeological Research.

Rescher, Nicholas. 2005. *Reason and Reality: Realism and Idealism in Pragmatic Perspective*. Oxford: Rowman & Littlefield.

Roberts, Russell, with Anthony Burnett-Brown and Michael Gray, eds. 2000. *Specimens and Marvels: William Henry Fox Talbot and the Invention of Photography*. New York: Aperture.

Robertson, Ian. 2001. Mapping the Social Landscape of an Early Urban Center: Socio-spatial variation in Teotihuacan. PhD diss., Arizona State University.

Rorty, Richard. 1979. *Philosophy and the Mirror of Nature*. Princeton, NJ: Princeton University Press.

Rosaldo, Renato. 1986. From the Door of his Tent: The Fieldworker and the Inquisitor. In *Writing Culture: The Poetics and Politics of Ethnography*, ed. J. Clifford and G.E. Marcus, 77–97. Berkeley: University of California Press.

Roskams, Steve. 2000. *Excavation*. Cambridge: Cambridge University Press.

Rothaus, Richard M. 2000. *Corinth, the First City of Greece: An Urban History of Late Antique Cult and Religion*. Leiden: Brill.

Rowlands, Michael. 2002. Heritage and Cultural Property. In *The Material Culture Reader*, ed. Victor Buchli. Oxford: Berg.

Rudwick, Martin. 1976. The Emergence of a Visual Language for Geological Science, 1760–1840. *History of Science* 14(3): 149–95.

Ruskin, John. 2001 [1849]. *The Seven Lamps of Architecture*. Cambridge: Electric Book Company.

Sackett, James. 1982. Approaches to Style in Lithic Archaeology. *Journal of Anthropological Archaeology* 1(1): 59–82.

———. 1985. Style and Ethnicity in the Kalahari: A Reply to Weissner. *American Antiquity* 50(1): 154–59.

Sahlins, Marshall, and Elman Service, eds. 1960. *Evolution and Culture*. Ann Arbor: University of Michigan Press.

Salmon, J.B. 1984. *Wealthy Corinth: A History of the City to 338 BC*. Oxford: Clarendon Press.

Scarre, Christopher, and Geoffrey Scarre. 2006. *The Ethics of Archaeology: Philosophical Perspectives on Archaeological Practice*. Cambridge: Cambridge University Press.

Schanche, Audhild. 2000. *Graver I ur og berg. Samisk gravskikk og religion fra forhistorisk til nyere tid*. Karasjok, Norway: Davvi Girji OS.

Scharff, Robert C., and Val Dusek, eds. 2003. *Philosophy of Technology: The Technological Condition*. Malden, MA: Blackwell.

Schiffer, Michael Brian. 1976. *Behavioral Archaeology*. New York: Academic Press.

———. 1978. Methodological Issues in Ethnoarchaeology. In *Explorations in Ethnoarchaeology*, ed. R.A. Gould, 229–47. Albuquerque: University of New Mexico Press.

———. 1987. *Formation Processes of the Archaeological Record*. Santa Fe: University of New Mexico Press.

———. 1988. The Structure of Archaeological Theory. *American Antiquity* 53: 461–85.

———. 2008. *Power Struggles: Scientific Authority and the Creation of Practical Electricity before Edison*. Cambridge MA: MIT Press.

———. 2011. *Studying Technological Change: A Behavioral Approach*. Salt Lake City: University of Utah Press.

Schiffer, Michael Brian, and Andrea R. Miller. 1999. *The Material Life of Human Beings: Artifacts, Behaviour, and Communication*. London: Routledge.

Schiffer, Michael Brian, Alan P. Sullivan, and Timothy C. Klinger. 1978. The Design of Archaeological Surveys. *World Archaeology* 10: 1–28.

Schlanger, Nathan, and Jarl Nordbladh, eds. 2008. *Archives, Ancestors, Practices: Archaeology in the Light of Its History*. New York: Berghahn Books.

Schnapp, Alain. 1997. *The Discovery of the Past: The Origins of Archaeology*. Translated by I.K. a. G. Varndell. London: British Museum Press.

Schnapp, Jeffrey T., and Michael Shanks. 2009. Artereality (Rethinking Craft in a Knowledge Economy). In *Art School (Propositions for the 21st Century)*, ed. Steven Henry Madoff. Cambridge, MA: MIT Press.

Schnapp, Jeffrey T., Michael Shanks, and Matthew Tiews, eds. 2004. *Archaeologies of the Modern*. Special Issue of *Modernism/Modernity* 11(1).

Scott, Sir Walter. 1814. *The Border Antiquities of England and Scotland; Comprising Specimens of Architecture and Sculpture, and Other Vestiges of Former Ages, Accompanied By Descriptions. Together With Illustrations of Remarkable Incidents in Border History and Tradition, and Original Poetry*. 2 vols. London: Longman, Hurst, Rees, Orme, and Brown.

Sennett, Richard. 2008. *The Craftsman*. New Haven, CT: Yale University Press.

Serrano Sánchez, Carlos, ed. 2003. *Contextos arqueológicos y osteología del barrio de La Ventilla (Teotihuacan 1992–1994)*. Mexico City: Universidad Nacional Autónoma de México.

Serres, Michel. 1982. *Hermes: Literature, Science, Philosophy*. Baltimore: Johns Hopkins University Press.

———. 1995a. *Genesis*. Translated by G. James and J. Nielson. Ann Arbor: University of Michigan Press.

———. 1995b. *The Natural Contract*. Translated by E. MacAuthur and W. Paulson. Ann Arbor: University of Michigan Press.

Serres, Michel, with Bruno Latour. 1995. *Conversations on Science, Culture, and Time*. Translated by R. Lapidus. Ann Arbor: University of Michigan Press.

Service, Elman. 1962. *Primitive Social Organization: An Evolutionary Perspective*. New York: Random House.

Shanks, Michael. 1991. *Experiencing the Past: On the Character of Archaeology*. London: Routledge.

———. 1992. Style and the Design of an Archaic Korinthian perfume jar. *Journal of European Archaeology* 1:77–106.

———. 1995. Art and the Archaeology of the Early Greek City-State: A Project of Embodiment. *Cambridge Archaeological Journal* 5:1–38.

———. 1996. *Classical Archaeology of Greece: Experiences of the Discipline.* London: Routledge.

———. 1997. Photography and Archaeology. In *The Cultural Life of Images: Visual Representation in Archaeology,* ed. B. Molyneaux, 73–104. London: Routledge.

———. 1999. *Art and the Early Greek City-State.* Cambridge: Cambridge University Press.

———. 2004. Three Rooms. *Journal of Social Archaeology* 4: 147–80.

———. 2007. Digital Media, Agile Design, and the Politics of Archaeological Authorship. In *Archaeology and the Media,* ed. Timothy Clack and Marcus Brittain, 273–89. Walnut Creek, CA: Left Coast Press.

———. 2008. Cultural Property. In *The New Oxford Companion to Law,* ed. Peter Cane and Joanne Conaghan, 288–89. Oxford: Oxford University Press.

———. 2012. *The Archaeological Imagination.* Walnut Creek, CA: Left Coast Press.

Shanks, Michael, and Lynn Hershman Leeson. 2007. Conversation. *Seed,* no. 12 (August 27, 2007). http://seedmagazine.com/content/article/michael_shanks _lynn_hershman_leeson (accessed April 15, 2012).

Shanks, Michael, and Randall McGuire. 1996. The Craft of Archaeology. *American Antiquity* 61(1): 75–88.

Shanks, Michael, and Christopher Tilley. 1982. Ideology, Symbolic Power and Ritual Communication: A Reinterpretation of Neolithic Mortuary Practices. In *Symbolic and Structural Archaeology,* ed. Ian Hodder, 129–54. Cambridge: Cambridge University Press.

———. 1987. *Social Theory in Archaeology.* Albuquerque: University of New Mexico Press.

———. 1992. *Reconstructing Archaeology.* London: Routledge.

Shanks, Michael, and Timothy Webmoor. 2012. A Political Economy of Visual Media in Archaeology. In *Re-presenting the Past: Archaeology through Image and Text,* ed. Sheila Bonde and Stephen Houston. Oxford: Oxbow Books.

Shanks, Michael, and Christopher Witmore. 2010a. Memory Practices and the Archaeological Imagination in Risk Society: Design and Long-Term Community. In *Unquiet Pasts: Theoretical Perspectives on Archaeology and Cultural Heritage,* ed. Ian Russell and Stephanie Koerner, 269–90. Farnham, UK: Ashgate.

———. 2010b. Echoes across the Past: Chorography and Topography in Antiquarian Engagements with Place. In *'Fieldworks': On Performance, Landscape and Environment,* special issue of *Performance Research,* ed. M. Pearson, H. Roms, and S. Daniels, 15(4): 97–106.

Shapin, Steven. 1984. Pump and Circumstance: Robert Boyle's Literary Technology. *Social Studies of Science* 14(4): 481–520.

Shapin, Steven, and Simon Schaffer. 1985. *Leviathan and the Air-Pump: Hobbes, Boyle, and the Experimental Life.* Princeton, NJ: Princeton University Press.

Shaviro, Steven. 2009. *Without Criteria: Kant, Whitehead, Deleuze, and Aesthetics.* Cambridge, MA: MIT Press.

Shennan, Stephen. 2006. From Cultural History to Cultural Evolution: An Archaeological Perspective on Social Information Transmission. In *Social Information Transmission and Human Biology,* ed. Jonathan C.K. Wells, Simon Strickland and Kevin Laland, 173–90. Boca Raton, FL: CRC Press/Taylor & Francis.

——. 2008. Evolution in Archaeology. *Annual Review of Anthropology* 37(1): 75–91.

Shepherd, Nick. 2003. 'When the Hand that Holds the Trowel is Black . . .'. Disciplinary Practices of Self-Representation and the Issue of 'Native' Labour in Archaeology. *Journal of Social Archaeology* 3(3): 334–52.

Sherratt, Andrew. 1990. The Genesis of Megaliths: Monumentality, Ethnicity and Social Complexity in the Neolithic North-West Europe. *World Archaeology* 14: 245–60.

Siewiorek, Dan, Asim Smailagic, and Thad Starner. 2008. *Application Design for Wearable Computing.* San Rafael, CA: Morgan & Claypool.

Simmel, Georg. 1978 [1900]. *Philosophie des Geldes.* Leipzig: Duncker & Humblot. Translated as *The Philosophy of Money* (London: Routledge).

Simondon, Gilbert. 1989 [1958]. *Du mode d'existence des objets techniques.* 3rd ed. Paris: Aubier.

Skeates, Robin. 2010. *An Archaeology of the Senses: Prehistoric Malta.* Oxford: Oxford University Press.

Skibo, James M., William H. Walker, and Axel E. Nielsen. 1995. *Expanding Archaeology.* Salt Lake City: University of Utah Press.

Sloterdijk, Peter. 2004. Anthropo-Technology. *New Perspectives Quarterly* 21(4): 40–44.

——. 2008. Excerpts from Spheres III: Foams. Translated by Daniela Fabricius. *Harvard Design Magazine* 29: 38–52.

——. 2009. Rule for the Human Zoo. *Environment and Planning D: Society and Space* 27: 12–28.

——. 2009. Inspiration. *Ephemera: Theory and Politics in Organization* 9(3): 242–51.

——. 2009. Spheres Theory: Talking to Myself About the Poetics of Space. Interview, Harvard University Graduate School of Design, February 17, 2009. Published in *Harvard Design Magazine,* April 4, 2010, http://beyond entropy.aaschool.ac.uk/?p=689 (accessed April 15, 2012).

Smiles, Sam, and Stephanie Moser, eds. 2005. *Envisioning the Past: Archaeology and the Image.* Malden, MA: Blackwell.

Smith, Claire, and Heather Burke. 2003. In the Spirit of the Code. In *Ethical Issues in Archaeology,* ed. Larry J. Zimmerman, Karen D. Vitelli, and Julie Hollowell-Zimmer. Walnut Creek, CA: AltaMira Press.

Smith, Laurajane. 2006. *Uses of Heritage.* London: Routledge.

Snodgrass, Antony, 1987. *An Archaeology of Greece: The Present State and Future Scope of a Discipline.* Berkeley: University of California Press.

Society of Friends of the Railway. 1998. Οι Ελληνικοί Εισηρόδρομοι: Η διαδρομή τους από το 1869 έως σήμερα [The Greek Railways: Their Journey from 1869 to Today]. Athens: Militos.

Solli, Brit. 2008. Fra test via tegn og tekst til ting. Eller: Pimp my site? *Primitive Tider* 10: 155–64.

———. 2011. Some Reflections on Heritage and Archaeology in the Anthropocene. With Replies from Mats Burström, Ewa Domanska, Matt Edgeworth, Alfredo González-Ruibal, Cornelius Holtorf, Gavin Lucas, Terje Oestigaard, Laurajane Smith and Christopher Witmore. *Norwegian Archaeology Review* 44(1): 40–88.

Solnit, Rebecca. 2010. *Infinite City: A San Francisco Atlas.* Berkeley: University of California Press.

Spence, Jonathan D. 1985. *The Memory Palace of Matteo Ricci.* New York: Penguin Books.

Star, Susan Leigh. 2009. Personal communication.

Star, Susan Leigh, and James Griesemer. 1989. Institutional Ecology, 'Translations' and Boundary Objects. *Social Studies of Science* 19: 387–420.

Star, Susan Leigh, and Martha Lampland. 2009. Reckoning with Standards. In *Standards and Their Stories: How Quantifying, Classifying, and Formalizing Practices Shape Everyday Life,* ed. Martha Lampland and Susan Leigh Star. Ithaca, NY: Cornell University Press.

St Clair, William. 1998. *Lord Elgin and the Marbles: The Controversial History of the Parthenon Sculptures.* Oxford: Oxford University Press.

Stengers, Isabelle. 1997. *Power and Invention: Situating Science.* Minneapolis: University of Minnesota Press.

———. 2005. Introductory Notes on an Ecology of Practices. *Cultural Studies Review* 11(1): 183–96.

———. 2010. *Cosmopolitics I.* Minneapolis: University of Minnesota Press.

———. 2011. Wondering about Materialism. In *The Speculative Turn: Continental Materialism and Realism,* ed. L. Bryant, N. Srnicek, and G. Harman, 368–80 . Melbourne: re.press.

Sterling, Bruce. 2005. *Shaping Things.* Cambridge, MA: MIT Press.

Steward, Julian. 1955. *Theory of Culture Change: The Methodology of Multilinear Evolution.* Urbana: University of Illinois Press.

Stewart, Susan. 1994. *Crimes of Writing: Problems in the Containment of Representation.* Oxford: Oxford University Press.

Stoneman, Richard. 2011 [1987]. *The Land of Lost Gods: The Search for Classical Greece.* New York: Tauris Parke.

Strathern, Marilyn. 1990. Artefacts of History: Events and the Interpretation of Images. In *Culture and History in the Pacific,* ed. Jukka Sikaka, 25–44. Helsinki: Finnish Anthropological Society, 1990.

Sugiyama, Saburo. 2005. *Human Sacrifice, Militarism, and Rulership: Materialization of State Ideology at the Feathered Serpent Pyramid, Teotihuacan.* Cambridge: Cambridge University Press.

Swidler, Nina, Kurt Dongoske, Roger Anyon, and Alan Downer, eds. 1997. *Native Americans and Archaeologists: Stepping Stones to Common Ground.* Walnut Creek, CA: AltaMira Press.

Taylor, Walter. 1983 [1948]. *A Study of Archaeology.* Memoirs of the American Anthropological Association 69. Menasha, WI: American Anthropological Association. Reprint. Carbondale: Southern Illinois University, Center for Archaeological Investigations.

Thomas, David Hurst. 2000. *Skull Wars: Kennewick Man, Archaeology, and the Battle for Native American Identity.* New York: Basic Books.

Thomas, David Hurst, and Kelly L. Robert. 2006. *Archaeology.* 4th ed. Belmont, CA: Thomson Wadsworth.

Thomas, Julian. 1991. *Rethinking the Neolithic.* Cambridge: Cambridge University Press.

————. 1993. The Axe and the Torso: Symbolic Structures in the Neolithic of Brittany. In *Interpretative Archaeology,* ed. Chris Tilley. Oxford: Berg.

————. 1996. *Time, Culture and Identity.* London: Routledge.

————. 1999. *Understanding the Neolithic.* London: Routledge.

————. 2001. Archaeologies of Place and Landscape. In *Archaeological Theory Today,* ed. Ian Hodder, 165–86. Cambridge: Polity.

————. 2004a. *Archaeology and Modernity.* London: Routledge.

————. 2004b. The Great Dark Book: Archaeology, Experience, and Interpretation. In *A Companion to Archaeology,* ed. J. Bintliff, 21–36. Oxford: Blackwell.

Tilley, Christopher. 1989. Excavation as Theatre. *Antiquity* 63: 275–80.

————, ed. 1990. *Reading Material Culture. Structuralism, Hermeneutics and Post-Structuralism.* Oxford: Blackwell.

————. 1994. *The Phenomenology of Landscape.* Oxford: Berg.

————. 2004. *The Materiality of Stone: Explorations in Landscape Phenomenology,* Oxford: Berg.

————. 2008. *Body and Image: Explorations in Landscape Phenomenology 2.* Walnut Creek, CA: Left Coast Press.

Trentmann, Frank. 2009. Materiality in the Future of History: Things, Practices, and Politics. *Journal of British Studies* 48: 283–307.

Trigger, Bruce. 2006 [1989]. *A History of Archaeological Thought.* 2nd ed. Cambridge: Cambridge University Press.

Tringham, Ruth, and Mira Stevanovic. 2000. Different Excavation Styles Create Different Windows into Çatalhöyük. In *Towards Reflexive Method in Archaeology: the Example of Çatalhöyük,* ed. Ian Hodder, 111–18. Cambridge: McDonald Institute for Archaeological Research.

Tufte, Edward. 1997. *Visual Explanations.* Cheshire, CT: Graphics Press.

————. 2001. *The Visual Display of Quantitative Information,* 2nd ed. Cheshire, CT: Graphics Press.

Turkle, Sherry, ed. 2007. *Evocative Objects—Things We Think With.* Cambridge, MA: MIT Press.

Tversky, Barbara. 1999. Spatial Schemes in Depictions. In *Schemas and Abstract Thought,* ed. Merideth Gattis, 9–112. Cambridge, MA: MIT Press.

Tylor, Edward B. 1881. *Anthropology*. London.

Ucko, Peter. 1987. *Academic Freedom and Apartheid: The Story of the World Archaeology Congress*. London: Duckworth.

Van Dyke, Ruth, and Susan E. Alcock, eds. 2003. *Archaeologies of Memory*. Oxford: Blackwell.

Van den Hoven, Elise, and Berry Eggen. 2005. Personal Souvenirs as Ambient Intelligent Objects. In *Proceedings of the 2005 Joint Conference on Smart Objects and Ambient Intelligence. Innovative Context-Aware Services: Usages and Technologies*, 123–28. New York: ACM.

Verbeek, Peter-Paul. 2009. Cultivating Humanity: Towards a Non-Humanist Ethics of Technology. In *New Waves in Philosophy of Technology*, ed. Jan-Kyrre Berg Olsen, Evan Selinger, and Søren Riis, 241–63. New York: Palgrave Macmillan.

Viveiros de Castro, Eduardo. 1996. Os pronomes cosmológicos e o perspectivismo ameríndio. *Mana* 2(2): 115–44.

WAC. *See* World Archaeological Congress.

Waldstein, Charles. 1901. The Argive Hera of Polycleitus. *Journal of Hellenic Studies* 21: 30–44.

Walker, William H. 2008. Practice and Nonhuman Social Actors: The Afterlife of Witches and Dogs in the American Southwest. In *Memory Work: Archaeologies of Material Practices*, ed. Barbara J. Mills and William H. Walker,. Santa Fe: School for Advanced Research Press.

Wandsnider, LuAnn. 2004a. Solving the Puzzle of the Archaeological Labyrinth. In *Side-by-Side Survey: Comparative Regional Studies in the Mediterranean World*, ed. Susan E. Alcock and John F. Cherry, 49–62. Oxford: Oxbow Books.

———. 2004b. Artifact, Landscape, and Temporality in Eastern Mediterranean Archaeological Landscape Studies. In *Mediterranean Archaeological Landscapes: Current Issues*, ed. E. F. Athanassopoulos and L. Wandsnider, 69–79. Philadelphia: University of Pennsylvania Museum of Archaeology and Anthropology.

Wardrip-Fruin, Noah, and Nick Montfort, eds. 2003. *The New Media Reader*. Cambridge, MA: MIT Press.

Watson, Patty Jo, Steven A. LeBlanc, and Charles L. Redman. 1971. *Explanation in Archaeology: An Explicitly Scientific Approach*. New York: Columbia University Press.

Weber, Steve. 2004. *The Success of Open Source*. Cambridge, MA: Harvard University Press.

Webmoor, Timothy. 2005. Mediational Techniques and Conceptual Frameworks in Archaeology: A Model in Mapwork at Teotihuacan, Mexico. *Journal of Social Archaeology* 5(1): 54–86.

———. 2007a. What About "One More Turn After the Social" in Archaeological Reasoning? Taking Things Seriously. *World Archaeology* 39(4): 547–62.

———. 2007b. The Dilemma of Contact: Archaeology's Ethics-Epistemology Crisis and the Recovery of the Pragmatic Sensibility. *Stanford Journal of Archaeology* 5: 224–46.

———. 2008. From Silicon Valley to the Valley of Teotihuacan: The Yahoo!©s of New Media and Digital Heritage. *Visual Anthropology Review* 24(2): 183–200.

———. 2009. Arqueología neo-procesual: Alive and Kicking . . . What? Theoretical Camps, Motivational Attitudes and Academic Amnesia. A Response to "Arqueología Neo-Procesual: 'Alive and Kicking'. Algunas reflexiones desde el Paleolítico." *Complutum* 20(1): 186–90.

———. 2012a. An Archaeological Metaphysics of Care: On the Isotopy of the Past(s), Epistemography and Our Heritage Ecologies. In *Modern Materials: Proceedings from the Contemporary and Historical Archaeology in Theory Conference 2009*, ed. Brent Fortenberry and Laura McAtackney, 13–23. Oxford: British Archaeological Reports.

———. 2012b. Symmetry, STS, Archaeology. In *The Oxford Handbook of the Archaeology of the Contemporary World*, ed. Paul Graves-Brown, Rodney Harrison, and Angela Piccini. Oxford: Oxford University Press.

Webmoor, Timothy, and Christopher Witmore. 2008. Things Are Us! A Commentary on Human/Things Relations under the Banner of a 'Social' Archaeology. *Norwegian Archaeology Review* 41(1): 53–70.

Webster, Graham. 1963. *Practical Archaeology*. London: Adam & Charles Black.

West, M.L., ed. 1992. *Iambi et Elegi Graeci*. 2nd ed. Oxford: Oxford University Press.

Whatmore, Sarah. 2002. *Hybrid Geographies. Natures, Cultures, Spaces*. London: SAGE

Wheeler, Mortimer. 1954. *Archaeology from the Earth*. Oxford: Clarendon Press.

White, Hayden. 1973. *Metahistory*. Baltimore: Johns Hopkins University Press.

White, Leslie A. 1959. *The Evolution of Culture: The Development of Civilization to the Fall of Rome*. New York: McGraw-Hill.

Whitehead, Alfred North. 1953 [1925]. *Science and the Modern World*. New York: Free Press.

———. 1964 [1920]. *The Concept of Nature*. Cambridge: Cambridge University Press.

———. 1978 [1929]. *Process and Reality: An Essay in Cosmology*. New York: Free Press.

———. 2006 [1920]. *The Concept of Nature. The Tarner Lectures Delivered in Trinity College November 1919*. Teddington: The Echo Library.

Whitley, James. 1987. *Style Burial and Society in Dark Age Greece: The Changing Face of a Pre-Literate Society 1100–700 BC*. Cambridge: Cambridge University Press.

———. 2002. Too Many Ancestors. *Antiquity* 76: 119–26.

———. 2003-4. Archaeology in Greece, 2003–2004. *Archaeological Reports* 50, 1–92.

Whittle, Alasdair. 2003. *The Archaeology of People: Dimensions of Neolithic Life*. London: Routledge.

Whittle, Alasdair, and Alex Bayliss, eds. 2007. Histories of the Dead: Building Chronologies for Five Southern British Long Barrows. *Cambridge Archaeological Journal* 17, suppl. S1.

Wiessner, Polly. 1983. Style and Social Information in Kalahari San Projectile Points. *American Antiquity* 48: 253–76.

Willey, Gordon. 1953. *Prehistoric Settlement Patterns in the Virú Valley, Peru.* Bureau of American Ethnology, Bulletin 155. Washington, DC.

Williams, Charles K. 1982. The Early Urbanisation of Corinth. *Annuario della Scuola Archeologica Italiana di Atene e delle Missioni italiane in Oriente* 60: 9–20.

Wiseman, James. 1978. The *Land of the Ancient Corinthians.* Göteborg, Sweden: Paul Astrom.

Witmore, Christopher. 2004a. Four Archaeological Engagements with Place: Mediating Bodily Experience through Peripatetic Video. *Visual Anthropology Review* 20(2): 57–72.

———. 2004b. On Multiple Fields. Between the Material World and Media: Two Cases from the Peloponnesus, Greece. *Archaeological Dialogues* 11(2): 133–64.

———. 2006. Vision, Media, Noise and the Percolation of Time: Symmetrical Approaches to the Mediation of the Material World. *Journal of Material Culture* 11(3): 267–92.

———. 2007a. Symmetrical Archaeology: Excerpts from a Manifesto. *World Archaeology* 39(4): 546–62.

———. 2007b. Landscape, Time, Topology: An Archaeological Account of the Southern Argolid Greece. In*Envisioning Landscape: Situations and Standpoints in Archaeology and Heritage,* ed. Dan Hicks, Graham Fairclough, and Laura McAtackney, 194–225. Walnut Creek, CA: Left Coast Press.

———. 2009. Prolegomena to Open Pasts: On Archaeological Memory Practices. In *Archaeology, Experience, Modes of Engagement,* ed. Krysta Ryzewski, special issue of *Archaeologies* 5(3): 511–45.

———. 2012a. The World on a Flat Surface: Maps from the Archaeology of Greece and Beyond. In *Representing the Past: Archaeology through Text and Image,* ed. Sheila Bonde and Stephen Houston. Oxford: Oxbow Books.

———. 2012b. The Realities of the Past. In *Modern Materials: Proceedings from the Contemporary and Historical Archaeology in Theory Conference 2009,* ed. Brent Fortenberry and Laura McAtackney. Oxford: British Archaeological Reports.

———. Forthcoming. Archaeology and the Second Empiricism. In *Archaeology into the 2010s,* ed. F. Herschend, C. Hillerdal, and J. Siapkas.

Witmore, Christopher, and Ted V. Buttrey. 2008. William Martin Leake: A Contemporary of P.O. Brøndsted, in Greece and in London. In *P.O. Brøndsted (1780–1842)—A Danish Classicist in His European Context,* ed. Bodil Bundgaard Rasmussen, Jørgen Steen Jenson, John Lund, and Michael Märcher, 15–34. Copenhagen: Royal Danish Academy.

Wittgenstein, Ludwig. 1922. *Tractatus Logico-Philosophicus.* New York: Harcourt, Brace.

World Archaeological Congress (WAC). 1989. The Vermillion Accord on Human Remains. www.worldarchaeologicalcongress.org/site/about_ethi.php #code2 (accessed April 12, 2012).

———. 1990. First Code of Ethics. www.worldarchaeologicalcongress.org/site /about_ethi.php#code1 (accessed April 12, 2012).

———. 2009 [2006]. The Tamaki Makau-rau Accord on the Display of Human Remains and Sacred Objects. www.worldarchaeologicalcongress.org/about -wac/codes-of-ethics/169-tamaki-makau-rau-accord (accessed April 12, 2012).

Wylie, Alison. 1996. Ethical Dilemmas in Archaeological Practice: Looting, Repatriation, Stewardship, and the (Trans)formation of Disciplinary Identity. *Perspectives on Science* 4(2): 154–94.

———. 1997. The Engendering of Archaeology: Refiguring Feminist Science Studies. *Osiris* 12: 80–99.

———. 2002. *Thinking from Things.* Berkeley: University of California Press.

———. 2006. Philosophy of Archaeology. Philosophy in Archaeology. In *The Handbook of the Philosophy of Science*, vol. 15: *Philosophy of Anthropology and Sociology*, ed. Stephen P. Turner and Mark W. Risjord. London: Elsevier.

Yablon, Nick. 2009. *Untimely Ruins: An Archaeology of American Urban Modernity, 1819–1919.* Chicago: University of Chicago Press.

Yarrow, Thomas. 2003. Artefactual Persons: The Relational Capacities of Persons and Things in the Practice of Excavation. *Norwegian Archaeological Review* 36(1): 65–73.

Yoffee, Norman, ed. 2007. *Negotiating the Past in the Past. Identity, Memory, and Landscape in Archaeological Research.* Tucson: University of Arizona Press.

Young, Julian. 2002. *Heidegger's Later Philosophy.* Cambridge: Cambridge University Press.

Zimmerman, Larry, Karen Vitelli, and Julie Hollowell-Zimmer. 2003. *Ethical Issues in Archaeology.* Walnut Creek, CA: Altamira Press.

# Index